John Clare and
the Bounds of Circumstance

As a working-class poet, born into an impoverished family in rural England in 1793, John Clare has often been considered of interest for the unusual nature of his life and career rather than for his poetry. In this book, Johanne Clare argues that Clare should be taken seriously both as a poet and as a representative figure in a period of social and agrarian upheaval. She discusses Clare's political attitudes and his views on the social issues which most affected him – poverty, economic inequality, class prejudice, and the enclosure movement – and shows how his social identity and experience were intricately related to his major writings.

The author suggests that the full significance of Clare's contribution to English literature is found, not in his social criticism, but in his refusal to dissociate himself from his past or to become assimilated into the mainstream of English culture at the expense of his class identity. She argues that a clear set of aesthetic principles informs his finest work and she provides the first thematic and structural classification of his poetry. Focusing on the major vocational poems and selected passages from the prose, she shows how Clare formulated the creative ideas and rhetorical techniques that allowed him to give unified expression to both his social and literary concerns. Clare's deep involvement with nature and rural England not only was the basis for his poetry, but also enabled him to articulate beliefs which opposed the inhumane values of his time.

Johanne Clare is a member of the Department of English at the University of Toronto.

John Clare
and the Bounds
of Circumstance

JOHANNE CLARE

McGill-Queen's University Press
Kingston and Montreal

Printed in Canada

This book has been published with the help of a
grant from the Canadian Federation for the
Humanities, using funds provided by the Social
Sciences and Humanities Research Council of
Canada.

Printed on acid-free paper

Canadian Cataloguing in Publication Data

Clare, Johanne, 1951-
  John Clare and the bounds of circumstance

  Bibliography: p.
  Includes index.
  ISBN 0-7735-0606-3

  1. Clare, John, 1793-1864 – Criticism and
interpretation.   2. Clare, John, 1793-1864 –
Political and social views.   I. Title.

PR4453.C6Z68 1987   821'.7   C87-094124-0

For my family

I began by seeing how man was formed by circumstances - and what are circumstances? -
but touchstones of his heart - ? and what are
touch stones? - but proovings of his hearrt? -
and what are proovings of his heart but forti-
fiers or alterers of his nature? and what is his
altered nature but his soul? - and what was
his soul before it came into the world and had
These provings and alterations and perfection-
ings? - An intelligence - without Identity - and
how is this Identity to be made? Through the
medium of the Heart? And how is the heart to
become this Medium but in a world of Circumstances?

Keats

Contents

Preface

This book is primarily concerned with John Clare's early poems (1809–21) and the writings of the middle years (1822–37). I refer occasionally to the work of the asylum period, but, as I make clear in my conclusion, the asylum verse does not really belong in a study of the social forces that helped to shape Clare's imagination and of their more subtle manifestations in his poetry. One could argue that the sense of deprivation and loss, the imagery of imprisonment, and the obsessive concern with the problematical nature of personal identity which are to be found in Clare's asylum verse can all be traced back to the traumas of his social experience. But having said this (and it is not a point, I think, that needs to be laboured), one can then say that the relationship between the poetry of the 1820s and 1830s and the asylum verse seems to be one of inversion. As Tim Chilcott has shown in *'A Real World & Doubting Mind': A Critical Study of the Poetry of John Clare*, Clare's loosening grip on the world and himself caused him to write a poetry so empty of the particular facts of experience that it can be characterized as a poetry of absence and (in Clare's terms) "sad non-identity." The fact that most Clare scholars now seem to focus on the pre-asylum verse has considerably less to do with questions of aesthetic preference than with the fact that what is definitively Clare is primarily to be found in the poetry he wrote when he was still able to face life with courage, curiosity, and hope.

The challenge all Clare scholars continue to face is that of producing work which will appeal in its intensity, focus, and detail to other specialists but which at the same time will make Clare accessible to those readers unfamiliar with him. Within the limits of what is a fairly integrated argument, I have tried to give as full an account of Clare's work as possible not by summarizing its every phase and aspect, but by discussing in depth only those poems that represent Clare at his best and best represent his major preoccupations, themes, and imaginative strategies. One of the reasons, I suspect, that there is so little consensus about the nature and quality of Clare's work is that the very basic work of cataloguing the poems – of grouping them, of saying what they are "about" – has only begun to be done. Everyone knows that Clare was affected by the enclosure of his village and wrote about it. I have tried to show that he wrote about it, not glancingly, here and there, but directly, specifically, almost systematically, in a group of poems that I have labelled the enclosure elegies. Everyone now knows that Clare was interested in questions of taste and aesthetic principle. I have tried to show that this is a major preoccupation of a major group of his poems that I have labelled the vocational poems. Fortunately, the work of grouping and labelling the bird poems had already been done. I have tried to continue this work by indicating some of the ways in which this group of poems possesses – as a group – the thematic and formal coherence of a lyric-sequence.

John Barrell, Timothy Brownlow, and Tim Chilcott, whose excellent book on Clare did not appear until after mine had been submitted for publication, have all contributed to this basic work. These three critics in particular have also encouraged readers of Clare to be more sceptical and more self-conscious about the evaluative biases of our critical procedures. Much of Clare's poetry does not invite ordinary interpretation; it seems to be without implication, to resist conventional forms of textual analysis. These three critics have been especially adept in playing with, rather than against, the sense of surface strangeness in Clare's work. In identifying and explaining the ways in which Clare's modes of perception are unlike our own and the ways his poetic techniques were necessarily different from those of his contemporaries, John Barrell, in particular, encouraged readers to bring to Clare a more sophisticated and nuanced sense of the connections between historicist and sociological awareness and textual interpretation. Tim Chilcott has also contributed to our appreciation of the underlying structures of awareness that shaped Clare's work. But he is much more sceptical about the nature of the relations between Clare's life and work and between what he calls "the writer's lived awareness" and "the 'awareness' embodied in the created work" (p. xv). The following chapters are based upon assumptions which directly counter such scepticism. One cannot resist being intrigued by Chilcott's suggestion that Clare's verse "may be non-transitive, generating a kind of fictive, surrogate consciousness through its very encoding in language" (p. xv). But I believe that before we can explore the epistemological possibilities raised by such a suggestion, we must understand the "fiction" of Clare's self in Clare's own terms. We must, that is to say, acknowledge the rhetorical and self-conscious element in his work but at the same time share his fundamentally unself-conscious belief that in his poetry he could speak his mind and tell the truth.

I am grateful to a number of friends, teachers, and colleagues who gave me advice during the writing of this book. My thanks are due, first, to W.J. Keith, who waited patiently and read several earlier versions of this study and gave me the benefit of his insights, his tact, his high intellectual standards and his good common sense. R.W. Malcolmson, Peter Morgan, and Milton Wilson also read earlier versions and offered useful and informed advice as well as many personal kindnesses. I wish to thank Hans de Groot for his interest in Clare and for providing a forum in which I could express my own interest. I am also indebted to Eli Mandel without whose help I would not have struggled with this book or begun other projects.

I wish to thank the librarians and staff of the British Library, Peterborough Museum, Northampton Public Library, and Carl H. Pforzheimer Library. I acknowledge with gratitude the fact that this book was written with the support of the Canada Council and published with the help of a grant from the Canadian Federation for the Humanities.

Abbreviations

I   *The Poems of John Clare*, ed. J.W. Tibble (London: J.M. Dent 1935), vol. I

II   *The Poems of John Clare*, vol. II

JCAW   *John Clare's Autobiographical Writings*, ed. Eric Robinson (Oxford: Oxford University Press 1983)

JCOA   *John Clare*, ed. Eric Robinson and David Powell (The Oxford Authors Series, 1984)

Letters   *The Letters of John Clare*, ed. J.W. and Anne Tibble (London: Routledge and Kegan Paul 1951)

LPJC   *The Later Poems of John Clare*, ed. Eric Robinson, David Powell, and Margaret Grainger, 2 vols (Oxford: Oxford University Press 1984)

MC   *John Clare: The Midsummer Cushion*, ed. Anne Tibble and R.K.R. Thornton (Mid-Northumberland Arts Group in association with Carcanet Press 1979)

Prose   *The Prose of John Clare*, ed. J.W. and Anne Tibble (London: Routledge and Kegan Paul 1951)

SC   *The Shepherd's Calendar*, ed. Eric Robinson and Geoffrey Summerfield (London: Oxford University Press 1964)

SPP   *Selected Poems and Prose of John Clare*, ed. Eric Robinson and Geoffrey Summerfield (London: Oxford University Press 1967)

John Clare and
the Bounds of Circumstance

Introduction

When Clare's first two volumes were issued from Fleet Street in 1820 and 1821, they bore on their title pages the designation "John Clare the Northamptonshire Peasant." The title pages have yellowed through the years, but the label has been more resistant to time; though Clare never spoke of himself in quite these terms, he is still known as the peasant-poet of Northamptonshire. As his most recent editors have observed:

The label of peasant-poet was attached to him by his publishers with the best of intentions, however ridiculous and irrelevant it may seem to us today – who ever thought of dubbing Wallace Stevens the insurance-broker-poet, or Carlos Williams the doctor-poet? The label had a distinct sentimental value, and served not only to proclaim a phenomenon but also as a guarantee of reliability; the son of the soil was unusually well equipped to appear before the reading public as the Child of Nature.[1]

The reading public showed considerable interest in the first volume of this "second Burns": two months after its publication one thousand copies of *Poems Descriptive of Rural Life and Scenery* had been sold, and by 1821 four editions had been printed. But Clare passed out of the mind of the reading public almost as quickly as he had passed in. Only a year later, *The Village Minstrel* was published, but the volume did not sell very well, and *The Shepherd's Calendar* (1827) hardly sold at all. His last book, *The Rural Muse* (1835), was scarcely noticed. His reputation as a peasant-poet had (to borrow Clare's phrase) "macadamized the way to popularity," but he was to spend the rest of his life paying the price for his early success (*Prose*, 206).

In a sense he is still paying for it today, since he is still better known for his anomalous situation as a peasant-poet than for his poetry. What Hazlitt said of Chatterton might well apply to Clare: he has suffered "an abstracted reputation which is independent of any thing we know of his works."[2] Yet it is easy to see why Clare's situation has continued to fascinate his readers. His dramatic early success and later insanity, his unpromising beginnings, his poverty, his lack of formal education, his experience of hard labour (for which he was both physically and mentally unsuited), his sense of grievous loss because of the enclosure of his native village, his economically necessary and psychically dislocating move to Northborough, his desperate and naive schemes to achieve financial security, his tortuous dealings with his patrons and publishers, his lifelong struggle against both subtle and overtly malicious forms of class-prejudice: these aspects of his life may explain why there have been to date more biographies of Clare than full-scale critical studies. And when one considers the difficulties that this formally uneducated working man had to overcome, one can hardly resist feeling that the qualities of the poet and his poetry must be less fascinating than the fact that he managed to be a poet at all.

In his early years, Clare himself encouraged just this kind of feeling by stressing the negative impact of his situation upon his creative achievement. One can see this in the "Prospectus" he drafted for his first projected volume: "It is hoped that the humble situation which distinguishes their author will be some excuse in their favour, & serve to make an atonement for the many inaccuracies & imperfections found in them."[3] This was at once an apology for his poetry and for his social circumstances, and one of the saddest elements of Clare's story is to be found in the fact that he believed both apologies were necessary. But this was Clare in 1818, and as early as 1821 he was to regret having encouraged his readers to approach his work with lowered expectations. He soon came to realize that little was gained and much lost by his confessions of inadequacy. Throughout the 1820s we find him writing very differently about his "humble situation," and by 1830 he was claiming the right to be judged "without any appeals to want of education lowness of origin or any other foil that officion [officiousness?] chuses to encumber my path with" (*Letters*, 267): "I wish not to have my difficulties trumpeted by everyone who chuses to pen his spleen in my favour ... officious interferences as to my adversity add nothing to my prosperity" (*Letters*, 271). "Such things," he argued, "can neither mar me nor make me & all I wish now is to stand on my own bottom as a poet" (*Letters*, 275). But the damage to his professionalism had been done, and Clare could no more undo it than he could erase the label that had adhered to him: the circumstances of the Northamptonshire peasant-poet continued to attract more attention than his poetry.

Yet, as Clare himself well knew, there was a difference between the "officious interferences" of those who found him merely interesting because he was a peasant-poet (an oddity akin to dancing dogs and lady-preachers), and the critical interest of those who hoped that because of his background he would contribute something of original importance to English literature. It was the condescending nature of the interest in his situation, not the interest *per se*, which was most injurious to his literary reputation. Indeed, to react against the appalling attitudes of many of his contemporaries by ignoring the particular circumstances which were the object of their condescension might well make us accomplices to that condescension. Such a reaction would also obscure many of the most significant thematic and formal elements in the poetry, for Clare's experience as a labouring man living in the small rural community of Helpston at the beginning of the nineteenth century commands our attention not from the distant reaches of "background," but from the foreground of his texts, in his chosen subject-matter and in the expressive significance of his imagery, rhetoric, language, types of character and self-characterization, and authorial point of view.

Clare's social identity was to assume enormous importance when he wrote about the prevailing values, historical events, and class conditions which shaped the world in which he lived. Almost all of his social criticism was written from the viewpoint of a rural labourer, and always his personal bias was openly declared. Registering this viewpoint was important to Clare, not only because it had not yet been adequately recorded in literature, but because it carried with it a presumption of veracity. Just as Jane Austen, writing in the same period about the same acquisitive values (but from the other side of the park-gates), published her novels under the protective but revealing pseudonym "a lady," in order to vouchsafe her reliability as an informed witness to the mating-for-money habits of her genteel contemporaries, so Clare emphasized his social identity and experience in order to establish his credibility as witness to the conditions of the rural labouring poor:

O Poverty! thy frowns were early dealt
O'er him who mourn'd thee, not by fancy led
To whine and wail o'er woes he never felt,

Staining his rhymes with tears he never shed,
And heaving sighs a mock song only bred:
Alas! he knew too much of every pain
That shower'd full thick on his unshelter'd head.   (*I*, 139)

Clare wrote about poverty as a poor man, about the worst effects of enclosure as a man who had suffered them, about class-prejudice as it affected his personal dignity and creative poise.

Indeed, even when he was not specifically addressing the questions of poverty, injustice, and exploitation, he continued to insist that his class-identity imbued his most personal responses with a representative significance. Many of the poems I shall be considering in this study appear to have little to do with the shared conditions of Clare's social peers or with the crucial historical events through which they suffered. In fact, many do not look like social poems at all, but appear to be intensely private explorations of the poet's imaginative life and creative aspirations – subjects which social historians may be forgiven for finding of less than staggering significance. These poems are concerned, though in remarkably diverse ways, with the poet's role and with the qualities of mind, feeling, and sensibility which Clare brought to his vocation, and for this reason I have called them vocational poems. From them we learn what he hoped to achieve in his poetry and what he would not attempt, what he thought was important to his work and what he believed to be essential to all forms of writing, why he felt alienated from the tradition and from his public and how he learned to trust his own creative instincts. These are, one might suppose, primarily aesthetic matters; and yet, as I hope to show, it is precisely these questions that reveal how impossible it is to disentangle Clare's aesthetic and his social preoccupations. When he wrote about poetry or the poet's calling, or set forth his ideas about the relationship between education, imagination, and creative achievement, it was not in the voice of a disembodied, denatured, desocialized character with no pretextual identity, but rather as a man whose values, whose ways of seeing and speaking and feeling, had been shaped by his experience as a poor, disenfranchised, formally uneducated labouring man. If there is a single theme which unites the disparate group of writings I shall discuss, it is to be found not only in Clare's persistent emphasis upon his social being, nor in his concern with the imaginative life, but rather in his attempt to mediate between these two commitments so as to make them one.

The first poems I shall examine are the early poverty poems and the enclosure elegies. Both these groups belong to the tradition of rural dissent, and both reveal the depth of Clare's understanding that his position in society decided not only the limits of his material expectations, but the quality of his relations to his physical and human environment. The enclosure elegies represent a consistent and well-organized response to one of the crucial developments of his period; several of the elegies are of high intrinsic value. But the same cannot be said of the poverty poems, and it may be argued that other works would better represent Clare's talents and the range and depth of his concern for the conditions of his class. *The Parish*, for instance, presents a much more extended analysis of the plight of the rural labouring poor and of their relations to the master class. *The Shepherd's Calendar* offers a fuller and more varied portrait of the rustic community at work and play. Finally, the "hard country sonnets" contain more striking images of life at the margins of society. But none of these are autobiographical poems, and though the social criticism they present was undoubtedly shaped and quickened by Clare's personal experience, that personal experience is not inscribed within their forms.[4] In *The Shepherd's Calendar* Clare wrote about rural labouring life in general, not about his own life in particular, and in *The Parish* he looked *at* the experience of poverty rather than *out from* the centre of that experience. In constrast, the early poverty poems and enclosure elegies are intensely personal works. In writing them, Clare was concerned not only with the social implications of poverty and enclosure but with the problem of how to present these issues, how to disclose his personal involvement with his themes. Because they are such self-conscious poems, they provide an opportunity to understand the relations between Clare's identity as poet and as working man which *The Parish* and *The Shepherd's Calendar* cannot provide.

After 1817 Clare ceased to write any poems which were solely concerned with his own poverty, and after the middle 1820s few works which were centrally preoccupied with the theme of enclosure. But the ideas about nature and society which he developed in response to these experiences, and the authorial point of view he first developed in writing about them, can be traced through all his poetry. The impact which poverty and enclosure had upon his life is too crucial and too complex to be neatly summarized: it would be difficult to say which hard truth hit Clare the hardest as he watched his native landscape being despoiled by "curst improvement" and felt his hopes for financial independence change into despair. But certainly one of those truths involved his recognition that he lived in a society in which "proud distinction makes a wider space / Between the genteel and the vulgar race" (*SC*, 69). This was a necessary and tragic recognition and one that was to have as profound an impact upon the way Clare saw himself as a poet as it had upon the way he responded to his circumstances as a labouring man. In the third, fourth, and fifth chapters I consider some of the ways Clare's sense of living in a divided society affected his relations to the tradition and to his reading public.

No professional writer of the early nineteenth century was placed as low as Clare in the social hierarchy of the period or given so few opportunities for intellectual advancement. He had little to cushion him – no alternative, deeply felt interests, no financial resources, few close friends – when his work broke against the prejudice and indifference of his contemporaries. Yet his personal circumstances might have remained in the background (if not in his social criticism, then at least in his nature poetry) had Clare not been so acutely aware of how his humble situation made him an unusual case – one of the few English poets who could not (through education, inherited position, or acquired prestige) ever call himself a gentleman. He felt keenly the differences between himself and the genteel poets of the eighteenth century he so admired. But, while these differences caused him to fear that in literature as in life he had been born on the wrong side of the "wider space," it was primarily his dealings with the publishing and reviewing machinery of his period that brought home to him with full force the truth that the "genteel race" held as strong a monopoly upon the official culture of the nation as it did upon the means of production. Clare fought that monopoly on many fronts, arguing that the genteel classes should not be seen as the sole custodians of the nation's literature, and claiming that "the commonest of the lower orders" had the "best feelings" for great poetry and were the "true arbiters" of English literature – "the veins & arteries that feed & quicken the heart of living fame" (*Prose*, 100). But such arguments were, to a considerable extent, founded upon Clare's belief in the potentialities of his class rather than upon the manifest character of the lower orders, for elsewhere he admitted that, even among those who could read, most of his social peers knew next to nothing of Spenser, Shakespeare, or Milton and "seldom [knew] how to value or appreciate what they [were] acquainted with" (*Prose*, 207). Clare had little reason for hoping that the men and women of his class would be purchasing and reading his volumes: they had neither the means nor the leisure-time to do so. And the gestures of deference so common in his early poems and the characteristic rhetoric of the later works give one no reason to suppose that Clare was addressing these men and women. He was writing for and about them, not to them, and his belief that his readers tended to be people with whom he had circumstantially little in common was to have an enormous though calculable effect upon the way he wrote.

It may be argued that in characterizing Clare's audience as a predominantly genteel company which looked upon the literary efforts of an English labourer with condescension or alarm, I show an insufficient understanding of the sociological formation of the reading public and of the rising numbers of lower-class readers in the early nineteenth century. One may suppose that among the four thousand readers who purchased Clare's first volume there were more grocers and printers' assistants than marquises or bishops.[5] Moreover, Clare was personally acquainted with at least a few men lacking both position and property who were centrally engaged in the work of reading and writing, publishing and reviewing the nation's literature. But in considering Clare's relations to his public I am not concerned with its sociological formation, but with the causes and consequences of his belief that (with scant exception) his readers – whatever their place in the hierarchy of status – tended to assess his poetry in terms prescribed by the culture of gentility. Conservative reviewers were not the only ones who undercut his best efforts by challenging his right to follow the poet's vocation. A grocer's son was as likely as the marquis of Exeter to remind Clare that he was merely a field-hand who wrote verses, and by some of his peers in his own community he was advised to leave literature to the gentlemen.

Critics have commented upon the ambiguous nature of Clare's relationship to his fellow-Helpstonians, and certainly several of his poems and letters suggest that Clare was very conscious of this ambiguity. In the third chapter I consider one such poem, the long autobiographical "Village Minstrel." "The Village Minstrel" has more than a few formal flaws: it is structurally haphazard, tonally inconsistent, and the metrical movement of its Spenserian stanzas is marred by syntactical muddles. But in spite of its obvious imperfections, this is a moving and important work which allows us to watch a poet-in-the-making, living with and fighting against the limitations of his situation. The struggle was against the circumstances of his class, not against his class. Though "The Village Minstrel" gives pointed emphasis to the ambiguous and at times strained nature of Clare's relationship to his peers – he could not share with them the writing and publishing experience – his need to proclaim his individuality was never exercised at the expense of his commitment to his class or to his own social being. His identity as one of the "vulgar race" was not for him something out there, never an external fact which he chose to obscure or avoid.

Few poets in the language wrote quite so emphatically as Clare about being victimized by his society. The difficulties and disabling fears he had to surmount before he could put pen to paper colour all his work and give even to his most blithe and spontaneous utterances a dark and serious quality. But it would be wrong to describe Clare as the passive victim of circumstance, still more wrong to suggest that he was always intoning his litany of just complaint. His first readers thought of him as a man who had, through the very act of writing, transcended his circumstances and found enough personal happiness to write upon the happiest of themes: the beauty of the natural landscape, the satisfactions of country life, the joys of childhood. There is some truth in the characterization, for Clare found much to celebrate in rustic life and village custom, and his delight in nature led him to write some of the most expansive and celebrative poems in the rural tradition. He thought of nature as his greatest creative resource and wrote of his excursions into its innermost recesses as journeys of escape from the push and shove of circumstance. Within the sphere of nature the differences and distances between "the genteel and the vulgar race" and his self-consciousness of his own place within the hierarchy of status no longer haunted him. He celebrated the landscapes of his locality not only for the aesthetic pleasure they gave him, but because in them he found images of generosity, freedom, and unity he couldn't find in English society as he knew it. To speak of Clare's celebrations in this way is to recognize from the outset that he connected his responses to nature and his responses to society. In the last two chapters of this study I indicate some of the ways this essential work of connection led Clare to develop his best ideas about the role of the poet and to write his finest and most original nature poems.

Clare escaped to the green woods and meadows to feel his emotional pulse and celebrate his creative resource, and one can scarcely imagine a figure so politically innocuous, so unthreatening to his rulers, as a poet who longed to

> pillow on the yielding rush
> And acting as I please
> Drop into pleasant dreams or musing lye
> Mark the wind shaken trees
> And cloud betravelled sky   (*JCOA*, 125)

But "acting as I please" strikes the chord of freedom and the pleasant dreams and musing had an unquiescent content. Indeed, in some respects Clare's poetry of nature represents as significant, though less pointed, a contribution to the tradition of rural dissent as the poverty poems: the landscape experience afforded Clare a way of escaping from society but it also allowed him to develop the poise and articulate the beliefs with which he resisted his society's most inhumane values. He was well aware that he was challenging the disciplinarian and utilitarian attitudes of political orthodoxy by writing "in the world's despite" of his longing for a place where

> I can live and at my leisure seek
> Joys far from cold restraints - not fearing pride
> Free as the winds that breath upon my cheek   (*JCOA*, 126)

He was also aware that by writing about his own aesthetic experience, by the sheer fact that he wrote at all, he was arguing for the creative potentialities of working-class men and women, bringing his class with him, as it were, as he tried to enter into the official mainstream of English cultural life. And he knew exactly what he was writing against: the attitudes of men and women who believed that the interests of society were best served by keeping the labouring poor in a state of ignorance and servility so profound that they could never know how to claim a share in this official culture.

CHAPTER ONE

The Nature of Society: The Thousands and the Few

CLASS CONSCIOUSNESS AND POLITICS

The occupational and social class into which Clare was born did not make up the entire contents of his social being, but Clare sometimes implied that it did. In his poetry, letters, and prose he referred frequently to his "humble station in life," sometimes apologetically and sometimes with pride. Often he used his humble station to justify his innocence, his rusticity, and his plain-speaking: he has always been "a stranger to the world," "a poor man," "a vulgar fellow that mimicked at no pretensions," he wrote, so he must be allowed to "ask you a few plain questions" and to answer "in the rough way of a thoroughbred clown."[1] He took pride in the fact that he would not be "improved," would not set foot on the path of upward mobility which Crabbe had so successfully travelled. He felt it was important to record that even in his most promising days he always kept company with his equals and kept his distance from "the betters" in his community. "Never," he claimed in a revealing choice of words, "was I at any time lifted up above my prosperity – I never attempted to alter my old ways & manners I [h]arboured no proud notions nor felt a pride above my station" (*Prose*, 66).

But pride *in* his station was not always easy to maintain. His letters and prose reveal that Clare himself never doubted that his social position affected his relations to all people of respectable or genteel status. His consciousness of his "coarse origins" influenced the way he conducted himself both in his long-standing relationships with his patrons and in his passing encounters with the various gentlemen who, after the success of the first volume, were always passing through or riding up from Cambridge or London to see for themselves this strange new figure in the literary scene. The autobiographical writings are filled with anecdotes which serve to highlight his vulnerability to the class-prejudices of these gentlemen; their high-handed behaviour, Clare was to say with characteristic understatement, "gave me a great deal of trouble & hurt my feelings" (*Prose*, 66). He despised himself for the "timidity that made me very awkward & silent in the presence of my superiors." But, with just cause, he despised some of those self-proclaimed "superiors" even more:

Among the many that came to see me there was a dandified gentleman of unconscious odditys of character that not only bordered on the ridiculous but was absurdly smothered in it / he made pretensions to great learning & knew nothing / On his first coming he began in a very dry manner to examine the fruits of experience in books & said he hoped I had a fondness for reading as he wished to have the pleasure to make me a present of some / he then begd my walking stick & after he had got it he wanted me to write my name on the crook / I really thought the fellow was mad / he then asked me insulting liberties respecting my first acquaintence with Patty & said he understood that in the country the lower orders made their courtship in barns and pigsties & asked me whether I did / I felt very vexd & said it might be the custom of the high orders for aught I knew ... but I assured him he was very wrong respecting that custom among the lower orders / here his wife said he was fond of a joke & hoped I should not be offended but I saw nought of a joke in it.   (*Prose*, 72)

It is difficult not to feel outrage when one considers the impertinence Clare had to endure. But the most painful reading in the *Autobiography* and the letters occurs not when Clare is detailing the appalling insolence of his "superiors," but when he is confessing his sensitivity about the angularities of his own conduct and appearance. We learn from these confessions that Clare was upset for weeks because he once cut short the intrusive questions of a passing stranger, who, he later discovered, was none other than the marquis of Exeter. He was mortified by his behaviour in the presence of General Birch Reynardson of Holywell, especially when he mistook the governess for the general's wife. He experienced discomfort when he had to deal with people who "looked with much surprise at my odd clownish appearance" (*Prose*, 84). When he dined with respectable people, he wished he were somewhere else. When the toasts went round, he kept silent. When the wines were poured he did not know which glass to raise. When he was called for an audience with the marquis of Exeter he would not go until the weather was fine: "I felt fearful," he writes, "that my shoes would be in a dirty condition for so fine a place." When the weather cleared he went to Burghley Park but his boots continued to be an awkward problem:

> his Lordship sent for me / I went upstairs & thro winding passages after the footman as fast as I could hobble almost fit to quarrel with my hard-nailed shoes at the noise they made on the marble & boarded floors & cursing them to myself as I set my feet down in the lightest steps I was able to utter / his Lordship recieved me kindly askd me some questions & requested to look at the MSS ... after I had been about half an hour eying the door & now & then looking at my dirty shoes & wishing myself out of danger of soiling such grandeur he saw my embarrassment as I suspect & said I shoud lose my dinner in the servants hall & had better go.
>
> (*Prose*, 69)

At Burghley Park, hobnails were cause for embarrassment; among the black-coated Londoners he met at John Taylor's table, it was his country green coat and yellow vest. In his own cottage at Helpston it was the "shabby & dirty" appearance, the "dull & silent" behaviour with which he met the various dandies who called him from the fields to answer their "gossipy questions."

But his class was not the only thing that separated Clare from the dandies who came up from London to gape at him. He lived in his society through mediations other than his station in life. He looked out upon the world not only as a labouring man, but as a country man, as an inhabitant of the Midland Fens, and as a member of a small village community. Without question these other ways of looking were decisive in shaping Clare's experiences, knowledge, and sensibility. If in this study I speak rarely of these specifically rural and local interests, it is not because I do not consider them important, but because their importance has been well recognized in recent criticism.[2] But I do not believe it possible to speak of Clare's country experience without also speaking of the low station in rural society from which he looked out upon country life and scenery. Nor do I consider it useful to discuss his sense of place and local attachment without also discussing the ways in which his localism was both determined and qualified by his social position within his locality. Clare did not forget - he was never allowed to forget - that within the structures of English society, whether national, rural or local, he had no power, no property, no privileged rights. And so, if we are to understand the rural experience and the local attachments to which he bore witness, we have to employ class terms.

In the autobiographical fragments we are offered an image of a young man who sat in the same church as the local farmers, looked out over the same landscapes as the local magistrates, sometimes even found himself rubbing shoulders with the greatest estate-owners in the country. Yet the distance which separated the prosperous and the powerful from this "boy / Among the vulgar and the lowly bred" was enormous (*JCOA*, 422). Clare's encounters with local merchants and farmers, and his meetings with the great county magnates, only served to emphasize that distance. In all of his writings there is nothing to suggest that Clare himself believed that he shared with the great or the smaller landowners in his locality anything more than the sky and the public roads. He was grateful for the small annuities which the marquis of Exeter and Earl Fitzwilliam had granted to him. He was delighted when Lord Milton showed him the library at Milton Park. But it is difficult to agree with Robinson and Summerfield when they claim that Clare "shared in the culture of the great house which descended by devious routes to the cottages through servants and servants' servants down to the poor."[3] If there really were such "devious routes" of access to patrician culture, then they were so devious that Clare could never find them: his uncomfortable audiences with the local aristocrats, the labour in their gardens, the cheques in the mail, the rare suppers with the kitchen staff, the brief tours of the Fitzwilliam library, and the friendship of men like Artis and Henderson who just happened to be servants at Milton Park do not add up to participation in the "culture of the great house." If anything, the very proximity of the Fitzwilliam estate to Clare's home would have served as a constant reminder of how little the patrician and the plebeian residents of his locality had in common.

Nor did Clare feel any strong identity of interest with the prosperous farmers in his locality simply because they too were, in the most limited sense of the word, his neighbours. Those readers who might hope to find in Clare lavish images of an organic community in which the labourer and the employing farmer joined together in the common experience of work and play will be sadly disappointed. For Clare did not write at all sympathetically about the farmer class. "The better sort," he claimed,

that imagine themselves gentry are dull money getting panders ignorant of the world & all that constitutes its glory / genius & talent & merit are greek words to them / the men of greatest merit in their eye is those that

have strength to do the most work & can keep from troubling the Parish
the longest – as to books they know as much about them as I do about the
Talmud or the Koran / they are exactly what Goldsmith fancies
the Dutch to be 'Dull as their lakes that slumber in a storm'.[4]

Two perspectives are offered here: the perspective of the poet who
sees the philistine as his natural enemy and that of the labouring
man who feels that his ability to produce and keep on producing is
all that matters to those who buy his labour. A singular disdain for
the kind of man who can value other men only for their economic
capacities animates both perspectives. And a single enemy con-
nects them: the "money getting" farmer. The anger and the disdain are characteristic. Indeed, in my reading of Clare's poetry, I
have been able to find no more than three complimentary references to the land-owning or the prosperous tenant-farmer, and it is
most significant that all of these references are emphatically retrospective. In one stanza from "The Village Minstrel," in a few introductory lines from *The Parish*, and in a brief passage from *The
Shepherd's Calendar*, Clare was to invoke a time when the harvest
feast "brought the masters level with the men," when the landowner cared about the men who worked for him, when the farmer
shared with those men certain interests and customs in common.[5]
But, as he made very clear in *The Shepherd's Calendar*, this
"dream of good" had dissolved, that spirit of community had been

> thrown aside
> And the old freedom that was living then
> When masters made them merry wi their men ...
> And joind the chorus while a labourer sung
> All this is past.   (*SC*, 68-9)

And what had passed for Clare was not only a time when the field-
hand could feel that he shared certain cultural customs and values
with the farmer, but also a time when he could feel that his economic interests were confluent with the interests of the man who
employed him to plough his fields and harvest his crops. *His* fields,
his crops: for Clare the farmer who could speak in this proud, proprietary way of the rural landscape and of the agrarian means of
production was not only outside the labourer's experience, but
antagonistic to that experience. The farmer's interests, he wrote,
"are always curses to the cottager & the poor man." And so,
whether the farmer's profits rose or fell, whether the cabal at Westminster attended to country interests, whether the Corn Laws were

repealed, were questions of little interest to Clare. For he understood that however these questions might be decided "the poor
man will be no better off":

he is so many degrees lower in the Thremometer of distress that such
benefits to others will not reach him and tho the Farmers should again be
in their summer splendour of 'high prices' and 'better markets' as they
phrase it the poor man would still be found very little above freezing
point - ... I wish the good of the people may be found at the end and that
in the general triumph the poor man may not be forgotten for the poor
have many oppressors   (*SPP*, 172-3)

The bias revealed in this passage from Clare's "Letter from a Poor
Man"; the awareness that the farmer and the labourer shared no
common grievances; the angry recognition that in times of general
prosperity the misery of the poor man could be obscured: all these
encourage one to argue that Clare's commitment to his class was of
preemptive significance.

The extent to which this commitment animated all of Clare's
poetry of protest must be recognized if we are to understand not
only for whom but against whom he was writing. To suppose that
in his poetry of humble and rustic life, in his celebrations of local
attachment, or in his protests against the effects of the enclosure
movement, Clare was writing on behalf of all countrymen, or
speaking for all his local neighbours, is to miss the specific causes of
his vehemence and the specific constituency he sought to represent. To suppose that Clare was first and foremost opposed to
metropolitan influence, urban values, or urbane statesmen is
to skate past the real object of his attack: the acquisitive values and
self-interested men he saw everywhere around him. His anger is not
directed, as Cowper's, Wordsworth's, and Cobbett's often was,
against "the Wen," "the monstrous heap," the "proud and gain-
devoted cities." For the improving farmers spurred on by "gain's
rude rage," the "petty gentry," and the landlords of "accursed
wealth" whom Clare challenges in his earliest poems do not live in
the cities; they live in the rural world, in the same locality as those
they exploit and oppress. Few poets have been so entirely devoted
as Clare to writing about country life and scenery, and few have
written so exhaustively and so fondly about the locality in which
they lived. But we should be wary of equating Clare's interest in
country life and in local customs and topography with an unex-
amined loyalty to all countrymen or to all members of his locality.
Clare had little reason to believe that the rural community in gen-

eral or his local community in particular existed as discrete social units on whose behalf he could challenge the policy-makers of the nation. He could find no set of common interests and grievances and aspirations that would allow him to speak for all members of these communities. At best, he could speak for a certain kind of countrymen, a certain class of Helpstonians, and to do so he had necessarily to speak out against other countrymen. Since it was his neighbours who initiated the process of enclosure and profited from the exploitation of the labouring poor, Clare had no reason to believe that rural or local loyalties softened the drama of contending classes which set countrymen against countrymen.

Although a vocabulary of political debate and denunciation figures in many of his protest poems – most notably in the enclosure elegies – it would be difficult if not impossible to claim that Clare intended to serve the cause of political radicalism: he was distrustful of and almost entirely disengaged from most forms of political dissent. Indeed, though the evidence is scattered and rare, he appears to have been willing, on at least a few occasions, to express an attitude not only of indifference to political radicalism but of outright condemnation. Far from endorsing an organized challenge to political authority, he appears to have associated such a challenge with the mutinous conspiracies of unprincipled men, and to have considered the arguments of political radicalism unworthy of serious consideration. "I have not read Tom Paine," he commented, "but I have always understood him to be a low blackguard" (*Prose*, 140). He thought that radicals were often both dangerous and despicable: "O'er-bearing fools," hypocrites, dispensers of cant, and "cunning knaves" who "bawl freedom loud and then oppress the free."[6] When questioned about his political views he was eager to give the right answers: "I am," he wrote, "as far as my politics reaches 'King & Country' / no Inovations on Religion & Government say I" (*Letters*, 72).

This was the right answer because the man who asked the question was Lord Radstock. And though Radstock was, to be sure, one of Clare's kindest and most loyal patrons, he was also a former admiral in the British navy, and appears to have had an obsessive interest in ensuring that the working-class poet he patronized expressed the quiescence, deference, and sense of unquestioning duty suitable to his humble station in English society. Unless we understand the real and oppressive power which a man like Radstock exerted over his protégé, and the particular contexts in which Clare's anti-radical sentiments were expressed, we shall be in danger of giving much more weight to these sentiments that they deserve. We must recognize that the main reason why Clare never read Paine is that he depended upon his patrons to furnish him with books, and their generosity did not extend to sending him any of Paine's writings. The books Radstock gave to him were for the most part written by such pious apologists for religious orthodoxy and political authority as William Paley, Hannah More, Hugh Blair, and Owen Feltham. [7] Naturally enough the bishops were well represented in Radstock's reading-list: Burnet, Wilson, and, of course, Watson with his famous answer to Paine. Clare was expected not only to read these authors but to accept their views. Any deviation from the correct line earned him the ominous "hints" and "cautions" which Radstock felt duty-bound to make.

Clare's letters to John Taylor reveal that he was appalled by the self-serving demands his patrons made upon him and was most reluctant to delete from his poetry the various passages of "radical slang" that Radstock found so objectionable. But Clare also knew that failure to meet these demands could cost him the support of his most active and influential patron. Especially in the crucial early years of his publishing career, this was support he could not afford to lose. And so, when Radstock demanded proofs of his good views and proper opinions, Clare said what he was expected to say. The following lines, taken from his "Labourers Hymn," indicate that our poet was even willing to rehearse the most defensive, counter-revolutionary, anti-Jacobin rhetoric:

Ye Peasantry of England support your hardy name
Nor leagued with cunning knaves grow infamous in fame
...
Hail ye no tempting symbols by tyrant hand unfurled
Who while they rave for liberty forge chains for all the world
Your own king is our sailor – then muster at the helm
& stand against all wrongs that all rights would overwhelm
...
For the king he is our sailor & the lion is our sign
& we'll ne'er disgrace our colours in a mutiny to form. [8]

Yet while his "Labourers Hymn" would certainly appear to be proof that no mutinous qualities lurked in Clare's character, it is precisely the naval imagery of his lines, with their reference to mutiny and pirate-attack, captains and helms, which raises one's suspicions about the attitudes expressed therein. Nowhere else in his letters or prose or poetry do we find Clare (who never in his life saw the sea) drawing upon the figure of the ship of state, and nowhere else did he employ naval or marine imagery. The imagery of the hymn is, indeed, so uncharacteristic of Clare that one is, I think, justified in suspecting that it was written primarily to please Radstock. It is a badly written piece, certainly no credit to Clare, but it would have been gratifying to a retired admiral of the British navy.

But though we should approach Clare's endorsements of the *status quo* ("no Inovations say I") with considerable scepticism, there can be no doubt that his distrust of political agitation and fear of the violence it might unleash were genuine enough. It was not Lord Radstock's hints and warnings but his own judgment and experience that prompted Clare to observe that "people with little reflection look upon no remedy better than force" and "with the mob freedom and plunder are synonomous" (*Prose*, 225-6). This reflective, peaceful, physically delicate man was frightened by violently radical talk and deeds. But he was no less frightened by extreme repressive actions. He knew that violence was just as likely to force its way down, as it were, from the top, as it was to burst upward from the discontented bottom ranks of society: the xenophobic panic engendered by Queen Caroline's trial and the anti-Gallican hysteria which swept through his locality in the second decade of the century gave him that knowledge.[9] But Clare was not only a witness to these forms of counter-revolutionary violence; wherever he turned, he saw evidence of the social violence which the landowning classes perpetrated against the labouring poor through poor laws, enclosures, rack-renting and rate-fixing. In *The Parish* and the enclosure elegies Clare was to write angrily against all these. Yet, in spite of his anger, he did not believe that this social violence either justified or could be redressed by violent political agitation. He was appalled by a society in which, as he was to say, "the prosperity of one class was founded on the adversity & distress of the other" (*TP*, 27). And he was to write of enclosure as a critical historical moment in which the individual had necessarily to take sides not only *with* but also *against* other men. But he appears to have drawn back from the revolutionary implications of this recognized social division.

He was frightened by any form of political activity which seemed to feed, and feed upon, the extreme polarizing drift of English political life. He believed that reform was needed, and well understood that there were extremists on both sides. But he blamed certain reformist initiatives for the worst polarizing tendencies of the early 1830s. It was, in fact, because of the extremely partisan spirit of Cobbett's writings, and because this great polemicist insisted upon the necessarily conflictual aspects of English political life, that Clare (who was a great admirer of his grammar-books) was so suspicious of Cobbett's political principles. "I look upon Cobbett," Clare wrote,

as one of the most powerful prose writers of the day - with no principles to make those powers commendable to honest praise - the Letters to farmers contain some very sensible arguments & some things that appeared to be too much of party colouring - there is no medicine in party matters / where there is excess it is always on one side - & that is the worst of it - I am no politician but I think a reform is wanted - not the reform of the mob were the bettering of many is only an apology for improving the few - nor the reform of partys where the benefit of one is the destruction of the other but a reform that would do good & hurt none / I am sorry to see that the wild notions of public spouters always keep this reform out of sight - & as extreams must be met by extreams - the good is always lost like a plentiful harvest in bad weather.

(*Prose*, 221-2)

Clare's desire for "a reform that would do good & hurt none" was based not only upon his longing for a political *via media* in which the ideas of the reflective progressive could be heard above "the wild notions of public spouters." It was also based upon his longing for a reform that would benefit the impoverished rural wage-earners who made up the constituency of his protest. This was the "plentiful harvest" he wanted to reap from the "bad weather" he saw ahead. But Clare had good reason to be less than sanguine about ever seeing that longing realized by parliamentary reform. In 1830 he wrote to his friend George Darley:

How the times have altered the opinions & views of the people / even here we have our villages mustering into parliaments & our farmers puffing themselves up into orators & there is scarcely a clown in the village but what has the assumption to act the politician & I hope this general stir may produce general good / but the farce of the thing is that our tory folks should be grown into radicals & be brawling after the reform which they alone have so long & so obstinately prevented - what is the reason - it is a known fact in natural history that foxes will do all they can to drive badgers out of their holes - that they may get in themselves.

(*Letters*, 244)

This passage allows us to understand one or two important aspects of Clare's relations both to the political agitations of the pre-Reform period and to political activity in general. There is, one feels, something a little too snobbish and aloof about Clare's disdain for the puffing farmers and oratorical clowns, and his references to the "general stir" and the "farce of the thing" suggests that we are dealing with a man who was never really comfortable with the brawling spirit of his time.[10] But there is also some evidence here that Clare was not lacking in political astuteness: the foxes and badgers might struggle and turn, but what had this to do with the beleaguered rural wage-labourers? "I fear all this bother about country-meetings & other rigmarole pretentions will not better them," Clare wrote in another letter of 1830,

tho there are many voices mixed up in the cry – common sense is seldom among them for self interests & individual prosperitys are the universal spirits that stir up these assemblages of reformers – the Farmer is on the look out for 'high prices & 'better markets' as he stiles them tho these markets are always curses to the cottager & the poor man – the Parson is now rather stirring into radicalism for a partial reduction of individual taxes merely because he sees something must be done & as he wishes to keep his tythes & his livings untouched he throws the burden on government / The Speculator – he is looking up to a paper currency which placed a false value on his bargains & thereby enabled the cunning to cheat the honest & the unprincipled to ruin those who had a principle / for so long as county banks are alowd to accumulate their three farthing bits of paper on the public as money without any other check than a trust on their honesty so long will a few build their prosperity on the ruin of thousands. (*Letters*, 242)

"A few build their prosperity on the ruin of thousands": the observation is characteristic of Clare, and it is just this kind of observation that reveals how clearly he saw through the conservative myth that English society was predicated upon a natural order. For Clare, there was nothing natural, nothing defensible, about a society in which the wealth and privileges of "a few" were based upon the exploitation of "thousands." Though he was frightened by the spectacle of men leaguing together to defend their political principles and self-interest, and though he was even more frightened by the violence that political confrontation could unleash, he did not often shirk the responsibilities of his own insight. He recognized and wrote against the unbreachable gap between "the few" and "the thousands," a gap so overwhelming that the argument between foxes and badgers, parliamentary reformers and the opponents of reform, seemed in comparison nothing more than a minor dispute.

But because he was so fearful of revolutionary and counter-revolutionary violence, and so distrustful of the whole machinery of parliamentary reform and political agitation, Clare did not leap from recognizing the harsh conditions of class conflict to advocating the harsher conditions of class struggle: "I am so little a politician that I would rather keep out of the crowd then that my hobnails should trample on the gouty toes of any one" (*SPP*, 173). This is Clare in his "Letter from a poor man," summing up his position precisely: refraining from political affiliation with "the crowd," refusing to be drawn into class struggle, but nonetheless making clear, through his signature and his metonymic hobnails, that if he was forced into the struggle he knew for whom and against whom he would fight. There is in the image of hobnails trampling on gouty toes a note of class-malice and comic violence that might lead one to suspect that, had Clare ever been drawn into organized radical agitation, he would have been ruthlessly effective. But he was not drawn in, and there is another much less combative tone in his social criticism which is more characteristic than the sound of trampling hobnails. We can catch this other tone exactly, in these brief lines:

> any wrong
> Some sort of right may seek
> And I am glad if een a song
> Gives me the room to speak   (*JCOA*, 148)

This is dissidence, but it is the modest, almost sweet-tempered dissidence of a poet who, while not wishing to alarm his genteel readers, wanted them to see the problems he saw, answer the plain questions he raised, and redress the wrongs he described. This is the voice of a man who pleaded for justice more often than he demanded it, who did not know precisely how injustice could be redressed, but knew that "some sort of right" must be obtained. Clare believed that the "oppression almost amounting to slavery" in which his class lived would feel lighter if there were "not so many idly looking on who have no burthens to suffer" (*Letters*, 243). He argued that "a universal reduction of tythes, clerical livings, placemens pensions & taxes ... is the only way to bring salvation to the country." "But," he added, "I am no leveller for I want not a farthing of any one's property." He would not commit himself to political radicalism, but by writing about his own social experience he was, nonetheless, contributing to the tradition of dissent.

THE POOR MAN'S PERSPECTIVE

Clare himself must have believed that there was an epitomizing significance to his life for before he turned thirty he worked on two separate autobiographies, the *Sketches in the Life of John Clare*, written and sent off to his publisher in 1821, and the unfinished *Autobiography*, probably written between 1824 and 1826. A good part of the story told in these two autobiographical pieces centres upon the experiences of a young man who was constantly plagued with financial worries and whose standard of living was determined and controlled by his landlord, his employers, and his parish officers. This part of Clare's story is also the story of his family and of the many difficulties that overcame them: few of the pertinent details of their hardship and privation are withheld. Yet the *Autobiography* is not a tragic document since these sad details are almost always presented with a curious impassivity, almost as though in writing about his difficult early years Clare was editing his narrative as he wrote it, testing his ability to tell his tale without arousing his readers' pity or his own anger. The poet's youthful aspiration, his early delight in nature and in poetry, the expense of hope which his parents invested in him, and the buoyancy of spirit with which they met their problems are emphasized in the work, and this emphasis is in keeping with the general purpose of the *Autobiography*, which was to tell the story of the making of a poet. It was meant to be a success story in which all that was most positive and enabling in Clare's early experience could be applauded and explored. The distressing events, the disabling circumstances, are not excluded but their emotional significance is rarely explored. Clare's tendency to offer the harder facts but then to abstain from commenting upon them with anger or bitterness is nowhere more apparent than in the brief description he gives of the family cottage and the cottage's landlord:

[Our cottage] was as roomy & comfortable as any of our neighbours & we had it for forty shillings while an old apple tree in the garden generally made the rent / the garden was large for a poor man & my father managed to dig it night & morning before the hours of labour & lost no time / He then did well but the young farmer that succeeded our old landlord raised the rent & the next year made four tenements of the house leaving

us a corner of one room on a floor for three guineas a year & a little slip of
the garden which was divided into four parts   (*Prose*, 12)

There is some leaven of humanity in the story as Clare explains: "as
my father had been an old tenant he gave him the choice of his
share & he retained our old apple tree Tho the ground was good
for nothing yet the tree still befriended us & made shift to make up
the greater part of our rent" (*Prose*, 12).

The event must have been disruptive for the child and his family, and later it was to have an emblematic significance for the
poet. But what is remarkable is Clare's fatalistic attitude to
the event, his apparent refusal to enquire too closely into the cause
or the effect of this particular deprivation. The landlord decides to
raise the rent; the family is deprived of three-quarters of their original living-space; and that is that. This is the voice of a man who
was resigned not only to poverty but to increasing poverty, to having little and ending with less: "In cases of extreeme poverty my
father took me to labour with him and made me a light flail for
threshing, learing me betimes the hardship which adam and Eve
inflicted on their children by their inexperienced misdeeds, ... I
resignd myself willingly to the hardest toils and tho one of the
weakest was stubbor[n] and stomachful and never flinched from
the roughest labour" (*JCAW*, 3).

And yet in another chapter of Clare's story we are told that he
had learned at an early age to cut his stoicism with a very different
attitude. He wished his readers to observe his unquestioning acceptance of his lot in life. But he also wished them to know that he was
quite capable of twisting and breaking the rules. When he was still
rather young, Clare explains, he was sent to work at Burghley Park
under the gardeners of the marquis of Exeter. There, in an aristocrat's park, as he worked for desperately low wages at tasks too
heavy for his delicate frame and too repetitive for his active mind,
he happened to see another boy, the future marquis of Exeter, "in
his jean jerkin and trousers shooting in the Park or fishing in the
river" (*Prose*, 27). Adam's sins were paid for apparently by only
some of his children, but Clare forbears to comment upon this
most telling contrast between his childhood experience and that of
a young aristocrat. Burghley Park appears to have been a wretched
place to work, for during the day the workers were confined in the
gardens, and at night they were locked up in the garden-house so
that they would not rob the very fruit-trees which they had pruned
or cultivated. Here Clare picked up the drinking habits which were
later to earn him so many lectures from his evangelical patrons who

feared that he resembled Burns in more ways than just his humble birth. Clare tells us that he was often persuaded to join his older companions who would escape over the high walls of the park to rendez-vous at a public house. He learned from this experience that "confinement sweetens liberty" and that strong ale made life a little easier to bear. But this is the closest he comes to revealing his own attitude to the wretched conditions of his employment. The episode at Burghley Park is told with the clean edges of a parable: two boys in a park, but a world separates them; the labourers locked up, let out only to do their work, but finding solidarity in escaping their masters.

Physical labour was never easy or pleasant for this delicate and rather dreamy youth. If he was "stubborn and stomachful" in his work it was because he had to be if he was to get and to keep his employments. And because his father was disabled and so unable to earn more than five shillings by working on the roads, Clare's wages were essential to the maintenance of the family. In 1817, when their valuable apple tree stopped bearing fruit, the family was deprived of the one resource which previously had enabled them to pay their rent. The family income was not suffi-cient to keep them, and so, with his father about to fall upon parish relief, Clare left Helpston to work at the lime-kilns in Casterton. The wages were better there, and Clare hoped that he might make enough to keep his parents from the ignominy of hav-ing to enter a parish house. But it was hard for him to leave his father at this time, when, as Clare wrote, "every misfortune as it were came upon him to crush him at once" (*Prose*, 66). The condi-tions of his work at Casterton were not easy, and his living-quarters were appalling. There he had no place and little time to write poetry, since he had to work "from light to dark (& in some emer-gencys all night) to get some money" (*Prose*, 54). When his employer offered him a position as his gardener, Clare left the lime-kiln to work for a season in the gardens. By this time he had grown fond of the place and its wild "fields & solitudes." But there was little reason to be away from his family when his employer chose to reduce his wages to what he could earn in Helpston (from nine to seven shillings), and so he left Casterton and returned home. In writing of this, Clare registers no protest against what must have seemed from his point of view to be the arbitrary logic of the market. In outlining the financial embarrassments of that difficult year he seems less anxious to arouse his reader's sympathy than to emphasize the fact that he managed to survive: "I was never utterly cast down / in adversity I struggled on." It is only when he recollects his feelings about the humiliations that his father had to endure at that time, that Clare contradicts himself and speaks, with a bitter edge in his voice, about his desperation:

as soon as he went to the parish for relief they came to clap the town brand on his goods & set them down in their parish books because he should not sell or get out of them / I felt utterly cast down for I coud not help them sufficient to keep them from the parish / so I left the town & got work at Casterton ... I felt some consolation in solitude for my distress letting loose my revenge on the unfeeling town officer in a satire on the 'Parish' which I forebore to publish afterwards.   (*Prose*, 67)

But long before Clare began work on *The Parish*, long before he had any reason to hope that he would some day see his poetry in print, he was writing with tangible bitterness and anger about the desperate conditions of his life as a common labourer:

O winter, what a deadly foe
Art thou unto the mean and low!
What thousands now half pin'd and bare
Are forced to stand thy piercing air
All day, near numbed to death wi' cold
Some petty gentry to uphold
Paltry proudlings hard as thee,
Dead to all humanity.   (*I*, 19)

This is Clare in his "Impromptu on Winter." Written in 1809, the poem begins as the lachrymose complaint of a labouring man against the cold of the winter in which he must work, but then rather abruptly settles into an attack upon the men for whom he works: it is not the "cutting winds" or the numbing cold which are to blame for the conditions of this labourer's life, but rather a social class which repays his labour with poverty and "killing scorn." The immediacy of its accusation makes this an interesting and revealing poem. The language which carries the accusation is both evocative and precise. In the fourth line "forced" conveys the necessity of the labourer's work, and in the sixth "uphold" is acutely sensitive to the economic sources of the gentry's social power. The structure of the poem is no less remonstrative than its language, for, while the poet begins the "Impromptu" by rejecting the idea that it is the cold of winter which is his "deadly foe," he then curves back to the elements so that his constant poverty is set against the liberality of the changing seasons. In the sphere of nature the arrival of spring represents hope and renewal, and the arrival of fall promises generous fulfilment and reward. But in the sphere of working-class life, hope and fulfilment never arrive. For the man who works to support a social order that is "dead to all humanity," every season is like winter:

> But why need I the winter blame?
> To me all seasons come the same:
> Now winter bares each field and tree
> She finds that trouble sav'd in me
> Stript already, penniless,
> Nothing boasting but distress;
> And when spring chill'd nature cheers,
> Still my old complaint she hears;
> Summer too, in plenty blest,
> Finds me poor and still distrest;
> Kind autumn too, so liberal and free,
> Brings my old well-known present, Poverty.   (*I*, 19)

In the same year in which he wrote the "Impromptu" Clare began "Helpstone," a poem which also blames men of property for victimizing labouring men, but which does so somewhat less directly. Clare's accusation carries less force in this poem, in part because he describes himself as a man who is willing to "put up with distress and be content," in part because he is less precise about locating the cause of his distress: the "petty gentry" of the "Impromptu" have been replaced as targets by the much less specific abstraction of "Accursed Wealth." He has borrowed Goldsmith's evasive explanation for the decay of the English peasantry, and by doing so has grown more distant from the felt conditions of his life. But in spite of the borrowings and the evasions the accusatory tone is fierce enough in these lines, and specially so in the second couplet which yokes together the antagonistic "me" of one class with the silent "thee" of another:

> Accursed wealth o'er bounding human laws
> Of every evil thou remainst the cause
> Victims of want those wretches such as me
> Too truly lay their wretchedness to thee
> Thou art the bar that keeps from being fed
> And thine our loss of labour and of bread
> Thou art the cause that levels every tree
> And woods bow down to clear a way for thee   (*JCOA*, 4)

But angry accusations are not all that one hears in Clare's poverty poems. There are also whines and signs and tearful references to the way poverty has affected his sensitive poetic spirit. One is remined, hearing this tone, of what Keats once wrote about Burns: "how sad it is when a luxurious imagination is obliged, in self-defence, to deaden its delicacy in vulgarity, and riot in thing[s] attainable, that it may not have leisure to go mad after thing[s] which are not."[11] Unfortunately, there are sadder things to observe about this sad theme as it is treated in Clare's early work. In listening to some of Clare's pitiful laments, one is also reminded of why Keats despised a poetry that has a palpable design upon its reader.[12] One cannot help but stir uncomfortably reading such lines as these, for their author is trying so obviously and so literally to put his hand in his reader's pocket:

> poor, shatter'd poverty,
> To advantage seen in me,
> With his rags, his wants, and pain,
> Waking pity but in vain,
> Bowing, cringing at thy side,
> Begs his mite, and is denied,
> ...
>
> Fortune! smile, now winter frowns:
> Cast around a pitying eye;
> Feed the hungry, ere they die,
> Think, oh! think upon the poor,
> Nor against them shut thy door;
> Freely let thy bounty flow
> On the sons of want and woe.
> ...
>
> 'Tis not great, what I solicit;
> Was it more, thou couldst not miss it:
> Now the cutting winter's come,
> 'Tis but just to find a home,
> In some shelter, dry and warm,
> That will shield me from the storm.
> ...
>
> And, to be possess'd of all,
> A corner cupboard in the wall,
> With store of victuals lin'd complete,
> That when hungry I might eat.   (I, 47)

This is the "Address to Plenty" in which Clare's intention was, presumably, to embarrass the genteel readers of his period out of their indifference and moral complacency. To the modern reader the poem may seem embarrassing for reasons Clare did not intend, but it is interesting because it gives us some sense of the extreme and various nature of his responses to poverty. Here we find no hint of the accusatory tone which characterizes the "Impromptu" or "Helpstone" (written eight years earlier). Here the demand for social justice is replaced by a pathetic appeal to charity; and like all appeals to the benevolence of a master class, this one implies the recreant and the bended knee: it fails to present any clear challenge to the structure of inequality or to those who flourish within it. But though the putative audience of the "Address" is not called to account for creating or benefiting from the poverty of others, there is a sense in which the pathetically anxious tone of the poem and the most basic human needs for which it begs – warmth, shelter, food, clothing – reflect much more severely upon that audience than the author.

If we compare the "Address to Plenty" with a much better poem written a year later, during Clare's period at Casterton, we find yet another variation in his treatment of the theme of poverty. In his "Elegy on the Ruins of Pickworth," Clare's disconcerting whine has vanished but so has his disconcerting anger. He has not yet settled into the impassive voice of resignation which characterizes the *Autobiography*. He does not turn away from the social implications of his own insight and experience, and his observations carry a cargo of "ungrateful sentiment." But the challenge to social inequality carried with that cargo is more muted than it was in the "Impromptu." For the central idea of the poem, the ostensible point towards which its social observation tends, rests in the affirming *consolatio* of traditional elegy: death takes the mighty and the lowly, and in death we are all equal. The structure of Clare's elegy enacts the movement of the poet's mind as he moves from observing the ruined habitations of the wealthy and the poor which mark the site of a deserted village, to imagining the social inequalities sustained in the village when it was filled with living men, then to pondering the levelling force of time and death, and finally to finding in this force ("that common lot") a consolation for the social inequalities of the past and the present:

These buried ruins, now in dust forgot,
    These heaps of stone the only remnants seen, –
'The Old Foundations' still they call the spot,
    Which plainly tells inquiry what has been –

A time was once, though now the nettle grows
    In triumph o'er each heap that swells the ground,
When they, in buildings pil'd, a village rose,
    With here a cot, and there a garden crown'd.

And here while grandeur, with unequal share,
    Perhaps maintain'd its idleness and pride,
Industry's cottage rose contented there,
    With scarce so much as wants of life supplied.
...

While vain extravagance, for one alone,
    Claims half the land his grandeur to maintain,
What thousands, not a rood to call their own,
    Like me but labour for support in vain!

Here we see luxury surfeit with excess;
    There want, bewailing, beg from door to door,
Still meeting sorrow where he meets success,
    By lengthening life that liv'd in vain before.   (*I*, 53)

The significance of the ruins to the poet's personal situation is
established when Clare speaks of himself as one of the thousands
who "labour for support in vain" beside the grating evidence of the
master class's ostentatious extravagance. But other details and
phrases also betray the poet's situation. The very title of the poem
in its manuscript version – "Elegy on the Ruins of Pickworth, Rut-
landshire, Hastily composed, and written with a Pencil on the
Spot" – reminds us that it was written during the time when Clare
was working at the lime-kilns of Casterton (close by the site of the
Pickworth ruins). One critic has suggested that this title places
the poem "in the topographical mode by implying that the author
is in transit, that this ruin is just another sought out for comparison
by a picturesque tourist, another Dyer with his sketch-book,
another Gray with his Claude glass, another Gilpin with his *camera
obscura*."[13] There are certainly topographical elements in this
poem, but Clare's attitude to the Pickworth ruins can hardly be
equated with that of a gentleman-traveller to the pleasing prospects he has decided to take in this season. On the contrary, Clare's
was the attitude of a thinking man towards the place in which he
had to work "from light to dark (and in some emergencys all night)
to get some money." If his poem was "Hastily composed, and written with a Pencil on the Spot," it was not because Clare was eager
to move on to still more sights on the picturesque circuit, but
because he had to get back to work. His poverty, the conditions of

his employment, the place where he worked, and the thoughts which arose while he worked formed a unity in Clare's mind. And it is this unity of experience and response which is recorded in his poem. When the poet stands before the ruins of Pickworth, imagining where the old habitation might have stood, his experience and expectations as a labouring man affect the very content of his imaginings:

> The ale-house here might stand, each hamlet's boast;
>   And here, where elder rich from ruin grows,
> The tempting sign – but what was once is lost;
>   Who would be proud of what this world bestows?
>
> How contemplation mourns their lost decay,
>   To view their pride laid level with the ground;
> To see, where labour clears the soil away,
>   What fragments of mortality abound.
>
> There's not a rood of land demands our toil,
>   There's not a foot of ground we daily tread,
> But gains increase from time's devouring spoil,
>   But holds some fragment of the human dead.
>
> The very food, which for support we crave,
>   Claims for its share an equal portion too;
> The dust of many a long-forgotten grave
>   Serves to manure the soil from whence it grew.   (I, 54)

This last line carries a knowledge of the land that we may find in the eighteenth-century georgic but are unused to meeting in nineteenth-century meditative-descriptive verse, and its deliberate and obtrusive vulgarity carries us back to an earlier coarseness that we may have missed: in the image of the past which the poet creates, he includes an ale-house with its "tempting sign" – but tempting, we may suppose, for only a certain class of men.

While Clare's social identity organizes his social and topographical observations, it also has an unsettling and subversive effect upon his elegiac meditations. His social observation is so sharply registered that when he attempts to connect philosophically social injustice and death by implying that both are natural and inevitable products of a "mysterious cause," his attempts ring hollow. He rehearses a received wisdom inadequate to explain or justify the extremes of poverty and wealth he sees before him:

Mysterious cause! still more mysterious plann'd
  (Although undoubtedly the will of heaven):
To think what careless and unequal hand
  Metes out each portion that to man is given ...

Almighty Power! – but why do I repine,
  Or vainly live thy goodness to distrust?
Since reason rules each provident design,
  Whatever is must certainly be just.   (*I*, 53)

It is impossible not to feel the irony in Clare's religiose acceptance
of the "will of heaven" and in his allusion to the central lesson of
An Essay on Man. But the irony remains undeveloped, and I doubt
that Clare set out to parody the Tory optimism of Pope or intended
to subvert his own elegiac meditation. On the contrary, I suspect
that he rehearsed Pope's philosophical belief for the same reason
he assumed the posture of the elegist: he hoped to find the poise
that would allow him to make moral and intellectual sense of social
injustice. But his personal knowledge of injustice undercut his
intentions. The idea that death is the common lot of humanity was
not sufficient consolation for the inequities in life, and while Pope
could find his reasons for trusting in "provident design," Clare
could only find reasons for distrusting it.

The ironies of the Pickworth Elegy, the cringing entreaties of
"The Address to Plenty," the detailed yet impassively recorded epi-
sodes in the *Autobiography*, the harsh and direct accusations in
the "Impromptu" and in "Helpstone": when we bring together
these works which deal with the issue of poverty we are confronted
with contradictions in tone, emphasis, and understanding. Above
all, we notice the tone as it wavers between anger, resignation, bitterness, and self-pity, almost as though Clare was playing with different points of view, trying to make up his mind about whether to
lament, protest, or accept his poverty. And in his indecisiveness,
his tendency to offer a radical insight in one line, but then in the
next line to succumb to a conservative myth of society, the young
Clare is very similar to the young poet of *The Village*. Like Crabbe,
Clare saw himself as Goldsmith's heir-apparent. Indeed, Clare
believed that he was at least in one respect better qualified than
either Goldsmith or Crabbe to contribute to the tradition of pastoral dissent. For he was willing to take Crabbe's claim – to "paint
the Cot, / As Truth will paint it, and as Bards will not" – into the
circle of his own experience;[14] in all the texts we have been examin-
ing, it is not only the truth about poverty but *his* truth he wants to

tell. For Crabbe the fact that he had himself experienced the conditions of the rural labouring poor seemed to complicate his act of protest. It is moral outrage which organizes the feeling and the observation in *The Village*, but Crabbe could allow his moral outrage to emerge only by dissociating himself from the miseries which "Labour's fair child" endured. He will not speak for himself, only for others, and so we find him suppressing his personal knowledge of the victimized labourers he describes, and trying desperately to keep himself out of his own poem. The only information he offers about his relationship to the impoverished village is that he was fortunate enough to escape from it. Clare was not so fortunate: he did not wish to escape from his native village but he did long to escape from poverty, and this he never managed. While Crabbe moved onward and upward, Clare stayed behind to deal not only with the experience of poverty but with the problem of how to write about it.

This complicated problem was complicated even more in 1817. For while 1817 was the most economically desperate year of Clare's life, it was also the year in which his fortune changed. It was while he was at Casterton working to keep his parents from parish relief that a plan was put forward to have his poems printed, and shortly after he was introduced by Edward Drury, a Stamford bookseller, to the man who was to be his publisher. In 1818 John Taylor agreed to bring out Clare's first collection of poems, and for the first time Clare began to see himself as a man with prospects. He began as well to think of himself, not as a rural labourer who wrote verses, but as a poet; and these new elements in his identity influenced his treatment of the theme we have been tracing. Between 1817 and 1821, in the first flush of his expectations and early success, Clare had some reason to believe that his poetry would provide him with an independent income and that he would never again have to live in poverty. He was encouraged in this belief by his patroness, Mrs Eliza Emmerson, though as the following letter would suggest this lady was less interested in Clare's independence than in the gratitude she expected him to feel for the various marquises and earls and lords of the Admiralty who had contributed to his annuity fund: "Your extraordinary patronage, will I hope remove from your mind those prejudices against the Great! - which your humble station had made you *too keenly* feel: you are now my friend - convinced that Greatness - goodness - kind heartedness and benevolence! dwell pre-eminent in the bosoms of the Rich and Great."[15] The rich and the great would not have missed the five, ten, fifteen-pound sums they settled on Clare for life. Perhaps

Clare knew this, and for this reason was never as convinced as Mrs Emmerson that goodness, kind-heartedness, or benevolence were the defining qualities of the English aristocracy. But there can be no doubt that the annuity of almost forty pounds which was given to Clare at first must have seemed to him a princely sum: with this and with the income from the sales of his books he would be able to work at his poetry in peace of mind, and leave the lime-kilns and threshing-barns for his neighbours. His expectations soon proved to be chimerical. In the early 1820s he was worrying again about how he would feed his family, and constantly comparing his situation with that of other poets: "Bloomfield had not a £100 a year to maintain 5 or 6 in the family," he noted in his journal, "why I have not £50 to maintain 8 with This is a hungry difference" (*Prose*, 126). And it was a hungry difference Clare was always to feel. For he never did receive income from the sales of his poetry, never could give up the hard necessary work in the fields and barns, and his annuity never did allow him enough funds to feel any financial security.

But perhaps some connection was severed in those brief early years of promise and change when Clare was encouraged to believe that if he was ever again to write upon this theme it would be through the pacifying structure of memory. His economic distress certainly continued to be a theme in his letters, and we know from them that he neither lost his sense of resentment nor succumbed to the blandishments of his patrons, who were forever telling him how grateful he should be. We know too that during the years (1820 to 1824) when he was working upon *The Parish*, he grew more, not less, willing to argue that the prosperity of one class was founded upon the distresses of another. But *The Parish* is almost the only poem of the 1820s which looks closely at the causes of poverty. Many of his vocational poems and enclosure elegies belong to the same period, and in these works Clare's own economic situation and that of his class are almost never singled out for special or detailed treatment. By the mid-1820s, when he was writing some of his best work, poverty had come to seem simply one in a long list of injustices he shared with his class. He continued to refer to the experience of poverty, but increasingly the references move to the background of his poems, becoming an aspect of their settings rather than a major theme, an element in Clare's point of view rather than the central object of his vision.

CHAPTER TWO

"Vile Invasions":
The Enclosure Elegies

In his excellent account of the enclosure of Clare's native village, John Barrell has concluded that there is simply not enough evidence to allow us to know for certain whether the landless labourers of Helpston became poorer as a consequence of the enclosure.[1] Of course, even if such evidence existed, we would have to be wary of assuming that we have in our grasp the real historical situation against which to verify the content of Clare's enclosure elegies. Not all of the elegies take Helpston for their setting, though there is definitely a local emphasis in several of them - most notably in "The Lamentations of Round-Oak Waters" and "The Lament of Swordy Well." But in writing even these most local poems, Clare may have been thinking not only of the rural labouring poor of Helpston, but of those in other villages, or in all the villages, which had undergone the same process. It may have been a wider scene and a more general reality - the alienation of a whole class and not merely the changes in one locality - that Clare was seeking to reflect.[2]

We should recognize too that the elegies do not focus upon the measurable economic effects of enclosure upon the rural labourers, but rather upon the losses they sustained in the immeasurable qualities of personal happiness, dignity, creativity, and freedom. Thus, knowing for certain whether or not the poor of Helpston really became poorer after the enclosure will not deepen our appreciation of the historical importance of the elegies. Such knowledge might, however, offer some explanation as to why Clare did not write more often and more specifically about the connection between enclosure and increasing economic deprivation. Barrell has raised the possibility that Clare did not write more fully about this connection because it did not exist to be written about.[3]

(Barrell suggests further that in the very few poems in which Clare in fact does imply that the rural labourer was impoverished by enclosure, he was merely following literary and political conventions.) But it is just as likely that such a connection between the enclosure of his village and the poverty of his peers did exist, and that Clare deliberately chose to ignore it because he did not want to threaten his most important argument against "curst improvement" in general and "vile enclosure" in particular: his belief that they had to be resisted because they created a dispensation in which economic values were allowed to prevail over all others. Had he conveyed the impression that he opposed enclosure primarily because it made his class poorer, he would have put in jeopardy the critical integrity of his whole case against the extreme economism of the enclosing class.

Clare's opposition to enclosure was most definitely a moral opposition. He invariably depicted the rural labouring poor as innocent victims – and innocent victims are usually justified in feeling morally superior to their victimizers. But the fact that his class had been victimized by (in Clare's characteristic terms) "spoilers," "destroyers," "philistines," and "knaves" explains only part of the reason he felt justified in taking a high moral tone in inveighing against improvers. In the first place, there was the question of their appalling motives. Though Clare was hesitant to focus upon the economic consequences of enclosure for his class, he was more than willing to pinpoint the economic motivations – in a word, the greed – of those who initiated and profited from the process. Any one of the elegies might serve to show that he saw enclosure as a manifestation of the acquisitive values of the master class, visible proof that the men who owned or managed the rural means of production wanted to

> glut their vile unsatiated maws
> And freedoms birthright from the weak devours   (*JCOA*, 98)

In the second place, there was the obvious evidence of the encloser's refusal to acknowledge any relationship between man and nature which was not predicated upon possession. To Clare, the inhumanity of the master class was nowhere more apparent than in the "lawless laws" it enacted to set its coercive and possessive rights to the land over what he deemed the more just and noble rights to access which the labourers had inherited as their birthright, earned through their work, and secured through their profound feelings of local attachment. This was not only a question of rights but of values, of whether the providential generosity of nature was to be used by the "thousands" or possessed by the "few"; and it was a question to which the encloser had given the wrong answer by claiming possession of the wastes and commons and ancient footpaths, areas which Clare felt no single person or group had a right to own:

> the rude philistines thrall
> Is laid upon them and destroyed them all
> Each little tyrant with his litte sign
> Shows where man claims earth glows no more divine   (*JCOA*, 169)

Finally, closely related to the sordid avarice of the encloser, but distinct from it, was his inability to recognize any reality which did not fit the shape of his own reductive, reified consciousness:

> Green paddocks have but little charms
> With gain the merchandise of farms
> And muse and marvel where we may
> Gain mars the landscape every day   (*JCOA*, 240)

Blind to the immense variety of interactions in which man with his capacity for aesthetic and spiritual experience could be involved, incapable of seeing the natural landscape as more than an economic resource to be possessed and exploited, the encloser had declared himself the enemy of everything in the realm of nature and society – ancient trees and ancient customs – which couldn't turn a profit:

> Inclosure like a Buonaparte let not a thing remain
> It levelled every bush and tree and levelled every hill   (*JCOA*, 260)

It should be clear from the lines I have quoted that invective figures significantly in everything Clare wrote about enclosure, and though I believe he wrote better poetry and ultimately better served the cause of dissent when he stopped inveighing against the values of the enclosing class and focused upon the kinds of human suffering it created, the invective is important for what it reveals of Clare's attitude towards that class: he may have feared its strategies, but he despised its morality. His sense of enclosure as a historical episode in which two sets of values clashed as violently as two classes of men gives to the elegies a radical significance which transcends the immediate object of their protest. But the specific effects of enclosure upon the well-being of his class remain very much at the centre of the poems and are in no sense obscured by Clare's more generalized pronouncements upon the morality of men "with plenty blest / So ankering after more" (*JCOA*, 23). Clare was particularly sensitive to the feelings of inefficacy and alienation suffered by the rural labourer when he lost his customary rights of access to the wastes and commons, and the most effective passages of the elegies are those in which he writes about such feelings and brings us close to the experience of people who must spend their lives working on the land but are made to feel that they do not belong in it save as the hired and managed labour of "them that own'd the field" (*JCOA*, 23). He believed that such an experience was akin to, perhaps even worse than, slavery. For whereas the man born into slavery had never known freedom nor possessed rights and customs to protect him from the cruelty of his masters, the labourer had known "freedom's birthright" and been forced to watch helplessly as it was taken from him:

> O England! boasted land of liberty,
> With strangers still thou mayst thy title own,
> But thy poor slaves the alteration see,
> With many a loss to them the truth is known:
> Like emigrating bird thy freedom's flown,
> While mongrel clowns, low as their rooting plough,
> Disdain thy laws to put in force their own;
> And every village owns its tyrants now,
> And parish-slaves must live as parish-kings allow.   (*I*, 157)

Labourers as slaves, enclosers as vile invaders, Napoleonic tyrants, imperial Turks: through this characteristic pattern of imagery Clare conveyed his belief that enclosure was a betrayal not only of his class, but of the character of the nation as a whole.[4]

"The Mores," written sometime in the early 1820s, provides an excellent example of the complexity and delicacy of Clare's understanding of what that betrayal involved. The poem is rich in the sort of natural observation for which Clare is famous: in painterly detail it describes the immense proportions and sweeping contours of the unenclosed landscape, and special attention is paid to the rich colours of the wild scenery – white daisies, yellow cowslips, red fallow fields, blue mists, and "uncheckt shadows of green, brown and grey." Yet these details, beautiful as they are, are in a sense only manifestations of what Clare found most beautiful about the unenclosed moor: nobody had claimed it for personal profit. This landscape, whose beauty had depended upon its "unbounded freedom," is then specifically related to the experience of the labourer before enclosure, and each descriptive detail presses the reader to infer that a landscape free of the "fence of ownership" was at once the cause and the sign of the labourer's sense of freedom:

> Unbounded freedom ruled the wandering scene
> Nor fence of ownership crept in between
> To hide the prospect of the following eye
> Its only bondage was the circling sky ...
> Cows went and came with evening morn and night
> To the wild pasture as their common right
> And sheep unfolded with the rising sun
> Heard the swains shout and felt their freedom won
> Tracked the red fallow field and heath and plain
> Then met the brook and drank and roamed again
> The brook that dribbled on as clear as glass
> Beneath the roots they hid among the grass
> While the glad shepherd traced their tracks along
> Free as the lark and happy as her song   (*JCOA*, 167-8)

The central argument of the poem is conveyed through the deliberate confounding of topographical and emotional realities: what was seen is what was felt. As long as part of the landscape remained free of the "hated sign" of the private owner Clare was able to feel that the power of the master class was not ubiquitous, and to feel this was to live without fear and with a sense of efficacy and belonging, spontaneity and hope. But once the grid of private ownership was everywhere imposed, these positive convictions could no longer be held.

>   a hope that blossomed free
> And hath been once no more shall ever be
> Inclosure came and trampled on the grave
> Of labours rights and left the poor a slave
> And memorys pride ere want to wealth did bow
> Is both the shadow and the substance now ...
> Moors loosing from the sight far smooth and blea
> Where swopt the plover in its pleasure free
> Are vanished now with commons wild and gay
> As poets visions of lifes early day ...
> And sky bound mores in mangled garbs are left
> Like mighty giants of their limbs bereft

Fence now meets fence in owners little bounds
Of field and meadow large as garden grounds
In little parcels little minds to please
With men and flocks imprisoned ill at ease   (*JCOA*, 168)

The phrase "ill at ease" may seem rather anticlimactic after the rhetorical force of the word "imprisoned," but this mixture of harsh, polemical words and terms sensitive to small and subtle ranges of feeling is characteristic of Clare and well suited to convey the quality of his insight into the meaning of freedom. For him freedom was both a reality and a "sweet vision" of human potentialities not yet realized, a "substance" based upon the historical rights of the labourer and a "shadow" in which the labourer could hope for new and better possibilities for himself. It was the substance which protected him from utter destitution, but it was the shadow that allowed him to feel like a free man in a free country.

Whether Clare wrote of life before enclosure or after, a social order and the labourer's experience within that order were always implicated in the landscapes he described. "The Mores" offers a clear example of the interconnectedness of Clare's topographical and social concerns; but this is a constant and obvious feature of all the elegies – indeed, to my mind, so constant and so obvious a feature that I find myself in sharp disagreement with critics who have implied that Clare's anxiety about what enclosure was doing to his local landscape far outweighed and even conflicted with his solicitude for what was being done to the labourer. As examples of this tendency, I can cite: Joanna Rapf who has suggested that Clare resisted enclosure for aesthetic rather than social reasons;[5] Kenneth MacLean who has claimed that in writing so often about the way enclosure changed the landscape, Clare chose "to mourn the plumage and forget the dying bird";[6] and, at a more extended level of argument, John Barrell, who has praised the loco-descriptive aspects of the elegies but finds their social criticism confusing and inadequate.[7] MacLean, in particular, concerned himself with Clare's failure to insist upon the causal connections between enclosure and increasing poverty, but has expressed this concern in terms which are, I believe, too broad and inevitably misleading. The absence of developed *economic* argument in the elegies does not justify the conclusion that Clare was indifferent to the *social* consequences of enclosure, and the notion that he was so obsessed by the purely topographical consequences that he "forgot" the human constituency of his protest simply does not bear up beside the evidence of the texts.

To be sure, he was obsessed by the way enclosure changed the face of the landscape and threatened the wild occupiers of the land. One sees evidence of this obsession everywhere: in "The Lamentations of Round-Oak Waters," for instance, when Clare responds so angrily to the sight of the once open fields now "all beset wi posts and rails / And turned upside down" (*JCOA*, 21), or in "The Lament of Swordy Well" when he has the personified land so plaintively beg the enclosers to "leave me as I am" (*JCOA*, 152), or again in "Helpston Green" where his indictment of enclosers is presented in the form of a casualty list of all they have destroyed:

> Not tree's alone have felt their force
>   Whole woods beneath them bow'd
> They stopt the winding runlets course
>   And flowrey pastures plough'd
> To shrub or tree throughout thy fields
>   They no compasion show
> The uplifted axe no mercy yields
>   But strikes a fatal blow   (*JCOA*, 62)

But many of the natural objects and scenes described in the elegies are invested with a human subjectivity of response which invites one to suspect that they signify more than physical nature. Certainly something more than the topographical consequences of enclosure pressed Clare to write in "The Mores" of the "bondage" which the "fence of ownership" had imposed upon the land, in "A Favourite Nook Destroyed" of the "poor outcast refugees of mother earth" whose lives had been disrupted by the "vile invasions of encroaching men" (*I*, 531), and in "Remembrances" of the "little homeless miners" (moles) who had been driven from their homes and trapped "as traitors" to the new regime of the encloser:

> I see the little mouldywharps hang sweeing to the wind
> On the only aged willow that in all the field remains
> And nature hides her face while theyre sweeing in their chains
> And in a silent mumuring complains   (*JCOA*, 259)

These images of suffering nature bring us into sympathetic contact with a local landscape, but they also take us into a political range of reference; in confronting them one's mind is thrown back to types of human suffering, specifically to the alienation, displacement, and oppression of the men and women for whom Clare spoke.[8]

I do not wish to give the impression that beneath every fallen tree in the elegies there lies the body of an exploited field-hand and in every bird's throat the cry of a dispossessed cottager. Not every scene and object in these poems invites symbolic interpretation, and I would be misrepresenting both the poems and the quality of Clare's resistance to enclosure if I were to imply that his natural imagery was merely functional – there only to symbolize or provide the settings for historical events and personal meditations. Long before it became fashionable to do so, Clare warned against the tragic consequences of a mode of production which violated the life-rhythms of natural species and destroyed the ecological balance and unity of a given region. There was an ecological specificity to his concern when he characterized the enclosed landscape through the imagery of starving birds, homeless animals, dying wildflowers, felled trees, and broken fields. And yet, in spite of this specific concern, in spite of the fact that in a quantitative sense they are taken up by line after line of natural description, the elegies resist easy classification as landscape poems or nature lyrics. If they are to be classified, it must be as poems of protest in which the social reasons, the social object, and the social constituency of the protest are clearly defined. I press this point because, I suspect, the mistaken assumption that they are simply landscape poems (with glancing historical allusions) has allowed for the even more mistaken idea that Clare cared more about the face of the landscape than the fate of his peers. In the end, whether Clare cared more about one or the other, whether his reasons for resisting enclosure were social or aesthetic, and whether his images are opaquely topographical or transparently political are questions which can and should be occluded by the recognition that the elegies are about the correspondence between a topographical and political order, about the relationship between the labourer and the land, and about the way a social process could intrude upon aesthetic experience.

The unity of Clare's concerns goes a long way towards explaining why the figure of *prosopopeia*, which he rarely used in his nature poetry, appears so often in the elegies. In the identification of the labourer and the land through the suffering they shared at the hands of a common enemy Clare found the theme which organized all his responses to enclosure, and in *prosopopeia* he found the figure to convey this theme. By writing poems in which in his own character as one of the beleaguered rural labouring poor he imagines hearing the "grievous murmurs" of a personified landscape despoiled by enclosure, he was able to portray with remarkable

economy this communion of suffering, and by having his eloquent
trees and accusant river-banks speak for his people, he gave ironic
emphasis to his belief that too few human voices were raised in
defence of the rights and needs of labour. As we can see in "The
Lament of Swordy Well" (1821-4), the ascription of human feelings and moral attributes to nature had the additional virtue of
ironically underscoring the inhumanity of the enclosing class. This
compressed and angular poem is a dramatic monologue spoken by
a personified section of the landscape which has recently been
"improved"; that the land and the labourer have gained nothing
from the improvement is its theme:

> Im swordy well a piece of land
> Thats fell upon the town
> Who worked me till I couldnt stand
> And crush me now Im down
> ...
> Alas dependance thou'rt a brute
> Want only understands
> His feelings wither branch and root
> That falls in parish hands.   (*JCOA*, 147-8)

The colloquial idiom and the priorities are clearly those of the
workingman. (The economic emphasis is unusual, and though
Clare in his own character as labourer makes no appearance in the
poem, it's worth recalling that his father mended roads until he
"couldn't stand" and then, crippled by rheumatism and destitute,
was forced to "fall in parish hands.") The indirection of the central
conceit does not obscure the feelings of anger and betrayal which
lie at the heart of the poem; rather, it enabled Clare to express
those feelings in a particularly tough and abrasive way. Thus while
the land carries the character of humanity, the "mongrel
men" responsible for its enclosure are reduced to their inhumane
motivations through metaphor and personified abstraction:

> Yet worried with a greedy pack
> They rend and delve and tear
> The very grass from off my back
> Ive scarce a rag to wear
> ...
> And should the price of grain get high
> Lord help and keep it low
> I shant possess a single flye
> Or get a weed to grow

I shant possess a yard of ground
To bid a mouse to thrive
For gain has put me in a pound
I scarce can keep alive   (*JCOA*, 150-1)

The figure of *prosopopeia* – and the whole situation it summons up of a rustic poet finding nature more humane than society – is turned to similar effect in an earlier work, "The Lamentations of Round-Oak Waters" (1818). As its title suggests this poem resembles "The Lament of Swordy Well," but here the personification – in this case, of the "genius" of a brook that has been destroyed – is more formally managed: whereas the brusque and colloquial Swordy Well speaks *as* a labourer, the more linguistically decorous spirit of Round-Oak Waters speaks on behalf of the labourer; and whereas the former boldly introduces itself ("Im swordy well a piece of land ..."), the latter is introduced to us by the poet. Because Clare first appears, lamenting his lot as a "shunned son of Poverty," the reader is provided with an immediate human context in which to place the dramatic monologue of Round-Oak Waters. At first, the predominant mood of the monologue is one of resigned suffering and nostalgic longing for a past in which the mutuality of the labourer and the land has been based upon more than a shared sense of betrayal. But towards the end, a note of hot recrimination cuts through this mood as Round-Oak Waters registers the changes which enclosure has brought about:

O then what trees my banks did crown
    What Willows flourishd here
Hard as the ax that Cut them down
    The senceless wretches were

'But sweating slaves I do not blame
    Those slaves by wealth decreed
No I should hurt their harmless name
    To brand 'em wi' the deed
Altho their aching hands did wield
    The axe that gave the blow
Yet 't'was not them that own'd the field
    Nor plan'd its overthrow

'No no the foes that hurt my field
    Hurts these poor moilers too
And thy own bosom knows and feels
    Enough to prove it true
...

'Ah cruel foes with plenty blest
  So ankering after more
To lay the greens and pastures waste
  Which proffited before   (*JCOA*, 23)

Had it been possible for Clare to publish this poem, the passage above, with its invective and its ironical play upon the catchwords of the improver ("plan'd" and "proffited") would have earned him the reputation of a radical. It was, he believed, a sign of the whole moral perversity of the enclosing class that it not only destroyed the labourer's access to the land, but made him act as the agent of the very process that victimized him, since, perforce, the labourer and not the property-owner had to do the actual work of draining, levelling, and fencing the old landscape.

But if "The Lamentations of Round-Oak Waters" deserves a place in the tradition of dissent, it is not only for its direct denunciations, but for the way it characterizes the rural labouring poor as people who think and feel and have been cast out of the landscape in which their culture is grounded. The spirit of Round-Oak Waters reminds the poet of the ranges of experience and quality of feeling which had been possible before enclosure:

How pleasures lately flourish'd here
  Thy self has often seen
The willows waving wi' the wind
  And here and there a thorn
Did please thy Mellancholly mind
  And did My banks adorn

'And here the shepherd with his sheep
  And with his lovley maid
Together where these waters creep
  In loitering dalliance play'd
And here the Cowboy lov'd to sit
  And plate his rushy thongs
And dabble in the fancied pit
  And chase the Minnow throngs

'There didst thou joy and love to sit
  The briars and brakes among
To exercise thy infant wit
  In fancied tale or song

And there the inscect and the flower
   Would Court thy curious eye
To muse in wonder on that power
   Which dwells above the sky

'But now alas my charms are done
   For shepherds and for thee
The Cowboys with his Green is gone
   And every Bush and tree (*JCOA*, 20-1)

The insistently repeated adverbs of place convey the immediacy
and the tangibility of the villagers' losses: "here" the rustic poet
could exercise his imagination and curiosity; "there" the shepherd
could choose freely the shape of his own contentment. An historian
might complain that, however catastrophic enclosure was for the
common labourer, life in an open-field parish was hardly the paradise of liberty and song depicted in these lines. But it should be
clear by now that the historical and, needless to say, literary significance of the elegies rests upon how vividly they express a particular
consciousness of loss, and not upon whether they describe the
socio-economic conditions of the rural labouring poor in a way that
can verify or be verified by what is known statistically of these
conditions.

It may be useful to anticipate another complaint that could be
made of "Round-Oak Waters" (and of the elegies in general), for
some readers may feel that Clare squandered the urgency of his
protest by focusing upon the lost aesthetic pleasures of labouring
life before enclosure. One might ask, for instance, in what rank in
the scale of human suffering are we to place people (whatever their
rank in society) who have lost their customary pleasures? If this is
what access to the land really meant to the labouring poor - places
where they could loiter in the grass, dally with their lovers, and
chase minnows in a stream - then how tragic was the loss of this
access? Certainly the relationship between the rustic and the land
depicted in "Round-Oak Waters" seems lacking in the profundity
which characterizes the same relationship as it is depicted in the
Lyrical Ballads. One thinks in particular of "Michael," in which a
georgic celebration of work, a catalogue of passions and heroic
acts, and a theory of association are offered to explain Michael's
feelings for his land. Yet it's important to notice that even in the
profound idiom of Wordsworth the emphasis falls upon the rustic's
right to find pleasure in life:

Those fields, those hills – what could they less? had laid
Strong hold on his affections, were to him
A pleasurable feeling of blind love,
The pleasure which there is in life itself. [9]

There is, of course, little to be gained by comparing the intrinsic merits of one of Wordsworth's greatest poems and one of Clare's earliest – especially if the criterion for comparison is profundity. But I would suggest that in spite of their obvious differences of quality and emphasis "Michael" and "Round-Oak Waters" are founded upon a common recognition: that the relationship between the rustic and his local landscape had a precious shape and meaning which far transcended the reasons of necessity or utility. Clare might write of his neighbours taking their pleasure by a country stream, Wordsworth of a shepherd's "pleasurable feeling of blind love" for his patrimony, but both poems may be read as local and precise enactments of the larger and more philosophical protest which Wordsworth expressed most succinctly in his sonnet "To the Utilitarians":

Avaunt this oeconomic rage!
What would it bring? – an iron age,
When Fact with heartless search explored
Shall be Imagination's Lord,
And sway with absolute controul
The god-like Functions of the Soul. [10]

In the end, by writing about the "dalliance" of a shepherd and his mistress, the cowboy's play, the labourer's delight in watching the unbounded freedom of the open fields, Clare was not squandering the urgency of his protest, but finding its centre. These activities were to him a living criticism of those who would transform all earthly goods into market commodities and judge all human experience by utilitarian values.

A living criticism? Rather, they were dying before his eyes. Yet we find in the elegies very little evidence of the introverted, resigned melancholy sense of an older order giving way to a new one which is so characteristic of the genre. That kind of melancholy depends upon the recognition of change and loss as inevitable and irreversible, whereas the changes and losses Clare lamented were far from inevitable. His mourning was always quickened by anger. Even when he wrote about scenes, objects, values, and customs which appeared to have been irrevocably destroyed by enclosure

("all plough'd and buried now, as though there naught had been,"
I, 161), he wrote with a dissenter's optimism, hoping that the losses
would be reversed and that his poems would help push back "the
vile invasions" of what Wordsworth called the "oeconomic rage"
and he, "gain's rude rage" (*I*, 124).

The informing connection between his posture as elegist and the
specific content of his protest against enclosure is most carefully
articulated in "To a Fallen Elm." Written sometime in the late
1820s, this is one of the last of the enclosure elegies and one of the
best. The poem breaks quite sharply into two parts – the first half
is epitaphic and the last half is declamatory – but the transition
between them is smoothly managed through the controlling image
of the elm-tree itself and through a beautifully realized pattern of
auditory imagery. The two-part structure is reminiscent of "The
Old Cumberland Beggar," and the imagery suggests that Clare
shared something of Wordsworth's ability to domesticate the most
sublime of feelings and to find sublimity in the habitual rhythms of
ordinary experience. But if "To a Fallen Elm" suggests Clare's affinity to Wordsworth, it's primarily because it recalls Wordsworth's
tenet that in the situation of low and rustic life "the passions of
men are incorporated with the beautiful and permanent forms of
nature."[11] This tenet is recalled, however, in a particularly tragic
and ironic way since the natural object Clare describes – and with
which his own passions are "incorporated" – is beautiful but far
from permanent: it has been cut down by an improver keen to turn
a profit from the ground where it once took root.

The poem is shaped by specific and unconsoling recollection;
here, as in all the elegies, Clare's ability to remember vividly what
enclosure has effaced only intensifies his sense of loss. The importance of the elm-tree's physical presence to the emotions of the poet
and his family is established in the intimate apostrophe with which
the poem begins:

Old elm that murmured in our chimney top
The sweetest anthem autumn ever made
And into mellow whispering calms would drop
When showers fell on thy many coloured shade
And when dark tempests mimic thunder made
While darkness came as it would strangle light
With the black tempest of a winter night
That rocked thee like a cradle to thy root
How did I love to hear the winds upbraid
Thy strength without while all within was mute   (*JCOA*, 96)

The impression created here of the elm-tree as an old, affectionate friend is developed in the lines which follow. But the note of sublimity caught in the image of the dark winter storm is also amplified:

> It seasoned comfort to our hearts desire
> We felt thy kind protection like a friend
> And pitched our chairs up closer to the fire
> Enjoying comforts that was never penned
>
> Old favourite tree thoust seen times changes lower
> But change till now did never come to thee
> For time beheld thee as her sacred dower
> And nature claimed thee her domestic tree
> Storms came and shook thee with a living power
> Yet stedfast to thy home thy roots hath been
> Summers of thirst parched round thy homely bower
> Till earth grew iron – still thy leaves were green
> The children sought thee in thy summer shade
> And made their play house rings of sticks and stone
> The mavis sang and felt himself alone
> While in thy leaves his early nest was made
> And I did feel his happiness mine own
> Nought heeding that our friendship was betrayed   (*JCOA*, 97)

Several of the images in these passages possess the qualities of the archetype and the oxymoron. Green leaves in an iron world, darkness strangling light, silence in a storm, a violent tempest rocking the elm maternally as though it were a cradle: these images of reconciled contraries celebrate the essential unity and awesome power of nature, and press the poem into a range of reference which encompasses more than a solitary tree and a single family. But the more personal, palpable, and domestic images of the chimney-top beside the protecting tree, the chairs pulled close against the fire, the makeshift toys of the children are no less striking and no less central to the argument of the poem. The comforting ordinariness of "her domestic tree" was for Clare as important an aspect of nature's "sacred dower" as the wild sublimity of her stormy night.

I don't wish to imply that the imagery is merely a device in the rhetorical pattern of the poem: it exists for its own sake, has its own discrete mimetic functions. But clearly it also has a rhetorical dimension and contains prescriptive as well as descriptive ele-

ments. It gives shape to Clare's perceptions and feelings about the
elm-tree, its place in nature and within his domestic experience,
but also allows him to express a set of convictions about man's
proper relationship to nature – convictions which directly counter
the creed of the improver. Against the lese-majesty of those who
would fragment and dominate the landscape, Clare posits the
power and unity of nature, and against the base instincts of
the profit-hungry encloser, he offers the comparative nobility of his
own passionate and tactful involvements. When "To a Fallen Elm"
moves from description into declamation, it does so smoothly and
forthrightly primarily because the images in the first part have
already given imaginative assent to the arguments which follow
them.

The grievances against enclosure presented in the second section
of the poem are essentially the same as those in the earlier elegies,
but here they are conveyed in a harsh, polemical language of
unprecedented pitch. Perhaps the most impressive aspect of this
section involves the way it justifies its own stridency by suggesting
that all forms of human communication are inevitably shaped by
the world in which they are uttered. The world before enclosure, as
Clare sees or rather hears it in "To a Fallen Elm," is filled with a
language – evocative, nuanced, rich in contrast – which unites the
song of the mavis, the thunder and wind, the "sweetest anthem" of
autumn, and the "mellow whispering" of the "music-making elm."
The elm-tree possesses no lexicon, but it knows

> a language by which hearts are stirred
> Deeper than by the atribute of words   (*JCOA*, 97)

Clare's sensitivity to this language is a sign of his communion with
nature, and his ability to give verbal shape to the wordless euphony
of nature is, to a considerable extent, the basis of his own eloquence. In the world after enclosure no such euphony and no such
eloquence are possible, not only because the symbol of nature's
language (and of the poet's own) has been cut down, but because
this new world is so filled with the ugly, self-proclaiming cant of
the enclosing class that no other forms of speech can be heard. In
such a situation, Clare would have us understand, his only recourse
is to put aside the gentle language of evocation and enter, with cor-
rosive intent, into the loud and empty rhetoric of his enemies. He
must listen attentively to the enclosers and their political lackeys as
they speak a language less human than the language of his beloved
elm-tree:

Thoust heard the knave abusing those in power
Bawl freedom loud and then oppress the free
Thoust sheltered hypocrites in many a shower
That when in power would never shelter thee
Thoust heard the knave supply his canting powers
With wrongs illusions when he wanted friends ...
With axe at root he felled thee to the ground
And barked of freedom – O I hate that sound

It grows the cant term of enslaving tools
To wrong another by the name of right ...
No matter – wrong was right and right was wrong
And freedoms brawl was sanction to the song

Such was thy ruin music making Elm
The rights of freedom was to injure thine
As thou wert served so would they overwhelm
In freedoms name the little that is mine   (*JCOA*, 97–8)

The parallelism, the repetitions, and the metrical discipline give
rhetorical emphasis to this passage. The tightness of rhythm and
rhyme in the final couplet ("... wrong was right and right was
wrong / And freedoms brawl was sanction to the song") and the
management of the internal pauses in the last five lines is impressive. But the most striking feature is the strong and simple diction
and, in particular, the variety of ways Clare uses the word "freedom." It appears nine times in the last half of the poem and, as
John Barrell has noted, Clare plays upon the different connota-
tions of the word as it was conventionally used by the advocates of
enclosure, the apologists for *laissez-faire*, the Tory and the Whig,
in order to convey his "more than conventional response" to the
term.[12] Clare well understood that those who most vociferously
"barked of freedom" were only using (abusing) the word to justify
the "right" (another abused term) of the few to exploit and oppress
the thousands. But he continued to have faith in the word and in
its power to assert its true meaning even within the discourse of
those who tried to preempt its meaning. When the encloser spoke
of "freedom" or "liberty" or "rights" in order to give "sanction to
the song" of his greed and self-interest, he stood condemned by his
own words.

The fact that "To a Fallen Elm" turns upon the issue of human
language and nature's euphony reminds us that Clare's responses

to enclosure were shaped not only by his experiences as a labourer but by his acute consciousness of his identity and resources as a poet. It is interesting to note that the parliamentary statute for the enclosure of his village was enacted in 1809 – the same year in which he wrote "Helpstone," his first extant poem – and the final Award was published by the commissioners of enclosure in 1820 – the year his first volume was published. The coincidence of these dates may not have held a special significance for Clare since most of the actual work of enclosing Helpston probably occurred between 1811 and 1816. [13] But the coincidence reminds us that during the very years Clare was learning to write about his local landscape, organizing his perceptions, and sounding the depths of his own feelings of local attachment, the landscape was taken from him. It may not have been transformed beyond recognition, but because his perceptions were so fine and because he was so concerned (even as a young man) to trace the line of continuity in his life, the most subtle changes caused by enclosure affected him dramatically; his world was turned, in his words, "upside down" and "inside out" at the very time that it began to mean so much to him as a poet. Moreover, because, like Wordsworth, Clare placed such great value upon the visions and experiences of his childhood, enclosure seemed to represent a special threat to the future poems he wanted to write: the scenes of his childhood epiphanies were no longer there to return to.

In "The Village Minstrel" Clare took pains to emphasize the harmful effects of enclosure upon the creative aspirations of Lubin, the young rustic hero of the poem and Clare's surrogate:

> But who can tell the anguish of his mind,
> When reformation's formidable foes
> When civil wars 'gainst nature's peace combin'd,
> And desolation struck her deadly blows,
> As curst improvement 'gan his fields inclose;
> O greens, and fields, and trees, farewell, farewell!
> His heart-wrung pains, his unavailing woes
> No words can utter, and no tongue can tell,
> When ploughs destroy'd the green, when groves of willows fell.
>
> (*I*, 155)

In may respects, Lubin is a representative figure and his grievances against enclosure are typical of his class. But the hero of "The Village Minstrel" also has a starring role to play as an aspirant poet, a solitary character, sharply individuated, who hates enclosure for reasons which depend specifically upon his literary life. Lubin had been preparing to write about the unbounded freedom of the open fields and untamed wastes, but enclosure has destroyed what he was going to write about, and we are meant to understand that this loss has almost silenced him ("No words can utter, and no tongue can tell ..."). Obviously Lubin's creator was not silenced by the effects of enclosure upon his imagination, but he was, nonetheless, seized by the idea that the enclosure of his village had irreparably altered the course of his development as a poet. Thus, in "To a Fallen Elm," the lament of the cottager for his lost domestic happiness is confluent with the dejection of the poet who has had the tutor of his eloquence stolen from him. Thus, in "The Mores," Clare vilifies the enclosing class not only for trampling upon "the grave of labour's rights" but for impinging upon the "poets visions of lifes early day."

Most of the references to his specific character as a literary man are very brief, but all of the elegies indicate that Clare confronted the effects of enclosure with a kind of hostility he could not entirely share with his rustic neighbours, not because they did not suffer the same aesthetic and emotional losses but because they did not suffer as poets. In "Round-Oak Waters," Clare presents himself as a victim of poverty and oppression. But he is also a young man with literary aspirations of which "the worlds made gamely sport and scorn" and because of these aspirations he has fears and doubts, pleasures and interests, which set him apart from his peers:

> And different pleasures fill'd thy breast
>   And different thy employ
> And different feelings thou possest
>   From any other Boy   (*JCOA*, 20)

In his discussion of the poem Barrell has suggested that Clare's emphasis upon his differentness and his lament for the social consequences of enclosure split "Round-Oak Waters" into two separate strands of meaning, and that these strands are not only unconnected but contradictory since Clare protests on behalf of a collectivity from which he takes pains to separate himself.[14] It is true that Clare often tried to have it both ways, wanted to be taken as both a choric and lyric poet. But in drawing attention to the poetical cast of his mind and aspirations Clare was not separating himself from the rural labouring poor; he was distinguishing himself *within* their collectivity. In all of the elegies, in "Round-Oak Waters" most of all, his need to proclaim his special interests and private sufferings as a poet did not conflict with his wish to make a direct political statement against enclosure on behalf of his class. The melancholy of the young poet obsessed with the problem of finding his subject was not simply contiguous but integrally connected to the outrage of the labouring man who was also struggling to be heard: enclosure was the cause of both feelings.

Clare was not always at one with his fellow-villagers – his solitude was dear to him – but he was one of them, and the political authority and urgency of the elegies depends upon the fact that their author was a member of the constituency of his protest, himself one of the "thousands," "a shunned son" of his society, "a poor moiler," a beneficiary of "labour's rights" before enclosure, and after it, a "parish-slave by wealth decreed." The act of writing, and the attendant work of poetic self-definition, did not erase that sense of shared identity, only brought it into closer focus. Because of his social experience, Clare was especially susceptible to the mystique of the alienated poet in a heartless world, and he sometimes wrote of the sphere of poetry as though it were a perfect haven, immune to the infections of society and innocent of its cruelties. But the active relations into which he entered as a working poet – with the language, the literary tradition, and the reading public – constantly brought him back to imperfect reality. As we shall see in the following chapter, there were elements within the poetic tradition which seemed as threatening to Clare's creative and emotional resources as the "vile invasions" of enclosure. Indeed, he had to struggle against the articulated values of the literary community he so admired as arduously and constantly as he struggled against the enclosers he so despised. The two struggles were of a different nature and took a different form, but both exercised Clare's capacity for protest, and in both the question of his social identity was of overwhelming importance.

CHAPTER THREE

The Struggle for Acceptance

THE TRADITION AND THE READING PUBLIC

Clare sat down to dinner more than once with such eminent figures as Coleridge, Hazlitt, and Lamb, and included among his regular correspondents such literary men as Alan Cunningham, Thomas Pringle, George Darley, Francis Cary, and his publishers, James Hessey and John Taylor.[1] In his own locality he had the companionship of Octavius Gilchrist, a Stamford grocer who also happened to be a published poet, an editor, a contributor to the major periodicals, and an authority on the Elizabethan dramatists. There was also living close by, at Milton Park, J. Henderson with whom he could share his botanical interests, and E.A. Artis who, as the discoverer of Durobrivae, was to play a significant role in the subsequent history of English archaeology. Yet in spite of these contacts, Clare's real and felt intellectual isolation cannot be overemphasized. In the early years, Gilchrist was his only immediate source of literary companionship and then in 1823, when Clare was most in need of that companionship, Gilchrist died, leaving Clare in what he was to call the "desert" of his community. From this time on, save for his infrequent visitors and his few trips to London, he had to depend upon his correspondence for literary companionship. There can be no doubt that several of his correspondents – his publishers in particular – gave Clare confidence in his own abilities and helped him to feel that he had at least a tenuous contact with the world where poetry was discussed, literary ideas were exchanged, and literary reputations were made. But their letters could not help him to break out of his intellectual isolation; they only punctuated it.

Because he was so isolated and because his formal education had been so meagre, Clare's reading necessarily played a profound and decisive role in shaping his creative life. He was a voracious and critical though unsystematic reader, and he was well aware of what his reading meant to him. By following the work of his contemporaries and by attending to the work of the great poets who had preceded him, he was able to find the literary mentors and colleagues who were, in an immediate sense, never part of his ordinary life. He was always asking his friends and patrons to send him this or that volume, always grateful when they sent books out to him, always anxious to air his opinions on what he was reading. He was forthright in offering his critical judgments. If he was not impressed by a poet or did not approve of certain aspects of his work then he said so, no matter how fashionable or prestigious the poet might be. He was also only too happy to praise the poets who most pleased him and to admit that he had been influenced by the poets he most admired.

Thomson, Collins, Gray, Goldsmith, Cowper, Burns, and Wordsworth were the major figures in the tradition of rural poetry to which Clare himself wanted to belong, and he felt no need to apologize for his early attempts to write like them - just like them, if he could. The apprentice to any craft need feel no embarrassment about following his masters, since it is by copying that we learn. But even after the early years Clare does not appear to have suffered from what Harold Bloom has called "the anxiety of influence," "the exhaustions of being a late-comer" to "a tradition grown too wealthy to need anything more."[2] Indeed, Clare appears to offer a definite and clamorous challenge to Bloom's theory that, if the poet is to be more than the copyist of another man's vision or style, he must clear "imaginative space" for himself by engaging in oedipal struggle with the fathers of his tradition. Far from feeling threatened by the powerful writers who had gone before him and struggling against the "embarrassments" of believing that everything that could be said about rural life and scenery had already been said, Clare was confident that he could contribute to the tradition new subjects and a new way of seeing them. Rather than feeling "the exhaustions of being a late-comer," he was exhilarated by his belief that the poetry of natural description could be as various and rich and inexhaustible as nature itself. He was encouraged in this belief not only by the poets and theorists he read - in particular, Thomson, Cowper, Hugh Blair - but also by friends and friendly critics: among others, by John Taylor who claimed that Clare had found "delight in scenes which no other poet thought of celebrating";[3] by Francis Cary, who praised his ability "to bring before us many objects in nature that we often have seen in her but never before in books";[4] and by a critic in the *Gentleman's Magazine* who likened Clare to Thomson in his ability to impart "the air of novelty to objects ... which until touched by his creative and fertilizing pencil, had appeared devoid of any thing which could impart dignity or grace to a literary description."[5]

Clare was even more exhilarated by the wide open spaces which the poetry of rural dissent challenged him to enter, though, insofar as his own experience was implicated here, his exhilaration must have been tempered by a sense of serious and urgent purpose. The lives and emotions of the rural labouring poor, and especially their reactions to the effects of the enclosure movement, had not yet been adequately chronicled, and to this important task, as we have seen, Clare directed his energies. He was, of course, aware that two senior and distinguished contemporaries had claimed the territory of humble and rustic life for themselves, but Clare appears to have been remarkably indifferent to Wordsworth's and to Crabbe's contributions to the tradition. His reading in Crabbe and Wordsworth, far from causing him to feel that his own poetry was superfluous or unnecessary, gave him reason to believe that by recording his perceptions and his way of perceiving the society in which he lived, he was offering an important and original contribution to the tradition. Clare heaped praise upon Wordsworth's lyrical and descriptive work and acknowledged that Wordsworth was the greatest poet of the age. But he disliked Wordsworth's poetry of humble and rustic life which was, in his estimation, too heavy in "affectations of simplicity."[6] He had nothing approving to say about Crabbe at all, disliked his pontificating tone, and felt that he had misrepresented the lives of the very people he ought (through his own humble origins) to have known well. Clare admitted that he liked Crabbe's *Tales* "here & there a touch," but as he wrote to Taylor:

there is a d-d many affectations among them which seems to be the favourite play of the parson poet – ... whats he know of the distresses of the poor musing over a snug coal fire in his parsonage box – if I had an enemy I coud wish to torture I woud not wish him hung nor yet at the devil / my worst wish shoud be a weeks confinement in some vicarage to hear an old parson & his lecture on the wants & wickedness of the poor. (*Letters*, 75)

Yet, whatever Clare might have said about Wordsworth and Crabbe, there is more than a little evidence (in the tone, form, theme, and title of *The Parish*; in the elegiac tone and structures of the enclosure poems) to indicate that Clare learned a great deal from both poets. My point, then, is not that Clare was not influenced by Wordsworth and Crabbe, but rather that he would not recognize, or at least was not willing to record his recognition of, their influence. Clare, usually so generous in his praise of fellow poets, normally so pleased to acknowledge his debts to the poets who had influenced him, refused to cast himself in the role of admirer or epigone to Crabbe or to the author of the *Lyrical Ballads*. He could not bring himself to attend to Crabbe's pious lessons in morality nor to follow Wordsworth in his experiments in ventriloquism. And perhaps with good reason. For Crabbe, writing from the secured respectability of his parsonage about the lives of common people, and Wordsworth, writing in what he supposed to be the language of those people, could not serve as models for a poet who happened to be one of them. The authors of *The Parish Register* and "Michael" could not help Clare to write from his own knowledge, in his own voice, about his own experience as an English rural labourer. For this task Clare had to be his own authority.

But, though Clare does not appear to have suffered from Bloom's symptoms, his relations to his precursors and contemporaries within the rural tradition were by no means comfortable or unproblematic, and there is good reason to suppose that these relations caused Clare something close to "embarrassment" and "anxiety." To say this is to slide back to Bloom's terms, but not to back into his theory. For what Clare had to contend with throughout his writing career was not the "anxiety of influence" but the anxiety of having few influences to claim. His was the "embarrassment" of a student who discovers that his most revered tutors cannot always answer his questions, cannot teach him what he needs to know. He did not have to clear "imaginative space" for himself; on the contrary, he had to find some way to annex the uncharted literary regions he wanted to inhabit to the central territory claimed by the genteel, educated, sophisticated poets who had inspired him to write in the first place.

The region of his song was not, of course, entirely uncharted: Burns and Bloomfield had gone there before him. And for this reason Clare shared with both poets an identity of interest he could share with no one else. Though Burns came from a more prosperous family and had received more formal education, and though Bloomfield had more stability in his life and met with more even success than Clare was ever to find, the three poets had nonetheless a great many things in common: humble background, financial difficulty, the experience of physical labour, roots in the village community, schooling that was abruptly ended by necessity, even the approximate shape of their careers – the early pleasures of being lionized in the capital cities followed by the long years of misfortune and neglect. Bloomfield and Burns were the first poets to place the lives and passions of the rural labourers at the very centre of their work. They wrote about labouring folk even when they wrote about themselves, for both laid great emphasis on their particular social origins and circumstance. Unlike George Crabbe, they neither tried to forget nor allowed their readers to forget where they had come from. Clare's sense of friendly mutuality was felt most strongly with Bloomfield, who lived in Shefford, Bedfordshire, no great distance from Helpston, and whose writing life was coming to an end just as Clare's was beginning. The two poets exchanged kind and complimentary letters, and after Bloomfield's death (in 1823) Clare wrote three sonnets to his memory.

It was Bloomfield, not Burns, who received Clare's most frequent and extravagant praise. But it may well have been from Burns that Clare learned the critical terms and values which shaped his moving tributes to Bloomfield. Whereas Bloomfield tended to emphasize the negative aspects of his situation – the lowly status, the limitations in his social, educational, and travelling experience that forced him "to sing with pinions tied" of "trifling incidents ... / That to the humblest menial belong" – Burns wrote with almost evangelical zeal of the creative advantages which accrued to him because of his circumstances.[7] He suggested that it was precisely because he was (by genteel standards) unsophisticated and impolite, and (by university standards) unburdened by scholastic learning that he was able to stand in original, unmediated relationship to nature and to the impassioned nature of poetic genius: "The Poetic Genius of my Country found me, as the prophetic bard Elijah did Elisha – and the PLOUGH, and threw her inspiring mantle over me. She bad me sing the loves, the joys, the rural scenes and rural pleasures of my natal soil, in my native tongue: I tuned my wild artless notes, as she inspired."[8] Burns was invoking the highest authority he could invoke, an authority that would enable him, as the obedient servant of "her dictates," to cut through the carping social and intellectual prejudice of any man: "Who are you, Mr. Burns? Will some surly critic say: at what university have you been educated? What languages do you understand? Whether has Aristotle or Horace directed your taste? ... In short, what qualifications entitle you to instruct or entertain us?"[9] Burns could reply with blithe assurance:

Gie me ae spark o' Nature's fire,
That's a' the learning I desire,
Then tho' I drudge thro' dub' an' mire
    At pleugh or cart,
My Muse, tho' hamely in attire
    May touch the heart.[10]

The notion that creative genius lies beyond the pale of learning's authority was hardly a new one, and we need not review the history of pastoral to understand W.L. Renwick's observation that among Burns's readers, "simpler men, accepting at its face value the common pose that should never mislead an artist, did not notice that

I never drank the Muses' stank
Castalia's stream an' a' that

is the commonest cliché in European poetry, inherited by the scholarly poets."[11] Clare, who could not claim acquaintance with the *topoi* of classical and European literature, was, we may be sure, one of those "simpler men." But Burns (in spite of his knowing reference to "Castalia's stream") was no classical scholar either, and "the commonest cliché in European poetry" became in his hands anything but a cliché. To suggest as Professor Renwick has done that Burns "misled" and "deceived" his readers by "his pose of the Inspired Ploughman" is to allow a weary critical sophistication to cut off access to what was most fresh and convincing in his poetry. This "Inspired Ploughman" was not merely reenacting the stale postures of classical pastoral when, in the "Preface" to the Kilmarnock edition, he described his poetic enterprise in these terms:

Unacquainted with the necessary requisites for commencing Poet by rule, he sings the sentiments and manners he felt and saw in himself and his rustic compeers around him, in his and their native language ... To amuse himself with the little creations of his own fancy, amid the toil and fatigues of a labourious life; to transcribe the various feelings, the loves, the griefs, the hopes, the fears, in his own breast; to find some kind of counterpoise to the struggles of a world, always an alien scene, a talk uncouth to the poetical mind; these were his motives in courting the Muses.[12]

If Burns was a glamorous figure to the Romantics, it was in good part because, as Wordsworth was to say, "on the basis of his human character he has reared a poetic one."[13] And if his poetry was of decisive importance to Clare it was in good part because that "human character" was itself grounded in a particular set of social attributes. The man who lacked the "necessary requisites for commencing poet by rule," but who found all the inspiration he needed in his "native language," "natal soil," and "rustic compeers," gave something to Clare that Thomson, Goldsmith, and Cowper could never give him: a sense of confidence in the creative resources of his own social identity and experience.

This was also Bloomfield's gift to Clare, a gift that would help Clare to see himself, with no dissociation of sensibility, as both the pastoralist and the humble swain in his poetry of celebration, and as both judge and victim in his poetry of dissent. And it was a gift that Clare tried to repay by claiming more for Bloomfield than he ought to have done. The simple act of remembering Bloomfield's poetry and of claiming it as an imaginative resource would have been compliment enough, sufficient memorial to the modest talents of his precursor:

The shepherd musing oer his summer dreams
The may day wild flowers in the meadow grass
The sunshine sparkling in the valley streams
The singing ploughman and hay making lass
These live the summer of thy rural themes
Thy green memorials these and they surpass
The cobweb praise of fashion   (*JCOA*, 108)

But Clare's praise of Bloomfield was usually more lavish than this, often extravagantly wrong. Two years after his death, Clare wrote that Bloomfield had "dyed ripe for immortality & had he written nothing else but 'Richard & Kate' that fine picture of Rural Life were sufficient to establish his name as the English Theocritus & the first of Rural Bards in this country" (*Letters*, 167). We have no reason to believe that Clare was anything but sincere in recording his admiration for Bloomfield. But recognizing the sincerity with which he pressed his exaggerated claims for the enduring value of Bloomfield's verse need not then preclude us from questioning Clare's motives. There is good reason to suppose that they were not entirely disinterested, for Clare must have recognized that by rallying to Bloomfield's reputation he was to some extent helping to lay the foundations for his own. If he could persuade his contemporaries that Bloomfield really was "the first of Rural bards," then his prestige might give a kind of sanctioning authority to the position and stance of other rustic poets. What he said of Bloomfield was what he hoped his readers some day would say of him: that in spite of his social situation – or perhaps because of it – he was an important and innovative poet *within* the famed tradition.

Clare was obsessively preoccupied with the idea of poetic fame, and this preoccupation can be felt, like a dull, slow ache, through-out his poetry and prose: one poet is unjustly sung, he would argue, another unjustly ignored; Combe is merely popular but will never be famous, while Keats is unpopular but will be famous; and Byron, the poet to be most envied, is popular and will be famous too.[14] Clare was always drawing up lists and calling the rolls of the great English poets, and Bloomfield was rarely excluded from these lists. His name might appear in any passing reference to the great poets of the tradition:

> I delight
> To read a pleasant volume, where the cares
> Of life are sweetened by the muse's voice –
> Thomson, or Cowper, or the bard that bears
> Life's humblest name, though nature's favoured choice,
> Her pastoral Bloomfield.   (*I*, 517)

It is true enough that, whereas Thomson and Cowper had only to be named, Bloomfield's inclusion in the triumvirate of favourite poets had to be justified. Bloomfield had to be explained, singled out for the limitations ("Life's humblest name") and the resources ("nature's favoured choice") which were at the very centre of Clare's identification with him. But the important point is that Bloomfield was included in the triumvirate as a poet worthy of Cowper's and Thomson's company. Clare could hardly have been indifferent to the fact that, because of his background and because he pushed that background into the foreground of his poems, Bloomfield was seen by others as an unusual case, an exception to those genteel, educated, sophisticated men who had always been able to assume that participation in the literary life of the nation was theirs by right. But Clare refused to accept the idea that because of his social circumstances Bloomfield should be approached with condescension or placed with Burns in some separate minor category outside the main tradition:

situations in life however humble afford no apology in this age when we turn to the sun burning excellence of a Burns & a Bloomfield two poets tho of very different powers yet inimitable & perfect in their own exellence for both of whom I feel more than admiration & I dont care who laughs or calls me fool for odd opinions but if I may judge from Pope's Translation (for I have no latin) I would sooner be the author of Tam O Shanter than of the Iliad & Odyssey of Homer.   (*Letters*, 215)

These wonderfully revealing comments from a letter to Thomas Pringle suggest that Clare never thought of Burns and Bloomfield as the founding fathers of a minor tradition, but looked to them for company and support within the shared loneliness of being anomalies *within* a genteel and learned tradition.

For Clare, it was never a question of ignoring their unusually humble situations in life, or his own. He drew attention often enough to his own lack of education, confessed his lack of authority ("I have no latin"), and admitted the singularity of his own "odd opinions" ("Tam O'Shanter" aligned against the *Iliad*). And he drew attention to the singularity of Bloomfield's position as "the bard that bears / Life's humblest name." He depicted Bloomfield as a poet who lacked the necessary requisites to follow "the dazzling fashions of the day." He compared his poems to "quiet brooks" that could not compete with "the prouder streams" of all those poets who had been better placed on Fortune's Hill. But he also said of Bloomfield, as Burns said of himself, that there was a transcending advantage in his apparent disadvantage: the advantage of standing in unmediated relationship not only to "Natures wild pictures field and cloud and tree" but also to the "sweet unassuming" nature of his creative psyche:

Sweet unasuming Minstrel not to thee
The dazzling fashions of the day belong
Natures wild pictures field and cloud and tree
And quiet brooks far distant from the throng
In murmurs tender as the toiling bee
Make the sweet music of thy gentle song
Well - nature owns thee let the crowd pass bye -
The tide of fashion is a stream too strong
For pastoral brooks that gently flow and sing
But nature is their source and earth and sky
Their annual offerings to her current bring
Thy injured muse and memory need no sigh
For thine shall murmur on to many a spring
When their proud stream is summer burnt and dry   (*JCOA*, 108)

This is as much a defence as a celebration, and in its lines of defence we glimpse not only a portrait of Bloomfield against the background of his time but also a partial character-sketch of Clare himself. This is Clare striking an attitude of disdain for "the crowd," not only because he wished to redress the shabby critical treatment that Bloomfield had received, but also because he feared that he too would achieve nothing more than a *succès d'estime*. "Well – nature owns thee let the crowd pass bye": Clare could say this of Bloomfield, and as the years passed he would say it, proudly, and bitterly, of himself. He had good reason to feel that both he and Bloomfield had been denied a fair reading. But what is most remarkable in this sonnet and, indeed, in all his writings on Bloomfield is the confidence with which Clare voiced his opinion that "the crowd" had been wrong, that when "the tide of fashion" had finally run out Bloomfield's "pastoral brooks" would be seen as contributions of enduring value to the mainstream of the English tradition. Clare's confidence in Bloomfield's greatness was, one need hardly say, misplaced. But what he had to say about Bloomfield is much less important than what he said, in speaking of Bloomfield, about his own relations to the reading public and to the tradition.

Almost all the great poets he celebrated in verse and prose, in particular Milton, Wordsworth, Byron, and Keats, are described as men who refused (like Bloomfield) to follow the dictates of the critic or to pander to the fashions of the reading public. Of Milton, he wrote:

> The critics' wrath did darkly frown
> Upon thy muse's mighty lay;
> But blasts that break the blossom down
>   Do only stir the bay;
> And thine shall flourish, green and long,
> With the eternity of song.   (*II*, 187)

And of the critical hostility and indifference with which Keats's poetry had been received, he wrote:

>   When these are past, true child of Poesy,
> Thou shalt survive. Ah, while a being dwells,
>   With soul, in nature's joys, to warm like thine,
> With eye to view her fascinating spells
>   And dream entranced o'er each form divine,
> Thy worth, Enthusiast, shall be cherish'd here,
> Thy name with him shall linger, and be dear.   (*I*, 283)

It is made clear, explicitly in the lines to Keats, implicitly in the natural imagery of his tribute to Milton, that the mark of the true poet is found not only in his refusal to submit to the arbitrary and ephemeral power of critical fashion, but in his creative identification with the spirit and the palpable forms of nature. Bloomfield's poems were to be distinguished from the verses of the mere poetaster because, Clare said, "Nature is their source." But he believed that all the major poets in the tradition "went to nature for their images," knowing that nature is "the very essence and soul of Poesy": this was the cause of their greatness. And the proof, Clare argued, was to be found in the fact that the man of sensibility could not observe nature without recalling Thomson's *Seasons*, or Milton's *Comus*, or Gray's "Ode to Spring." He could not think of the morning without recalling Thomson's beautiful lines on that theme, or walk out under the evening moon without recalling Milton's "Il Penseroso" or Collins' "Ode to Evening." "The man of taste," Clare wrote, "looks on the little Celandine in Spring & mutters in his mind some favourite lines from Wordsworths address to that flower / he never sees the daisy without thinking of Burns" (*Prose*, 175).

Milton's natural imagery and Wordsworth's natural description are not necessarily the first things, certainly not the only things, that come to mind when one thinks of the greatness of these poets. And to avoid giving the impression that Clare was lacking in critical acumen, I must insist that he saw more in Milton than his evening moon, more in Wordsworth than his celandine. He was by no means indifferent to the theist and humanist assertion, the visionary and the philosophical system-building, of the finest poets in the language. But none of these qualities stretched and fascinated Clare as much as the great poet's ability to evoke the resonant spirit of nature and to describe with great precision the specific forms of nature. Whether it was a case of Clare finding what he was looking for or of finding what to look for, his reading in the great poets gave him confidence in the centrality of his own literary project. To the questions – what could he as an uneducated workingman have in common with the great classicist or the sublime egotist of the tradition, and what could he, with his slim resources, contribute to the tradition of Milton or Wordsworth? – Clare found necessarily large, unqualified answers: love of nature, poetry, language, creative integrity. These were the articles of pragmatic belief – so essential to Clare's confidence in his own work – that allowed him to find some common ground between "the genteel and the vulgar race" of English poets. They were formulated and sustained only with great effort. When one considers that Clare could not even take for granted that the literary tradition belonged to him as part of his inalienable birthright as an Englishman, then his very belief that he belonged in that tradition must be seen as an achievement of faith:

> I've heard of Parnass Hill, Castalia's stream,
> And in my dreams have worshipped beauty long;
> I've heard, alas, but never could I dream
> That aught of birthright did to me belong
> In that rich paradise of sacred song.   (*I*, 454)

Against the feeling recorded here that he had no right to partici-pate (as reader or author) in the "rich paradise of sacred song," the very fact that Clare employed the same terms to compliment Mil-ton and Bloomfield, to speak of Wordsworth and himself, must be seen as evidence of his moral courage. This uneducated working man had the nerve to express his hope that the muse that had inspired Milton would also inspire him:

> Poet of mighty power, I fain
> Would court the muse that honoured thee,
> And, like Elisha's spirit, gain
>   A part of thy intensity;
> And share the mantle which she flung
> Around thee, when thy lyre was strung.   (*II*, 187)

But, as we shall see, Clare rarely expressed his literary aspira-tions quite so proudly or explicitly. He was, in many ways, as unassuming a man as Bloomfield, and he lived in a time when deference was expected from a person of his class. He was expected to be modest about his creative resources, and social tact and per-sonal inclination made him modest about his creative aspirations. Indeed, at least until 1821, Clare was not simply modest about his literary aspirations and capacities; he was painfully diffident and constantly self-abasing. It was, paradoxically, only after the failure of his second volume that he began to speak with confidence about his right to "sing as well as greater men" (*I*, 435). He believed (not always with good cause) that his very failure to succeed with the reading public had given him something in common with the great poets of the tradition. And from this initial point of identification all the other crucial identifications were to be established. Yet even when Clare was in fullest possession of his talents and his self-confidence, his claims for the significance of his creative project were pronounced with some strain and hesitation. He did not have an exalted vision of his importance in literary history:

> Oh! when I view the glorious host
>   Of poets to my country born –
> Though sorrow was the lot of most,
>   And many shared the sneers of scorn,
> That now by time and talent tried,
>   Give life to fame's eternal sun –
> Oh! when I mark the glorious pride
>   That England from her bards hath won,
> E'ven I, the meanest of the throng,
> Warm into ecstasy and song.   (*II*, 73)

These lines reveal, however, that he claimed the right to follow the poet's calling and to aspire to a place, however humble, within "the glorious host / Of poets to my country born." Perhaps he would never be more than "the meanest of the throng," but he saw himself, nonetheless, as a member of that illustrious company, and preferred to be seen as a minor figure within the mainstream of English poetry rather than as a major figure in the brackish back-waters of a minor tradition. Burns and Bloomfield had demonstrated, it seemed to Clare, that there was no correlation between a man's education or social status and his creative capacities, and so he saw no reason why his own lack of formal education and humble place within the social hierarchy should preclude him from being compared to the major English poets. The comparisons might be unflattering (Clare himself offered some of the harshest evaluations of his talents), but he wanted the chance to be so compared.

Certainly he did not wish to be grouped with the Thresher-poet, the Washerwoman of Petersfield, the Water-Poet, the Poetical Bricklayer, the Poetical Milk-woman of Bristol, and all the other uneducated poets who were to find a rather distinguished publicity agent in the person of the Poet-Laureate. We have no record of Clare's response to their work (we cannot even be certain that he ever read any of them), and so, when I say that he did not wish to be identified with the group of poets Robert Southey was to write about, I do not mean to imply that he was scornful of them, but rather that he did not willingly submit to the condescension and prejudice which met their literary efforts. Nothing brought home to him the dangers of being identified with the various uneducated poets who had appeared in print quite so clearly as Southey's essay on the poetry of John Jones. We have no evidence that Clare ever read *Lives and Works of the Uneducated Poets*, but we do know that he read the essay on Jones which was to serve as the main chapter in Southey's more extended study. This essay appeared in the *Quarterly* of 1831, and when Clare read it he was appalled by the condescending tone of the piece:

Mr Southey seems to hold uneducated poets in very little estimation & talks about the march of mind in a sneering way – as to education it aids very little in bringing forth that which is poetry – & if it means [a] humble situation in life is to be the toleration for people to praise him I should say much admiration is worth but little / the whole review for a leading journal exceeds all the twaddle I ever met with.   (*Letters*, 254)

Thus Clare dispensed with the opinions of the Poet-Laureate, published in the leading journal of the day. But if Southey's essay was just so much "twaddle," it was not only because of its condescending tone, but because it did not even pretend to be a piece of serious literary criticism. As Southey made abundantly clear, his essay was meant as a charitable intervention which might "render some little service" to his protégé. The main thing, he explained, was to get "a little money" for the "old servant," and Southey, who no doubt meant to be kind, felt that the best way to accomplish this was to commend Jones's character rather than to recommend his poetry for whatever literary qualities it might possess.[15] Jones, with his "thankful and thoughtful mind," was held up to the reader's scrutiny, not as a writer, not even as a literary personality, but as a fine specimen of his class. And such a specimen, Southey argued, ought to be encouraged to write for no other reason than that writing was of "moral benefit" to his character. The fact that Clare himself might have found it difficult to argue for the literary merit of Jones's poetry is quite beside the point. What upset him was the thought that genteel readers would approach his work in the same way that Southey had approached Jones's. It was, perhaps, his fear of being belittled as Jones had been, of having his serious work undermined by the frivolous though well-intentioned postures of *noblesse oblige*, that prompted Clare to write so harshly of Southey's essay.[16] He was deeply offended, he was later to say, by any writer or critic who "would force it down the throat of the world that I am evoking charity when I am only seeking independance" (*Letters*, 262).

No writer revealed the injury that could be done in the sweet name of *noblesse oblige* quite so forcefully and unwittingly as

Hannah More, whose self-justifying comments upon her protégé, Anne Yearsley, were quoted approvingly by Southey in his essay:

"It is not intended," said the patroness, "to place her in such a state of independence as might seduce her to devote her time to the idleness of poetry. I hope she is convinced that the making of verses is not the great business of human life ... Pressing as her distresses are, if I did not think her heart was rightly turned I should be afraid of proposing such a measure, lest it should unsettle the sobriety of her mind, and, by exciting her vanity, indispose her for the laborious employments of her humble condition."[17]

What was considered to be noble and important work for a gentleman (and for Hannah More) was, for this bright and courageous milkwoman from Bristol, mere idleness and vanity. It was not simply that Anne Yearsley was not to be given the bare decencies of financial security so that she could develop her talents with some peace of mind but that financial and creative independence were to be deliberately withheld from her for her own moral good.

One can feel the drift of this kind of attitude duplicated by many of Clare's early reviewers, of whom we can take as an example the critic of the *Eclectic Review*, who recommended with capacious good will that what would be "most conducive to [Clare's] happiness" would be "a situation of honourable industry, in which, while elevated above the fear of want, he should not be discharged from the necessity of daily exertion, in which poetry should still continue to be, not his occupation, much less his trade, but his solace and his pride."[18] Clare should not be "tempted to play the idler," this gentleman concluded, but should "still be suffered to live, and to labour too." For, of course, the proper business for his life was not to write poetry, but to work in the fields. He was not to enjoy the free play of the mind freed from necessity, but was to spend his energies within the relentless cycle of "daily exertion." Not all Clare's reviewers thought this way, but most of them did. "The calamity of his fortune," his "hopeless lot," his "privation" were remarked upon with sympathy, but also with a chilling fatalism. His creative abilities could be tolerated, encouraged, even in small ways supported by patronage, but he was not to think of himself as a poet but rather as a workingman who happened to write poems in the hours or minutes after his duties had been done. And he was expected to be grateful for this. As early as 1817 Clare was thinking very seriously about what he wanted to write in the future. But his plans were shadowed by fears that this future would never arrive. "All that hurts me," he wrote in that year, "is the Nessesity of taking to hard Labour again – after all my hopes to the Contrary" (*Letters*, 25). And in this we can hear the voice of a young poet anxious to get ahead with his chosen work. But to many of Clare's patrons and reviewers, to Hannah More or Robert Southey, it might have sounded like an unsettled man ready to give himself up to idleness and vanity. Such a man must not be allowed to forget his place, nor to hold expectations which were unreasonable, improper, and threatening to many aspects of the *status quo* – in particular, to its system of work-discipline and to its separation along the lines of class of the functions of labour and culture.

Yet Clare received very conflicting signals from the critics who reviewed his first volumes. For if he was always being reminded that his destiny was the destiny of his class, he was also constantly being invited to dissociate himself from his class. On the one hand, he was not to be allowed to forget that because of his class-identity and his particular circumstances he had no right to commit all his energies to what could never be more than an avocation. Literature was, after all, a gentleman's vocation. On the other hand, his first published poems were usually praised because, so it was said, in the act of writing he had managed to transcend the circumstances in which his social being took shape. It was remarkable that certain poetic talents had "discovered themselves" in the person of a common day-labourer, but for the critic of the *Eclectic Review* the merits of this day-labourer's poems were "quite independent of the circumstances of their author."[19] For the critic of the *Quarterly Review*, Clare was interesting because he was one of those "examples of minds highly gifted by nature, struggling with, and breaking through the bondage of adversity."[20] For the critic of the *Gentleman's Magazine* Clare's poetry was evidence that "the teeming images of a mind finely oppressed by a generous enthusiasm, will burst forth in spite of the rustic garb and the inauspicious circumstances which, perchance, environ and obscure it."[21] Finally, the critic of the *Anti-Jacobin Review* found it necessary to draw attention to Clare's "distressing circumstances" and to observe with approval that "resignation to his lot appears to be a prominent feature in his character." "No envious spirit, no carking discontent is to be traced in Clare's poems," he wrote, and for this anti-Jacobin this was reason enough to commend a working-class man.[22] But Clare's poetry was to be praised not because he wrote about his circumstances, but because he had managed to "burst through the fetters" of circumstance:

This little volume is the production of a second Burns; a poet in humble life, whose genius has burst through the fetters with which his situation had surrounded it; and astonished the neighbouring villages with the brilliancy of his song. Amidst all the privations attendant on the life of a labouring peasant, this genuine child of poesy has written a volume, many articles in which would reflect no disgrace upon a far nobler name.

Clare's "humblest station in society" was the first thing to be noticed, yet when the compliments were handed out Clare was not seen as a class-type. His lack of schooling was often remarked upon and it was said that his work represented "the efforts of the uncultivated mind – the outpourings of genius unmoulded by scholastic system and unimbued with scholastic lore."[23] Yet it was never suggested that his best poems and "the sensibility, the keenness of observation, and the imaginative enthusiasm which they display" might be adduced as evidence of the intellectual and creative potentialities of working-class men and women. For, as the knowing critic of the *Gentleman's Magazine* was to say, Clare demonstrated "a range of thinking vastly superior to the standard of his ordinary compeers" and possessed "a heart cast in a fine mould and fired by emotions far above those of his own level and occupation."[24]

The critics from whom we have been quoting at least gave Clare the advantage of reading his poetry *as* poetry. Or at least they appeared to do so. And this was certainly preferable to the sort of condescending interventions with which Hannah More and Robert Southey had busied themselves. It may be that in putting Clare forward (in his character as thinking and writing man) as the "genuine child of poetry," and not as a child of the labouring poor, the reviewers thought that they were paying him the highest of compliments. The fact remains, however, that Clare was stigmatized as much as he was praised for the efforts of his "uncultivated mind" ("rising, as it were, from the clods and the dunghill").[25] It was clear to all concerned gentlemen that, because he was "equally unacquainted with the art and reserve of the world, and with the riches, rules, and prejudices of literature," this "genuine child of poetry" was not likely ever to grow up.[26] (Clare was twenty-seven years old when his first volume was published.) The critics might have congratulated themselves on the fatherly benevolence with which they spoke of Clare's "efforts." But the only way they could approach his work was to see him as an exception in literature and as an exception to his class. They dissociated Clare from his "rustic compeers," separated his social and his poetical experience, and by doing so served the ideology of caste far better than they served Clare. For precisely because he was seen to be exceptional, the ideologically potent questions raised by this living instance of low-born genius were turned aside. The reviewers were not compelled by this particular exception to question the exclusiveness of their definitions of culture, nor to reconsider their notions about plebeian character, nor to wonder whether it was not time for the walls of genteel prejudice to come down. John Clare, the common labourer who was expected to accept unquestioningly "the bondage of adversity" in which he lived, and John Clare, the exceptional man who struggled and broke past those bonds through the very act of writing, existed in separate categories of human experience, calling forth different responses from his critics.

GESTURES OF DEFERENCE

The critical commendations Clare received as a man whose mind had been "borne up by the elasticity of genius, above the vulgarizing influence of his circumstances and employment"[27] were commendations that carried a request: let us hear as little as possible about the vulgar circumstances and vulgarizing influences. His initial celebrity was founded upon the fact that he was seen as an oddity – a workingman with the heart of a poet. Yet even his publisher discouraged Clare from thinking that there could be an informing connection between his literary work and his labour in the fields. "To describe the occupations of Clare," Taylor wrote, "we must not say that Labour and the Muse went hand in hand: they rather kept alternate watch, and when Labour was exhausted with fatigue, she "cheer'd his needy toilings with a song."[28] Since he was so often seen, and encouraged to see himself, in this radically dissociative way, it is hardly surprising to discover Clare writing of himself as

A Peasant in his daily cares
A Poet in his joy   (*LPJC*, 845)

What is more surprising is how rarely Clare allowed Labour and the Muse, the workingman and the working poet, to part company. For by encouraging Clare to put aside his "rustic garb" and thence to allow his "fire of genius" to erase the evidence of his social character and experience, his critics and his publisher were offering him a way of slipping through the net of genteel prejudice. Why did Clare refuse to purchase this bargain? Perhaps he realized that by discarding his "rustic garb" he would be condoning the hypocrisies of his critics; perhaps he saw that what he was being asked to give up was not only his identity but the very provenance of his poetry; perhaps he understood all along that the contribution he wanted to make to the English tradition was bound up with his perceptions, feelings, and experience as a rural labourer. Perhaps for all these reasons, Clare did not take advantage of the option that was offered to him. It is not that he was constantly pointing towards the social grievances of his class but, rather, that he refused to point away from them.

If we are to understand the nature of Clare's achievement, and so take the true measure of his integrity, then we must do so against the whole set of attitudes we have been considering: the condescension, the indifference, the refusal to allow the working-class poet to take his writing life seriously, keep his creativity *and* his class, and reconcile the social position into which he was born and the literary place to which he aspired. Integrity is not, perhaps, the first word that comes to mind when one tries to characterize the tone and spirit of much of his early work. In many of the poems which went into his first two collections, Clare was quite capable of begging, apologizing, bowing and scraping, not for a fair hearing, but for any hearing he could get. His gestures of deference towards his audience suggest that he had succumbed, and was anxious to show that he had succumbed, to the pressures of genteel prejudice. Yet, because these gestures were only necessary because his class-identity was always confessed, they may be offered as evidence that Clare would not allow himself to be assimilated into the mainstream of English culture at the expense of that identity.

His deference is also proof that Clare was much better acquainted with the "riches, rules and prejudices of literature" than his first critics were willing to recognize. Long before he submitted his work to the public, he knew that a certain cast of experience, sophistication, and gentility was expected of a man who called himself a poet, and that, since he couldn't meet these expectations, the least he could do was to admit his inadequacies. His early poems are filled with the confessions of inadequacy of a poor, humble, obscure, luckless, despised, artless, unskilled, uncultured, rough, rude, presumptuous clown. The words are not mine but Clare's, and they were chosen, I suspect, with calculation. As a general rule it is better to admit one's failings and plead for mercy before, not after, one is indicted for them, and in his early work Clare followed this rule without hesitation. He was always belittling himself, anticipating the worst that could be said of him and saying it first. Did his harshest critics think that the workingman's experience was too common or limited or brutal to nourish the poetic imagination? If so, Clare was the first to agree, writing of the "low paths of poverty" in which he belonged, the "mean little village" in which he was confined:

> a village full of strife and noise,
> Old senseless gossips, and blackguarding boys,
> Ploughmen and threshers, whose discourses led
> To nothing more than labour's rude employs.   (*I*, 140)

Did his first readers assume that he was an ignorant man? Clare was again the first to agree:

> Learning scowls her scornful brow,
> And damps my soul – I know not how.   (*I*, 82)

Did Hannah More say that the working-class poet should not be allowed to forget his place? Clare was happy to admit that he knew his place very well. In "To My Oaten Reed" he addressed his "rough, rude" muse in these terms:

> How oft I've woo'd thee, often thrown thee by!
> In many a doubtful rapture touching thee,
> Waking thy rural notes in many a sigh:
> Fearing the wise, the wealthy, proud and high,
> Would scorn as vain thy lowly ecstasy,
> Deeming presumptuous thy uncultur'd themes.   (*I*, 127)

Did Southey think the uneducated poet was unworthy of serious critical attention? Clare was willing to defer to his judgment too:

> Then will it prove presumption thus to dare
> To add fresh failings to each faulty song
> Urging thy blessing on an idle prayer
> To sanction silly themes it will be wrong
> For one so lowly to be heard so long   (*JCOA*, 107)

The self-castigating terms and pleading, apologetic tone of such passages might lead one to suppose that Clare was unable to challenge the firmly entrenched prejudice of his detractors. I am not convinced, however, that any of these passages offers a true indication of Clare's self-image as man and poet, nor that he was quite as deferential as he appears to have been to forms of prejudice so hostile to his creative practice. When he wrote of his mean experience, lowly ecstasy, lowly dreams, little soul, faulty songs, silly themes, presumptuous longings, it was to disarm prejudicial comparisons before they were made. In many ways his deference was not the consequence of his capitulation to the power of genteel opinion but the product of his understanding that he would have to gain the favour of his audience before he could hope to challenge its values. All the same, it's clear that his deference was more than a calculated pose or clever tactic to win over his readers. Indeed, to suggest that Clare was not really modest or deferential, but only wanted to appear so is to ignore the very real anxieties with which he had to contend. Perhaps the greatest difficulty he had to surmount in his early years was that he had himself internalized some of the values of cultural hegemony so that, even as he voiced his right to "sing as well as greater men" (*JCOA*, 155), he felt a sense of impropriety and personal inadequacy in claiming that right. He had to struggle not only against an uncongenial environment, but also against a part of himself.

We can feel the weight of this problem in "The Progress of Ryhme," a poem which reveals the extent to which Clare felt that his place in English society was a hindrance to his creative poise, the main ingredient in his extreme self-consciousness. It is about a young peasant-poet who believes that he is capable of creative and original work, but fears that his imagination is unguided, his intellect untutored. He wants to write in his own voice about his own experience as a rustic, but for this he has few precursors and no great tradition to draw upon. He fears that he lacks the skill to express what he imagines and feels, that gentle readers will repay his work with rudeness and scorn. But the problem of class prejudice is not only felt as an external pressure: it has been internalized so that the act of utterance, and his very capacity to recognize beauty, are seen as shameful presumptions – "the right of bards," Clare says, but "nought to me." If he dares to speak aloud, outside the solitude of nature and beyond the circle of his family, his mind must strain to oppose this sense of his own impropriety:

> I glowered on beauty passing bye
> Yet hardly turned my sheepish eye
> I worshiped yet could hardly dare
> To show I knew the goddess there
> Lest my presumptious stare should gain
> But frowns ill humour or disdain
> My first ambition was its praise
> My struggles aye in early days

Had I by vulgar boldness torn
That hope when it was newly born
By rudeness gibes and vulgar tongue
The curse of the unfeeling throng
Their scorn had frowned upon the lay
And hope and song had passed away
And I with nothing to attone
Had felt myself indeed alone ...
No friends had I to guide or aid
The struggles young ambition made
In silent shame the harp was tried
And raptures guess the tune applied
Yet oer the songs my parents sung
My ear in silent musings hung
Their kindness wishes did regard
They sung and joy was my reward
All else was but a proud decree
The right of bards and nought to me
A title that I dare not claim
And hid it like a private shame
I whispered aye and felt a fear
To speak aloud tho' none was near
I dreaded laughter more than blame
And dared not sing aloud for shame   (*JCOA*, 154, 159)

The fact that Clare felt impelled to defend not simply how or
what he wrote about, but that he wrote at all, helps to explain why
his commitment to the poet's calling supplied the major theme for
almost all the poetry in his first two volumes. In his meditations on
poverty, love, hope, death, in his depictions of humble life and village customs, even in his descriptive landscape verse he was always
turning back to this theme, relating what he saw or felt or thought
to his vocational aspirations:

When on pillow'd thorns I weep,
And vainly stretch me down to sleep,
Then, thou charm from heav'n above,
Comfort's cordial dost thou prove:
Then, engaging Poesy!
Then how sweet to talk with thee ...
And poor, and vain, and press'd beneath
Oppression's scorn although I be.
Still will I bind my simple wreath,
Still will I love thee, Poesy.   (*I*, 82)

Yet it was precisely these aspirations that left him vulnerable to the charge of plebeian vanity. For wasn't it presumptuous of Clare to commit himself to a profession normally followed by educated gentlemen, to do something more with his life than his family and neighbours had been able to do? And wasn't he challenging the natural order of society by assuming the right to choose for himself the work he wanted to do? Clare may have felt that such questions deserved to be answered by a sullen and impertinent "so what":

> A poor, rude clown, and what of that?
> I cannot help the will of fate.   (*I*, 82)

But generally he answered his detractors carefully. Just how carefully can be seen from the title of the poem from which these lines are taken – "An Effusion to Poesy, On Receiving a Damp from a Genteel Opinionist in Poetry, of Some Sway, as I am Told, in the Literary World." There's a touch of scorn and bravado in the title, but the poem as a whole is deferential and nowhere more so than in its reference to the "will of fate."

Fate is an excellent excuse, and Clare often leaned upon it heavily, suggesting that just as he could not be blamed for the circumstances of his birth, so he could not help the fact that he had been called to the poet's work. If he was committed to what was properly thought of as a gentleman's profession, his commitment had little to do with personal volition or ambition. Poetry (that "charm from heav'n above") had chosen him and he could not help but respond to the call. There was something almost Calvinist about the idea of vocation which he articulated. Just as the Calvinist believes that by no good works and no natural tendencies to righteousness can a person earn his way into a state of grace, so Clare wanted his readers to understand that he had become a poet through no personal longings or natural tendencies:

> O soul enchanting poesy
> Thoust long been all the world with me
> When poor thy presence grows my wealth
> When sick thy visions give me health ...
> And but for thee my idle lay
> Had neer been urged in early day
> The harp imagination strung
> Had neer been dreamed of but among
> The flowers in summers fields of joy
> Id lain an idle rustic boy   (*JCOA*, 153-4)

To invoke the miracles of fate, to speak of poetry as a form of enchantment, to emphasize his own unfitness for the vocation to which he had been called, were ways for Clare to disclaim all personal responsibility for his aspirations and so disarm those genteel opinionists who questioned the propriety of his literary intentions.

But some readers refused to be disarmed even by Clare's most deferential poems. The critic for the *Monthly Magazine*, for instance, objected to "The Village Minstrel" because the poet's "mention of himself" was altogether "too egotistical and querulous."[29] The criticism is revealing. Since it is difficult to think of any writer in the language who is quite as self-effacing as the author of "The Village Minstrel," or as careful to avoid appearing egotistical about his talents, one wonders if anything John Clare could have written would have pleased this particular critic. Probably not. For this gentleman, convinced that literature ought to belong only to "the favoured few" and that those men with "defects" in their education ought to have the discretion to keep quiet, was alarmed by the whole idea of a labouring poet. If a man like Clare (of "consummate ignorance" and "vulgarity") was tolerated, his example might encourage "the *canaille* throughout the kingdom" and bring forth "the evil of incompetent intruders into the walks of literature."[30] For such a critic, the only guarantee of Clare's genuine deference would have been his silence. Other critics, less fastidious in their neoclassical standards and less vigilant in their service to genteel values and privileges, received Clare's work more courteously. The reviewer for the *New Monthly*, far from finding Clare impertinent or intrusive, noticed the modesty with which he spoke of his own poetic talents. "The Village Minstrel," he wrote, should be read by all readers who took pleasure "in the artless expression of pure and virtuous feelings, - and, above all, in the delightful contemplation of the heavenly gift of genius, yielding good and happiness to its possessor, even amid the pressure of poverty, hunger, anxiety, and almost every ill that flesh is heir to."[31] John Clare was not for this reviewer to be seen as an intruder into the walks of literature: he was to be invited in, if only as a temporary guest. But if the door was opened by some critics, one suspects that this was not only because Clare exemplified "pure and virtuous feelings," but because he suggested through his gestures of deference that he would be a most grateful and ingratiating guest.

I don't wish to create the impression that Clare's doubts and fears and his tendency to offer insult to his own creative work can be explained solely by reference to the class-prejudice that confronted him. He was addressing not only the genteel reader when he spoke of his unworthiness, compared himself unfavourably to other poets, emphasized his coarse origins and lack of formal education, and confessed his fear that he was incapable of more than "lowly dreams" and "artless themes." He was also, as the title and the structure of "To the Rural Muse" make very clear, addressing his muse which was, of course, another name for his own creative imagination. Indeed the issues of social alienation and cultural elitism, and the problem of how the working-class poet was to breach or bypass the "wider space / Between the genteel and the vulgar race" are less central to the psychic crises enacted in several of Clare's vocational poems than the specifically Romantic and socially unmediated problem of creative failure and renewal. "To the Rural Muse," for example, does not ask, or does not appear to ask, the question: how is the working-class poet to live and write in a class-divided society? Rather it asks: how is the poet to write when he is divided against himself? How is the imagination to protect itself against emotional loss, dejection, and self-doubt? These were the very questions which Clare's contemporaries raised in the greatest lyrics of the Romantic period, and they seem to bear little relation to Clare's social identity and experience.

"To the Rural Muse" is couched in the rhetoric of address but, like the famous crisis-lyrics of his contemporaries, Clare's poem is dramatic in structure: it enacts the conflict between the poet's will to write and his inhibiting self-consciousness about what he writes.[32] Its tone of sustained supplication, its courtly diction, its shifting moods of enchantment and dejection, and its imagery of wind and cloud, harp and bird, suggest that Clare had read Shelley's work closely – though we have no concrete evidence that Clare had ever read Shelley at all. The hero of the poem and the lyric situation are also Shelleyan. A young poet doubtful of his prowess, believing himself to be dwarfed by the shadows of his famous precursors and fearful that inspiration has deserted him forever and left him to a "hopeless silence," is emboldened by his memories of "the raptures of life's early day" to believe that he is still championed by his muse, and so "with warm courage calming many a fear" brings his votive offerings to her shrine.[33] Like the prophetic spirit that Shelley addresses in his "Ode to the West Wind," Clare's muse is first glimpsed on land, in water, and through fire, though Clare's images are a rusticated version of Shelley's Heraclitean imagery:

Muse of the Fields oft have I said farewell
To thee my boon companion loved so long

And hung thy sweet harp in the bushy dell
For abler hands to wake an abler song
Much did I fear mine homage did thee wrong
Yet loath to leave as oft I turned again
And to its wires mine idle hands would cling
Torturing it into song - it may be vain
Yet still I try ere fancy droops her wing
And hopeless silence comes to numb its every string

Muse of the pasture brooks on thy calm sea
Of poesy Ive sailed and tho the will
To speed were greater then my prowess be
Ive ventured with much fear of usage ill
Yet more of joy - tho timid be my skill
As not to dare the depths of mightier streams
Yet rocks abide in shallow ways and I
Have much of fear to mingle with my dreams
Yet lovely Muse I still believe thee bye
And think I see thee smile and so forget I sigh

Muse of the cottage hearth oft did I tell
My hopes to thee nor feared to plead in vain
But felt around my heart thy witching spell
That bade me as thy worshiper remain
I did and worship on O once again
Smile on my offerings and so keep them green
Bedeck my fancys like the clouds of even
Mingling all hues which thou from heaven dost glean
To me a portion of thy power be given
If theme so mean as mine may merit aught of heaven   (*JCOA*, 104)

The series of epithets in these opening stanzas suggest that Clare's muse takes for her domain not the entire territory of human life, nor even the whole range of country life, but only the country life as it is known best to a certain class of countrymen. She guards over the places where the rural workingman lives, works, and relaxes. She is a muse cut to the shape of Clare's own experience, the tutelary spirit of the fields, pasture brooks, and cottage hearths. Yet despite this perfect compatibility between the poet and his muse, the poet has felt doubts about his worthiness to serve her, and his doubts have been strong enough to produce periods of creative failure, from one of which, at the beginning of the poem, he is just emerging.

We never learn what specific experience has caused his dejection nor what force has precipitated the process of creative recovery. We only know that the poet has recovered or, rather, in the act of writing his poem is in the process of recovering. In the central stanzas Clare speaks of himself as an exile returning to a beloved homeland. He begs his muse to welcome his return and entreats her never again to part from him. Yet Clare is evasive about the place, or the state of mind, from which he has returned. It is not difficult to understand why Clare should be so evasive, for "To the Rural Muse" is written as a testament to his ability to evade the anxieties of the recent past, to avoid the "gloom thrown around by cares oershading wing," and to transcend the conditions which caused his dejection. Only by distancing himself from the immediate past, by nimbly throwing a retrospective arch over the years which have silenced him, can he find the necessary connection between the springtime of his life, when inspiration "found an early home," and his present in which he has desperate need of that inspiration. To ignore the immediate past and return to the distant past is thus not so much an evasion as a way for Clare to come home to his muse:

With thee the spirit of departed years
Wakes that sweet voice that time hath rendered dumb
And freshens like to spring - loves hopes and fears
That in my bosom found an early home
Wooing the heart to extacys - I come
To thee when sick of care of joys bereft
Seeking the pleasures that are found in bloom
And happy hopes that time hath only left
Around the haunts where thou didst erst sojourn
Then smile sweet cherubim and welcome my return

With thee the raptures of lifes early day
Appear and all that pleased me when a boy
Tho pains and cares have torn the best away
And winters crept between us to destroy
Do thou commend the reccompense is joy
The tempest of the heart shall soon be calm
Tho sterner truth against my dreams rebel
Hope feels success and all my spirits warm
To strike with happier mood my simple shell
And seize thy mantles hem O say not fare thee well

Still sweet enchantress youths stray feelings move
That from thy presence their existance took
The innoscent idolatry and love
Paying thee worship in each secret nook
That fancied friends in tree and flower and brook
Shaped clouds to angels and beheld them smile
And heard commending tongues in every wind
Lifes grosser fancys did these dreams defile
Yet not entirely root them from the mind
I think I hear them still and often look behind   (*JCOA*, 105)

But there is in these lines a quality of desperate fragility ("O say not fare thee well"), of muted consolation rather than of triumphantly secured recovery ("the reccompense is joy"). And so, though the poem itself exists as circumstantial evidence that Clare had found again the "sweet voice that time hath rendered dumb," his tone and language suggest that he is not entirely certain that he has recovered his creative resources ("I think I hear them still and often look behind").

We hear the same fragile, desperate, supplicating tone in the last stanzas of the poem. Here the poet voices the very same fears and doubts with which his poem begins, but now with a precision that permits us to understand more clearly the nature of his extreme self-consciousness:

Then will it prove presumption thus to dare
To add fresh failings to each faulty song
Urging thy blessing on an idle prayer
To sanction silly themes it will be wrong
For one so lowly to be heard so long
Yet sweet enchantress yet a little while
Forgo impatience and from frowns refrain
The strong are not debarred thy cheering smile
Why should the weak who need them most complain
Alone in solitude soliciting in vain   (*JCOA*, 107-8)

"It will be wrong / For one so lowly to be heard so long": this statement makes us fully aware that the poet's social identity is implicated after all in his self-consciousness, and that his social experience obtrudes even into this most private dialogue between his will to write and his imagination. He is convinced that it "will be deemed as rudeness" for him to offer his poetry to the muse or to the public, for compared to the men with "birthright" to the "rich paradise of sacred song" Clare has no rights at all. To pursue his vocation against this conviction is to be guilty of a presumption which cannot be overlooked, but only excused if he confesses his own guilt. In the end he can only ask to be admitted to the muse's shrine on special terms:

> Not with the might to thy shrine I come
> In anxious sighs or self applauding mirth
> On mount parnassus as thine heir to roam
> I dare not credit that immortal birth
> But mingling with the lesser ones on earth
> Like as the little lark from off its nest
> Beside the mossy hill awakes in glee
> To seek thy mornings throne a merry guest
> So do I seek thy shrine if that may be
> To win by new attempts another smile from thee   (*JCOA*, 107)

Like the society in which he lives, Mount Parnassus has its status-hierarchies, and, as the poet is the first to admit, his place on Parnassus corresponds to the same lowly one he inhabits in society: compared to the mighty poets of the tradition Clare sees himself as one of "the lesser ones on earth." The poem is rife with such comparisons: other poets have "abler hands" than he; they are strong, he is weak; their themes course through "the depths of mightier streams," while his themes flow in "shallow waves"; the great poets are likened to eagles in the sun, but he is only a "little lark from off its nest." These persistent references to his comparatively lowly status in the tradition may, of course, be taken as the findings of a painful self-scrutiny, of Clare's honest appraisal of his own poetic gifts. One notices, however, that the very terms and metaphors he employs to describe his poetry in "To the Rural Muse" are those he uses to describe his social circumstances in the introduction to his *Autobiography*: "As to the humble situation I have filled in life it needs no appology for all tastes are not alike / they do not all love to climb the Alps but many content themselves with wandering in the valleys – while some stand to gaze on the sun to watch the flight of the towering eagle – others not less delighted look down upon the meadow grass to follow the fluttering of the butterflye" (*Prose*, 11).

"Humble," "lowly," "mean," "unpresuming": the fact that Clare's self-valuation in "To the Rural Muse" is offered in the language of class suggests that his sense of himself as a poet and his consciousness of his place in English society were so intertwined that he could not separate one from the other. Thus, though there is a specifically Parnassian theme in this poem, though it may be useful to compare "To the Rural Muse" with the well-known crisis-lyrics of the major Romantics, the emotional centre of the poem, the fears and doubts the poet strives to muffle or overcome, must be related to a particular situation which Clare believed he could not share with his famous contemporaries or precursors. We must approach this and all the vocational poems with the understanding that, if we try to disentangle the workingman from the working poet, to separate Clare's creative experience from his social experience, then we will tear apart what Clare wove together.

CHAPTER FOUR

"The Village Minstrel"

Excluding the Byronic poems which Clare wrote in the asylum, he composed only three long poems and of these three – *The Parish*, *The Shepherd's Calendar*, and "The Village Minstrel" – only in "The Village Minstrel" does he speak at any great length about himself and his crucial formative years, or rather about those years as they were passed by a character named Lubin who is a projected version of Clare. I propose in the following pages to read "The Village Minstrel" as an autobiography, as a sort of *Prelude* in which Clare traces the growth of his creative mind up to the point when he begins to write for publication. There are, however, one or two difficulties posed by approaching the poem in this way, and these must be considered. In the first place, in the few written comments he offered about the poem, Clare himself appears to have been rather indifferent to its autobiographical shape and content. What he liked best about the poem was its treatment of rustic customs and those passages which contained, he thought, "some of the best rural descriptions I have yet written" (*Letters*, 74). The only evidence that he was consciously expressing his own feelings in writing about the feelings of the fictional character Lubin comes to us in a comment written after the poem had been published: "I began the Village Minstrel a long while before attempting to describe my own feelings and love for rural objects and I then began in good earnest ... but I was still unsatisfied with it and am now and often feel sorry that I did not withold it a little longer for revision / the reason why I dislike it is that it does not describe the feelings of a ryhming peasant strongly or localy enough" (*SPP*, 66). The "ryhming peasant" was Clare, of course, but in this comment, as in the poem itself, Clare does not absolutely identify himself as the hero of "The Village Minstrel." Indeed, because his poem is autobiographical but – unlike *The Prelude* – does not purport to be, Wordsworth's poem may be a less suggestive analogue than *Childe Harold's Pilgrimage*, or *Alastor*, or the work from which Clare's title is partly borrowed, *The Minstrel* by James Beattie. The subtitle of Beattie's poem is "The Progress of Genius," and, as Beattie wrote, the intention of his poem was to "trace the progress of a poetical genius ... from the first dawnings of fancy and reason."[1] This subtitle and statement of intention might also serve to explain the themes with which Clare's poem is centrally concerned.

Placing "The Village Minstrel" in the tradition of Romantic narrative rather than in the autobiographical tradition may, then, be critically more accurate. It may also remind us that we are dealing with a literary text and not merely a biographical document, though this is a fact the poem itself calls to our attention often enough. There is no doubt that if "The Village Minstrel" is read as a narrative of Clare's early years, only a very selective and highly edited version of those years is given in the poem. Many of the crucial experiences and developments which would be essential to a full biography of Clare's poetical career are not recounted in the story of Lubin's progress. These experiences, especially the anxieties and struggles, would have to be gleaned from Clare's *Autobiography*, his *Journal*, and his letters. Only from these can we gain some understanding of the real strength of character Clare must have possessed and some idea of how arduously he struggled for the public acceptance, not only of his poems, but of his identity as a poet. In the *Autobiography* he speaks emphatically about his longings for recognition, a theme which rarely surfaces in the vocational poems: "I always had that feeling of ambition about me that wishes to gain notice or to rise above my fellows / my ambition then was to be a good writer & I took great pains on winter nights to learn" (*Prose*, 19). Still more conspicuously absent from the vocational poems is any reference to Clare's attempts to educate himself after leaving the village school where, he explains, it was assumed that "my scholarship was to extend no further then to qualify me for the business of a shoemaker or stone-mason" (*Prose*, 18). Qualifying for the business of a literary life was something Clare had to do on his own, within the contrivances of a grab-as-grab-can process. The few educational opportunities and literary tools which fell to him through luck – finding a neighbour who was a "decent scholar," discovering Shakespeare on a broadsheet and Chatterton on a pictured pocket-handkerchief found at Deeping May fair, later having the intellectual company of Artis and Henderson close by at Milton Park – had to be supplemented by careful and

resourceful planning. Discovering who possessed books in his locality and finding ways to borrow them; learning by heart every bal-
lad that he had heard recited; reading every penny book, broadsheet, or pamphlet that came to hand; learning the vocabulary of a
genteel tradition by guessing at the meaning of words he had never
heard before; staring into booksellers' windows; reading catalogues
of books he could not afford to buy; working overtime and walking
miles in order to purchase a cherished copy of Thomson's *Seasons*;
saving pennies for paper and ink, and, when there were no pennies
to spare, using shop-paper and making ink with rainwater, blue-
stones, and nuts: these are the detailed activities which make up
the central narrative of the *Autobiography*. It is a story, like those
told by Bamford, Lovett, and Cobbett, of the making of a self-
made man. But this story rarely worked its way into the vocational
poems, least of all into "The Village Minstrel."

The fact that Clare omitted a particular theme which was not
only central to his own experience but also, one might assume, central to a poem about "the first dawnings of fancy and reason" in its
main character, does not disqualify "The Village Minstrel" as an
autobiographical text. All forms of autobiography and confession
are artful in the sense that they conceal as well as reveal certain
truths about their authors. And this is as true of Clare's *Autobiography* as it is of Newman's *Apologia*. The *Autobiography* cannot
be held up as the authority against which to measure the ways that
Clare is faithful to or deviates from the truth of his own experience
in "The Village Minstrel," for the *Autobiography* has to be read as
a text edited and censored by the poet *as* he wrote it, and despite its
apparently ingenuous tone, it is in some respects as evasive and
partial a piece of self-portraiture as "The Village Minstrel." Both
works may be ransacked for their autobiographical information
and eloquent misinformation, and the most important difference
between them is not to be found in terms of their autobiographical
content – they are both literary texts in which particular aspects of
Clare's experience are structured and reconstructed, evaded and
revealed – but rather in terms of their formal motive.

Why did Clare choose to project himself and selected aspects of
his experience through the fictional character of Lubin? We can
probably best answer this question first by recalling the sort of
reception given to Clare by the critic of the *Monthly Magazine*,
and secondly by remembering that in 1819 when Clare began his
poem, *The Prelude* was thirty-one years away from being published and that Wordsworth himself had observed that it was "a
thing unprecedented in literary history that a man should talk so

much about himself.''[2] In writing "The Village Minstrel" Clare was well aware that he already had several precedents to create, and so did not wish to add to them by appearing to indulge in the unseemly business of talking entirely about himself. By projecting his own experiences, perceptions, and epiphanies into Lubin's story, he was able to maintain a necessary and decorous distance between his life and his self-portrait, and hence comment upon his rustic hero, in his capacity as narrator, in a way that would have been quite impossible had he been narrating his own story. Though Clare could not and did not choose to conceal his authorship of the poem, though his origins and circumstances were well known to his readers, and though the narrator's style and language are obviously those of a formally uneducated countryman, the narrator never actually reveals himself or the nature of his relationship to Lubin. Unlike Wordsworth's "Michael" or "The Ruined Cottage," where the relationships between the narrators and main characters are clearly established, in Clare's poem we are never told how the narrator has access to his knowledge of Lubin's life and character. I would venture to suggest that Clare wanted his narrator and his hero to remain formally separate because they represented entirely different ways of projecting himself: in Lubin he offered an image of the way he assumed he was seen by his critics; through the narrator's commentary, an image of the way he saw himself.

It is difficult to think of any "progress poem" which has so unpromising a hero as Lubin, not only because of the poverty, the absence of educational opportunity, the obscurity, the "coarsest" of origins which inhibit his chances of writing and publishing anything, but also because he appears to be almost incapable of personal agency. In the opening stanzas he is associated with all that is "artless," "luckless," "oblivious"; he will not presume to "snatch to light the muse's fires" nor to sing beyond his swale; he submits to "fate's controlling will," and throughout the poem is described as a kind of human will o' the wisp wandering through his local landscape guided by strange longings and led on by a "wild enthusiasm" he does not entirely understand. He is less hero than victim, a creature of circumstance whose life is the sum of the many places he is fated to inhabit. And he is placed in every possible way: in a location (unspecified but characterized as "the swale where poverty retires"), in the lowest stratum of society, in the worst economic situation, far away from the world of learning, outside a sublime literary tradition, under the thumb of "fate's controlling will," and quite beyond the reach of the genteel reader. "Swale" in the usage of Clare's region had a very precise meaning: not simply a hollow or depression in the terrain but a place that was low, cold, and sunless.[3] These characteristics are repeated throughout the stanzas below in the references to "the black neglect," "oblivious night," and "constant winter cold and chill" which describe the conditions in which Lubin lives:

> WHILE learned poets rush to bold extremes,
> And sunbeams snatch to light the muse's fires,
> An humble rustic hums his lowly dreams,
> Far in the swale where poverty retires,
> And sings what nature and what truth inspires:
> The charms that rise from rural scenery,
> Which he in pastures and in woods admires;
> The sports, the feelings of his infancy,
> And such-like artless things, how mean soe'er they be.
>
> Though, far from what the learned's toils requite,
> He unambitious looks at no renown,
> Yet little hopes break his oblivious night,
> To cheer the bosom of a luckless clown,
> Where black neglect spreads one continual frown,
> And threats her constant winter cold and chill,
> Where toil and slavery bear each fancy down,
> That fain would soar and sing 'albeit ill,'
> And force him to submit to fate's controlling will.
>
> Young Lubin was a peasant from his birth;
> His sire a hind born to the flail and plough,
> To thump the corn out and to till the earth,
> The coarsest chance which nature's laws allow –
> To earn his living by a sweating brow;
> Thus Lubin's early days did rugged roll,
> And mixt in timely toil – but e'en as now,
> Ambitious prospects fired his little soul,
> And fancy soared and sung, 'bove poverty's control.   (*I*, 133)

The bell of injustice is rung here more than once, but one couldn't claim very much for these lines as social protest because the impact of their social observation is so sharply undercut by the pathetically accepting reference to "the coarsest chance which nature's laws

allow." The note of dissent is choked, cut off before it is fully articulated by the poet's argument, not with the reasons of his society
but with the "mysterious cause" of "fate's controlling will." There
is deference in this kind of arguing: a prosperous gentleman of
Clare's period would not fear or distrust a man who put all his
questions to fate and left English society alone – even the fiercest
anti-Jacobin could agree that fate worked in mysterious and
powerful ways.

But it is in describing Lubin's poetic aspirations that Clare's
deference is most elaborately enacted. In the passage above,
"fancy" is the subject of the third alexandrine and, though it might
be argued that in using this abstraction Clare was simply drawing
upon a venerable eighteenth-century convention in order to speak
decorously of his own creative imagination, his diction does not
encourage us to see the figure of fancy as though it were a constitu-
tive part of Lubin's character. One notices for instance that
throughout the poem the possessive adjective almost never pre-
cedes the terms used to signify creative capabilities (fancy, genius,
taste, poesy), almost as though Clare was trying to make the point
that Lubin's fancy isn't his at all, but rather a redemptive force
that visits him in his "black neglect," lifts him up to the light of the
"muse's fires," and so frees him momentarily from the "coarsest
chance which nature's laws allow." Lubin, with his "little soul," his
"little hopes," his "lowly dreams," his "mean" and "artless" concerns, hardly seems capable of imaginative flights of transcendence. He does not possess fancy; he is possessed by it. And so, if he
writes poetry and has "ambitious prospects," he is not to blame.
He knows what he was born to do: "To thump the corn out and to
till the earth." But fancy has claimed him for other work. Thus
fancy serves the same function in "The Village Minstrel" that was
served by "poesy" in "The Progress of Ryhme": it is the peg upon
which Clare hangs a vocational story in which the hero's ambitions
and capabilities are deliberately obscured.

Despite significant developments, Lubin never does take full
possession of his own capabilities, and remains to the end a creature determined by all the forces, benign and malevolent, that
stand over and against him. Fate, nature, poverty, fancy, and
finally, time itself control his past and present, and if he struggles
against or on behalf of any of these determining forces, it is with
little sense of personal efficacy. In the concluding stanzas of the
poem, he is no closer to reaching and no more certain as to how to
reach his "wisht-for prospects" than he was at the beginning:

Ah, as the traveller from the mountain-top
Looks down on misty kingdoms spread below,
And meditates beneath the steepy drop
What life and lands exist, and rivers flow;
How fain that hour the anxious soul would know
Of all his eye beholds - but 'tis in vain:
So Lubin eager views this world of woe,
And wishes time her secrets would explain,
If he may live for joys or sink in 'whelming pain.

Fate's close-kept thoughts within her bosom hide;
She is no gossip, secrets to betray:
Time's steady movements must her end decide,
And leave him painful still to hope the day,
And grope through ignorance his doubtful way,
By wisdom disregarded, fools annoy'd.
And if no worth anticipates the lay,
Then let his childish notions be destroy'd,
And he his time employ as erst it was employ'd.   (*I*, 162-3)

Still caught in his own passivity, unwilling to claim his future or to
demand the recognition of his contemporaries, he awaits the dis-
closure of "Fate's close-kept thoughts," wondering if he will be
allowed to *be* a poet or if he must "his time employ as erst it was
employ'd." Thus "The Village Minstrel" ends as it begins without
resolving the conflict it enacts. We are not to know whether the
enabling imagination will triumph over the disabling circumstances in which Lubin lives, whether fancy or fate will finally
claim him. We take our leave of a character whose mind is filled
not with plans and resolutions but with anxiety and doubt. And it
is difficult not to believe that in Lubin's state of mind we may find
some reflection of Clare's own longing and uncertainty in the early
years of his career.

The introductory and concluding stanzas provide the clearest
access to the deferential project of the poem and to the problematical situation of its hero. But their tone is by no means characteristic of the rest, and I do not wish to represent "The Village
Minstrel" as an anxious, gloomy, or even wholeheartedly deferential poem. It is in many ways a merry poem with a happy hero,
celebrating childhood and innocence, natural landscape and rustic
culture. The most cheerful passages are those which describe

Lubin's experience in the natural landscape, and his character there is quite different from the one who confronts us in the opening and concluding stanzas: not a suffering victim but a countryman with keen eyes and high spirits, often too preoccupied with the emotional and sensual pleasures he takes from the local landscape to worry about his future. The poet we encounter in these passages also seems different. His tone is more blithe and assured, and the quality of his writing more relaxed and polished, as though Clare, like his character, had been transformed by the new and animating emotions which attend the landscape moment. These are differences worth remarking upon, for in them we may find both a structural metaphor for Lubin's experience and a paradigm of Clare's creative practice. When Lubin enters the landscape he leaves behind him the low, cold, dark facts of circumstance and enters a situation so rich, immediate, and delightful that there is no reason and no room left for sorrow or complaint. This situation engenders in Lubin a poised and happy state of mind, a new and sturdier sense of his own identity, and these changes illuminate the happy transformation Clare underwent, not only in composing "The Village Minstrel," but in all his writing, when he turned away from the grave and perplexing issues of poverty, alienation, and class prejudice to write about the natural world he knew best.

The landscape stanzas of "The Village Minstrel" are the least diffident and most encomiastic ones in the poem, though one cannot always be certain whether the main subject of Clare's encomium is Lubin or the landscape. In a sense, of course, both are, since the point of the natural description throughout the poem is to celebrate Lubin in relation to nature, natŭre in relation to Lubin. These relations are often characterized by a mutuality of response so pronounced that Wordsworth's notion of an "ennobling interchange" between the mental and material categories does not quite catch the quality of the relation. In many of his landscape stanzas, Clare manages to discourage us from thinking in terms of the distinction between mind and matter, subject and object, so equally are the attributes of subjectivity shared by both Lubin and the natural world. Lubin enters the landscape, but the landscape seems to meet him half way; he speaks to nature but is also silenced by its eloquence; he is a contemplative observer of nature, but nature is at the same time a compassionate witness of his watching; he walks through the landscape and learns from it, but the landscape is no less capable of movement and growth:

When summer came, how eager has he sped
Where silence reign'd, and the old crowned tree
Bent with its sheltering ivy o'er his head;
And summer-breezes, breathing placidly,
Encroach'd upon the stockdove's privacy,
Parting the leaves that screen'd her russet breast:
'Peace!' would he whisper, 'dread no thief in me,'
And never rose to rob her careless nest;
Compassion's softness reign'd, and warm'd his gentle breast.

And he would trace the stagnant pond or lake,
Where flags sprang up or water-lilies smil'd,
And wipe the boughs aside of bush and brake,
And creep the woods with sweetest scenes beguil'd,
Tracking some channel on its journey wild,
Where dripping blue-bells on the bank did weep:
Oh, what a lovely scene to a nature's child,
Through roots and o'er dead leaves to see it creep,
Watching on some moss'd stump in contemplation deep.

And he would mark in July's rosy prime,
Crossing the meadows, how a nameless fly
Of scarlet plumage, punctual of its time,
Perch'd on a flower would always meet his eye;
And plain-drest butterfly of russet dye,
As if awaken'd by the scythe's shrill sound,
Soon as the bent with ripeness 'gan to dye,
Was constant with him in each meadow-ground,
Flirting the withering swath and unmown blossom round.   (*I*, 141-2)

We should note, however, that in some landscape stanzas this
mutuality of action and reaction is given up for another structure
of relationship, in which Lubin is not quite an equal but rather the
passive partner shaped by the strong and active influence which
nature exerts upon him. His passivity should not be overemphasized for in none of the landscape stanzas does Lubin give
up his freedom and agency to nature in quite the same way that he
submits in the opening stanzas to "fate's controlling will." In the
following passage, for example, Lubin is still the agent of his own
actions, pursues natural beauty, sees it, thinks about it, and then
tries to articulate the "wild sensations" it evokes in him. Indeed he
not only acts, he changes, and in ways that may be directly related
to the vocational theme of the poem. For what we are asked to

observe is a rustic not merely communing with nature but becoming a poet, finding what will be the material of his writing, learning to see nature not only as a pleasant place through which to wander but as a world he must know in every way, and finally discovering the impulse to move out of silent watching into expressive statement – though his expression is as yet no more than a matter of repeated "mutterings":

> Sequester'd nature was his heart's delight;
> Him would she lead thro' wood and lonely plain,
> Searching the pooty from the rushy dyke;
> And while the thrush sang her long-silenc'd strain,
> He thought it sweet, and mock'd it o'er again;
> And while he pluck'd the primrose in its pride,
> He ponder'd o'er its bloom 'tween joy and pain,
> And a rude sonnet in its praise he tried,
> Where nature's simple way the aid of art supplied.
>
> The freshen'd landscapes round his routes unfurl'd,
> The fine-ting'd clouds above, the woods below,
> Each met his eye a new-revealing world,
> Delighting more as more he learn'd to know,
> Each journey sweeter, musing to and fro.
> Surrounded thus, not paradise more sweet,
> Enthusiasm made his soul to glow;
> His heart with wild sensations used to beat;
> As nature seemly sang, his mutterings would repeat.   (*I*, 136)

While Clare could never quite bring himself to portray Lubin as an especially intelligent or resolute character – he would not presume to claim so much for the "little soul" of a village child – in describing Lubin's relationship to nature he shows him to be a youth abundantly endowed with a capacity for subtle perception, delicate sentiment, and a naturally fine taste for natural beauty – gentle qualities possessed by someone who is far from being a gentleman. Indeed, in the stanzas above, there is something quite subversive in the claim that nature is the poet's best guide and tutor and can supply all "the aid of art" that the artless Lubin lacks. It is subversive not only because it suggests that nature, in choosing her favourite sons, is alarmingly indifferent to the business of social classes, but because it sweetly intimates that formal education and the acquisition of specific literary skills are, however useful, not at all necessary to the tasks of the apprentice-poet. All he need do is follow "nature's simple way." This was the sort of claim that caused the critic of the *Monthly Magazine* to worry about "the *canaille* throughout the kingdom" intruding into "the walks of literature," demanding the right to take over his job or Robert Southey's.

Yet Clare's emphasis upon the artless, nature-inspired character of his poet-hero could also be construed as a gesture of deference. For "artless" is an ambiguous and value-laden word which might mean one thing to the follower of Wordsworth or Burns, but a very different thing to the follower of Dryden and Pope. Because of its ambiguity it was a term well chosen to determine the way Clare wanted his rustic hero to be received: artless because he was unpractised, devoid of skill and learning, but also in the more positive sense: innocent, simple, sincere, untainted by artifice. To emphasize Lubin's artlessness (and so, implicitly, the artlessness of his own character and writing) enabled Clare to defer to genteel standards, to acknowledge the uneducated poet's limitations, but at the same time to move outside the circle of deference and to suggest that genteel standards and prerequisites were merely relative. Why should his lack of education, sophistication, and "art" matter to a man who had been inspired by "fancy," "nature," and "truth"? There is an argument hovering about this emphasis, an intimation that the rustic poet might have something to offer to the English tradition, might contribute, for example, a new territory or a new way of seeing an old one. But the argument is never explicitly registered in "The Village Minstrel" because Clare kept himself so busy trying to show that Lubin is inspired by truth, called by fancy, chosen by nature, that he never quite got around to defining Lubin's personal talents and capabilities. Passivity, susceptibility, and humility are the keynotes of Lubin's character, so much so that even the poetic sensibility with which he is gifted is, so to speak, a negative capability, a matter of responsiveness and sensitivity to whatever happens to come his way. Like "The Progress of Ryhme," "The Village Minstrel" leans heavily upon the Christian paradigm of vocation. The Christian, possessing only faith, is redeemed by grace, and Lubin, possessing nothing more promising than his sensibility, is redeemed by his inspirers. But just as there is paradox in the Christian paradigm, so there are paradoxical shadings in the idea that Lubin's ignorance and commonness are the cause of his humility but also the source of the artlessness in which he takes pride. There is another paradox in the idea that in his susceptibility to the influences of nature rests his potential power as a poet, and yet another in the suggestion that, though Lubin is nothing in himself, nevertheless, as the instrument of fancy he is in possession of the poet's noble purposes. Within these paradoxes the deference and impertinence of his creator can be seen to mingle and contend.

In drawing this analogy between Lubin's experience and the Christian's, I do not mean to suggest that "The Village Minstrel" is in any sense a Christian work. On the contrary, it is a remarkably irreligious piece of writing, and nowhere more so than when Clare uses a religious structure of feeling to describe Lubin's relationship to nature. The most amiable evangelist would fear for the soul of a man who returns as often and as reverentially as does Lubin to the scene of nature: his interest in the natural landscape is un- abashedly sensual and he worships the "unsullied dew" of the natural world (*I*, 137) without raising one thought to its maker. Moreover, he remains untroubled by any pangs of conscience, unperplexed by any sense of sin. He finds in the landscape a natural paradise and within himself a natural innocence which were contrary to the doctrines of both church and chapel (and Clare underwent both forms of religious experience).[4] If at the end of the poem Lubin has lost some of his innocence and has been cast out of the paradise of childhood joy, his losses are not connected to Adam's sin but to the very particular evils of enclosure:

> Lubin beheld it all, and, deeply pain'd,
> Along the paled road would muse and sigh,
> The only path that freedom's rights maintain'd';
> The naked scenes drew pity from his eye,
> Tears dropt to memory of delights gone by;
> The haunts of freedom, cowherd's wattled bower,
> And shepherds' huts, and trees that tower'd high,
> And spreading thorns that turn'd a summer shower,
> All captives lost, and past to sad oppression's power,   (*I*, 156)

But before enclosure, in their original nature, the landscape and the character who loves it had no need of the interventions of Christian grace. The natural landscape is the only church Lubin needs to enter, the laws of nature the only ones he wants to obey, and the book of nature the only one he longs to know. In fact, there is not one theological reference in "The Village Minstrel," and the descriptive passages of the poem explain why: Lubin is indifferent to the consolations of conventional religion since the landscape experience allows him to "Edens make where deserts spread before" (*I*, 443). And he has no wish to be redeemed by grace since his relationship to the spirit of nature and to its palpable manifestations in the local scenery allows him to believe that

> From Eve's posterity I stand quite free,
> Nor feel her curses rankle round my heart   (*II*, 515)

These lines properly express Clare's attitudes rather than Lubin's as they are not from "The Village Minstrel" but from later poems, and we should, no doubt, be a little less cavalier in allowing the poet's experience recorded in one poem to obtrude upon the experience of a character from another. Nevertheless, these lines convey in specific terms the unorthodox ideas and the aura of radical innocence which hover about "The Village Minstrel." They also remind us that in substituting devotion to nature for Christian forms of devotion Lubin resembles his creator:

I was never easy but when I was in the fields passing my sabbaths and leisure with the shepherds & herdboys as fancys prompted sometimes playing at marbles on the smooth-beaten sheeptracks or leapfrog among the thymy molehills sometimes running among the corn to get the red & blue flowers for cockades to play at soldiers or running into the woods to hunt strawberries or stealing peas in churchtime ... we heard the bells chime but the fields was our church & we seemd to feel a religious poetry in our haunts on the sabbath while some old shepherd sat on a molehill reading aloud some favourite chapter from an old fragment of a Bible which he carried in his pocket for the day.   (*Prose*, 12–13)

This statement suggests that, though he was unconventional, Clare was not without piety. But, as though he feared he had misrepresented the true motives for his retreat into nature, Clare returned to the same theme later in the *Autobiography*, and we learn then that his motives were very different indeed from those of his Sabbatarian neighbours: "I got a bad name among the weekly church goers forsaking the churchgoing bell & seeking the religion of the fields tho I did it for no dislike to church for I felt uncomfortable very often / but my heart burnt over the pleasures of solitude & the restless revels of ryhme" (*Prose*, 32).

Lubin is as devout a follower of the profane "religion of the fields" as was his creator, and since more than half of the 155 stanzas which make up "The Village Minstrel" are concerned with the depth and constancy of his devotion to nature, Lubin demonstrates a piety which is consistently put to impious use. Yet, however misplaced his piety may be, Lubin gave to more than one of Clare's critics the impression of being a character of "pure and virtuous feelings."[5] This was an impression that I suspect Clare worked to create by portraying the collective village in such a way that it appears in some passages as the foil which casts into sharp relief the ways in which Lubin is more sensitive, more thoughtful, and also a little more proper than his fellows. To the relentless advocate of an exacting work-discipline, of course, Lubin would not have appeared an especially admirable specimen of his class: he spends too much time in idle pursuits, is always following birds and being distracted by flowers, seems to be less industrious and productive than his fellows. And to the hawk-eyed evangelist his values and conduct would have seemed far from virtuous: Hannah More would probably have been horrified by this portrait of a young labourer so appallingly indifferent to questions of his own sinfulness and redemption, so concerned with pleasures and excitements which led him far away from his real duties.

Nevertheless, the pleasures that Lubin seeks are more temperate than those of his fellow-villagers, and in contrast to some of the amorous, drunken, rowdy pleasures in which they choose to indulge, Lubin's notions of pleasure make him seem a paragon of innocence, sobriety, and circumspection. The recreational pastimes of the village, its feasts, dances, rites of courtship, games, and sports, provide the theme for several passages in "The Village Minstrel." And though the pastimes are not described in great detail, the details presented are well chosen. We learn much more from Clare than we do from other observers of rustic pastimes about what actually happens when cudgels are taken up or greased pigs set loose in the village, because Clare offers many things which men like William Howitt could not:[6] a description of rustic play seen from within (as an experience both grotesque and lovely); an evocation of the "glad animal movements" of the playing participants; access to the serio-comic emotions of contestant and spectator, emotions which are always an important ingredient in any game well played; and finally an image of a people who lose themselves in recreation in order to recreate themselves as a community, who take their Dionysian revelry seriously because they are bound together by it as much as by the economic functions and hardships they share.

The attitudes Clare expresses and the particular pastimes he describes are precisely the kind which alarmed those men of property in the early nineteenth century who valued and understood in very precise ways the value of a labour force whose productive energies were not wasted, whose strength and endurance were not tested in any area but that of work, whose pride was not aroused by riotous sport and violent competition.[7] It may have been to fore-

stall at least one of the arguments these rural Gradgrinds might
offer as to the iniquity of village games that Clare points out in the
following passage that the villagers, bound to the cycles of agricul-
tural labour, rarely have the chance to indulge themselves and can
commence their play only when their work has been done. But
the enthusiastic tone, the vivid and colourful manner in which the
games are described, and the fact that Clare focuses upon some of
the rowdiest and most violent rustic pastimes suggests that, far
from wishing to placate disciplinarian obsessions and prejudices,
he took a perverse delight in ignoring them altogether. Men of
property do not figure in the tableaux of "The Village Minstrel,"[8]
and so the villagers play on as they will:

> And monstrous fun it makes to hunt the pig,
> As soapt and larded through the crowd he flies:
> Thus turn'd adrift he plays them many a rig;
> An pig for catching is a wondrous prize,
> And every lout to do his utmost tries;
> Some snap the ear, and some the tunkey tail,
> But still his slippery hide all hold denies,
> While old men tumbled down sore hurts bewail,
> And boys bedaub'd with muck run home with piteous tale.
>
> And badger-baiting here, and fighting cocks –
> But sports too barbarous these for Lubin's strains:
> And red-fac'd wenches, for the holland smocks,
> Oft puff and pant along the smooth green plains,
> Where Hodge feels most uncomfortable pains
> To see his love lag hindmost in the throng,
> And of unfairness in her cause complains,
> And swears and fights the jarring chaps among,
> As in her part he'd die, 'fore they his lass should wrong.
>
> And long-ear'd racers, fam'd for sport and fun,
> Appear this day to have their swiftness tried;
> Where some won't start, and 'Dick,' the race nigh won,
> Enamour'd of some 'Jenny' by his side,
> Forgets the winning-post to court a bride;
> In vain the rout urge on the jockey-clown
> To lump his cudgel on his harden'd hide,
> Ass after ass still hee-haws through the town,
> And in disgrace at last each jockey bumps adown.

And then the noisy rout, their sports to crown,
Form round the ring superior strength to show, ·
Where wrestlers join to tug each other down,
And thrust and kick with hard revengeful toe,
Till through their worsted hose the blood does flow:
For ploughmen would not wish for higher fame,
Than be the champion all the rest to throw;
And thus to add such honours to his name,
He kicks, and tugs, and bleeds to win the glorious game.

And when the night draws on, each mirthful lout
The ale-house seeks, and sets it in a roar;
And there, while fiddlers play, they rant about,
And call for brimming tankards frothing o'er:
For clouds of smoke ye'd hardly see the door;
No stint they make of 'bacco and of beer;
While money lasts they shout about for more,
Resolv'd to keep it merry when it's here –
As toils come every day, and feasts but once a year.   (*I*, 153-4)

But however indifferent the poet himself appears to be to evangelical niceties and disciplinarian values, his character evinces a slightly priggish attitude towards rural pastimes, finding them "too barbarous" to participate in. He watches, listens, knows the games well, is even enthusiastic about them, but he remains a sober witness. Lubin's refusal to participate is not, I think, to be taken as a sign of moral disapproval, but is meant to underscore his personal inclination for solitary and contemplative pleasures over more active and communal ones. Nevertheless, since Lubin appears to be the only character in the poem who does not relish drinking, gambling, or wrestling, his conduct reflects badly upon the conduct of his peers. While the villagers lose themselves in revelry "too barbarous" for Lubin to enjoy, he finds himself in revery. He may be impious, but at least he is capable of contemplative and reverential modes of thought. He has too little reverence for what is worshipped in the churches and so too much for what he worships in the fields, but at least his reverence is genuine enough. In contrast to the "true-going churchman," he is no pharisee, and unlike the village threshers and ploughmen who never reach beyond the grasp of prices and wages, work and unemployment, Lubin is capable of devotion to more than material life and materialist longings:

Folks much may wonder how the thing may be,
That Lubin's taste should seek refined joys,
And court th' enchanting smiles of poesy;
Bred in a village full of strife and noise,
Old senseless gossips, and blackguarding boys,
Ploughmen and threshers, whose discourses led
To nothing more than labour's rude employs,
'Bout work being slack, and rise and fall of bread,
And who were like to die, and who were like to wed:

Housewives discoursing 'bout their hens and cocks,
Spinning long stories, wearing half the day,
Sad deeds bewailing of the prowling fox,
How in the roost the thief had knav'd his way
And made their market-profits all a prey.
And other losses too the dames recite,
Of chick, and duck, and gosling gone astray,
All falling prizes to the swooping kite:
And so the story runs both morning, noon, and night.   (I, 140)

As Clare well knew, a rather significant distinction can be drawn between the material preoccupations of the needy and the material self-interest of the greedy, but this is not a distinction that he chose to emphasize here. In writing "The Village Minstrel," he felt it more important to stress the differences which exist between the man who is concerned with feeling and beauty and matters of the spirit and the man who is, however desperate his cause, concerned only with the business of making a living.

The idea that because of his unworldly preoccupations Lubin judges and is harshly judged by his neighbours is essential to the vocational theme of the poem. Towards the end of his career, Clare wrote:

Despised and hated all along
The bard has nothing but a song.   (II, 374)

But the theme of the beleaguered poet had been developed years before in the complicated story of Lubin's relationship to his community. Because this community is the world to which Lubin belongs by the "coarsest laws" of fate, it is a mirror in which he cannot find the image of what he might become, but can only see the reflection of who he was born to be. If he is to assume the vocation of the poet, it must be in spite of his neighbours who undermine his idea of himself as a poet-in-the-making. They refuse to respect the ways in which he is different from them, and their contempt, whether affectionate or malicious, creates an environment hostile to his aspirations. His failure to conform, to join in their sports and conversations, earns him his reputation as an "uncouthly lout." (I suspect that Clare used the term "uncouthly" in both its senses: to specify Lubin's awkward and ungainly behaviour, but also to signify that he is to the villagers a strange and unfamiliar creature, touched with prophecy.)

A more uncouthly lout was hardly seen
Beneath the shroud of ignorance than he;
The sport of all the village he has been,
Who with his simple looks oft jested free;
And gossips, gabbling o'er their cake and tea,
Time after time did prophecies repeat,
How half a ninny he was like to be,
To go so soodling up and down the street
And shun the playing boys whene'er they chanc'd to meet.   (*I*, 141)

Yet though Lubin is as different from his neighbours as "a cornflower in a field of grain" (*I*, 162), he remains a part of his community: the cornflower grows from the same soil as the grain. And though in some ways the community seems to hinder his "progress," in other more crucial ways it exerts a positive and enabling influence upon the young poet's mind. For it is within the community that Lubin first learns the art of narrative and song and first discovers that through language and story the life of the imagination can be expressed and given shape. This is indeed a rudimentary kind of knowledge, gleaned from the ballads and fairy-tales which the old women of the village tell the children. But mastering this knowledge constitutes the major part of Lubin's education. Clare admits that his character has attended school, and though his attendance must end abruptly (as with Clare, so with Lubin, lessons are a luxury his parents can no longer afford to give him) he presumably stays in school long enough to master the art of reading and to learn that beyond the bounds of his knowledge there exists a great literary tradition:

Yet oft fair prospects cheer'd his parents' dreams,
Who had on Lubin founded many a joy;
But pinching want soon baffled all their schemes,
And dragg'd him from the school a hopeless boy,

To shrink unheeded under hard employ;
When struggling efforts warm'd him up the while,
To keep the little toil could not destroy;
And oft with books spare hours he would beguile,
And blunder oft with joy round Crusoe's lonely isle.   (*I*, 140)

Significantly, the only reference in the entire poem to literary texts
of any kind is to *Robinson Crusoe*, that parable of self-reliance in
which a character like Lubin or a poet like John Clare might find
much to comfort him.[9] Crusoe's entrepreneurial habits of mind,
his aggressive materialism, would not, we may be sure, have
impressed Clare, but it was doubtless not Crusoe's values but the
circumstances in which he was compelled to live which led Clare to
cite his story, and his alone. In Crusoe's isolation he would have
found a reflection of his own sense of isolation from the great world
and its learned literary traditions. For Crusoe, alone except for a
man who does not know his ways or his language, cut off from civi-
lization, manages to thrive in his circumstances, comes to prosperity because he is free of social restrictions, and learns to make a virtue of his necessity. In his situation Crusoe represents the polarities
of Clare's own situation: on the one hand, his alienation from the
prevailing culture of his time; on the other hand, his espousal of a
creative solitude in which the cold hand of social prejudice could
not touch him.

The allusion to "Crusoe's lonely isle" is, then, an apt and knowing one. The fact remains, however, that this is the only book cited
in "The Village Minstrel," that books don't figure in any significant way at all in the story of the growth of Lubin's poetical mind.
It is not a textual culture which first leads him toward literary habits of mind but rather the oral culture of the collective village, and
this culture is described by Clare in considerable detail. Names,
examples, summaries are given of the tales and ballads, legends
and superstitions which make up this oral tradition. Though some
of the stanzas which describe what he hears from the old village-
sibyls have the dull, inexorable beat of the catalogue, the stanzas
which place this tradition in the lives of the villagers and in Lubin's
own emotional life are perhaps the most impressive in the poem.
They convey the sense that this tradition is for the villagers at once
ordinary and extraordinary. The old women may recite a story at
any time, by the hearth or in the fields, but the tales never lose
their aura, remain wondrous events to both teller and listener. It
may be a happy coincidence, or perhaps no coincidence at all, that
in describing this oral culture Clare "sounds" better than he does

anywhere else in the poem. Many passages in "The Village Minstrel" indicate that Clare had difficulty coping with the metric and stanzaic requirements of his form: words are thrown into a line just so that it will scan, phrases are seized upon only because they are metrically pragmatic. But in this stanza Clare seems to have surmounted his difficulties, perhaps because he felt confident and enthusiastic in writing about the oral tradition:

> And when old women, overpower'd by heat,
> Tuck'd up their clothes and sicken'd at the toil,
> Seeking beneath the thorn the mole-hill seat,
> To tell their tales and catch their breath awhile,
> Their gabbling talk did Lubin's cares beguile;
> And some would tell their tales, and some would sing,
> And many a dame, to make the children smile,
> Would tell of many a funny laughing thing,
> While merrily the snuff went pinching round the ring.   (*I*, 144)

Earlier stanzas describe the effect of these tales upon Lubin's young mind:

> And tales of fairy-land he lov'd to hear,
> Those mites of human forms, like skimming bees,
> That fly and flirt about but everywhere,
> The fly-like tribes of night's un'scerning breeze,
> That through a lock-hole even creep with ease:
> The freaks and stories of this elfin crew,
> Ah, Lubin glories in such things as these;
> How they rewarded industry he knew,
> And how the restless slut was pinched black and blue.

> And thousands such the village keeps alive:
> Beings that people superstitious earth,
> That e'er in rural manners will survive,
> As long as wild rusticity has birth
> To spread their wonders round the cottage-hearth.
> On Lubin's mind these deeply were imprest;
> Oft fear forbade to share his neighbour's mirth:
> And long each tale, by fancy newly drest,
> Brought fairies in his dreams, and broke his infant rest.   (*I*, 135)

Here, as so often in the poem, Clare cannot resist drawing our attention to Lubin's different way of seeing things; what is amusing to his neighbours is awesome to this impressionable child. But the emphasis does not really fall upon the recognition that Lubin is different, but upon the fact that he participates fully in the oral tradition of the village. He may hold himself aloof from the games of the village children, but when stories are being told all Lubin's energies are engaged in the common experience. These stories break "his infant rest" in more ways than one. They are remembered and relived, they haunt his sleep, but they also lead him out of infancy because they teach him that the imagination may be exercised not only within the lonely stretches of the individual mind but also within the community.

The imaginative life of the collective village is sustained by the tradition of "wild rusticity." But the last of the stanzas quoted above suggest that the continuing survival of their tradition is not something the villagers take for granted; rather, they work to ensure its preservation through formal and dedicated participation. The telling of the stories appears to be a sufficiently spontaneous experience, but there are, nonetheless, elements of ritual in the context of their narration. These may be glimpsed in the almost theatrical separation of teller and audience, in the collective suspension of disbelief, and in the villagers' adherence to the unchanging forms of their tales, unchanging because they belong to the past and future generations of the village as much as to the present one. The old and young guard their traditions well, perhaps because it is the only form of knowledge they possess which cannot be bought or sold in an economic system: it means nothing to the men who buy their labour and skills, and so means everything to them. Many of the stories which Clare invokes have a historical content which is local and particular, speculative and incomplete, more legendary than factual. But this, of course, doesn't matter at all to the villagers since it is *their* knowledge, to be shared among themselves and not meant to be submitted to the sceptical scrutiny of gentlemen-scholars. Lubin, no longer seen as a self-proclaimed outsider, is a willing student of the shepherds' version of history. In the following stanzas, the village assumes a new character: not merely the place in which Lubin has to live, but a community in the profoundest sense, the *locus* in which Lubin may express his inner life and share in the accessible inner lives of others:

Where ling-clad heaths and pastures now may spread,
He oft has heard of castle and of hall;
And curiosity his steps hath led

To gaze on some old arch or fretting wall,
Where ivy scrambles up to stop the fall:
There would he sit him down, and look, and sigh,
And bygone days back to his mind would call,
The bloody-warring times of chivalry,
When Danes' invading routs made unarm'd Britons fly
...
And oft, with shepherds leaning o'er their hooks,
He'd stand conjecturing on the ruins round:
Though little skill'd in antiquated books,
Their knowledge in such matters seem'd profound;
And they would preach of what did once abound,
Castles deep moated round, old haunted hall –
And something like to moats still 'camp the ground
Where beneath Cromwell's rage the towers did fall;
But ivy creeps the hill, and ruin hides it all.   (*I*, 154–5)

In earlier stanzas Lubin is described as a sort of changeling connected only by threads of circumstance to a world which offers him neither inspiration nor moral support nor (worse still) subject-material for his poems. But here he is portrayed as a devout follower of a rich tradition, fully engaged in the life of his community, consciously seeking out its most articulate members. He may refuse to participate in many of the village customs, but the oral tradition has a rich and active influence upon his developing imagination. Thus, we are led to understand, if he must pursue his solitary way, it is not because his rustic neighbours have so little to offer him, but because there is something in the nature of his vocation that makes it impossible for him to be entirely at one with them.

In discussing the relationship between Lubin and his community there are several good reasons to invoke Beattie's *The Minstrel* and Shelley's *Alastor*, the one as an analogue, the other as a source. In its own way, Clare's work is as preoccupied as Beattie's with the "great Romantic dilemma of being a poet among men," and Clare himself was, no less than Shelley, an anxious and obsessed late-comer to that literary theme.[10] An exercise in the comparison of Beattie's and Shelley's work to Clare's poem might be useful in demonstrating that Clare was a poet of his time, working very consciously within a major literary tradition. But this kind of exercise should not obscure the specific nature of the project which Clare set himself in composing his poem, which was to write, with no sanctioning tradition and few friendly texts to draw upon, as a working-class poet about a working-class youth who longs to be a poet. Though Lubin is as tender-minded, ardent, and poised for solitude as the youthful heroes of Beattie and Shelley, he is otherwise quite different from them in character and in the manner of his characterization. As one of Clare's first critics well observed, Lubin, "a living wight ... a substantial English labourer, a consumer of bread and cheese and porter," seems to exist in a different order of reality from that which Beattie's hero inhabits.[11] For Edwin is less a character than the half-realized embodiment of a "half-allegorical idea." Lubin is not only more earthly but earthier than the elegant Edwin. The reviewer for the *Eclectic Review* may have been right to note that Lubin appears to possess a mind that has been borne up "by the elasticity of genius, above the vulgarizing influence of his circumstances and employment." But he was wrong to say that Lubin "is no vulgar boy," for Lubin is refreshingly vulgar, and Clare seemed eager to emphasize that fact by careful description of his appearance and behaviour: the noble-minded Lubin is also an "uncouthly lout" who talks to himself, "soodles" rather than walks, wears patched clothing, and is not too particular about matters of personal hygiene. In constrast the gentle and inexplicably genteel Edwin, like the frail luminary hero of Shelley's poem, seems more fitted for the company of angels than the society of men.

Both these characters are made of finer stuff than the "selfish, blind, and torpid ... unforeseeing multitudes who constitute," Shelley claimed in the preface to *Alastor*, "the lasting misery and loneliness of the world."[12] But since the same unforeseeing multitudes tend to constitute the bigger if not the better part of humanity, it is difficult for each of these poetic figures to be an angel without also being something very like a misanthrope. Thus sweet Edwin, a little too good and pure of heart to walk the common paths of men (his sole companion is a hermit), longs to feel his own pulse undistracted by any human pulses beating around him. Thus the idealistic visionary of *Alastor*, driven to find a companion with whom to share his visions and ideals, leaves "his cold fireside and alienated home," but is doomed to languish and then to die in a "self-centred seclusion": no one is quite good enough for him either.[13] Lubin on the other hand is neither a misanthrope nor an angel, and in comparison with Beattie's hero or Shelley's is a much less rigorous follower of the discipline of solitude. Though he is forever leaving the company of the village to follow the " 'witching eye" of nature, he is also always coming back to it, as though to find out what he might be missing. In fact, he misses out on very little that occurs within the bounds of the village. And this is one of the most paradoxical aspects of this paradoxical poem. For Lubin, the devout young follower of the solitary way, who holds himself aloof from the talk and play of his neighbours, is always there, always manages to be back in time to hear the conversations and to watch the revels take place. Thus the controlling physical image of "The Village Minstrel" is not of a long journey out and away, but of commutation back and forth between life in the village and life in the landscape. It is the counterpointing of these two kinds of experience, of being with and being apart from the community, of joining and separation, which determines the prevailing rhythm of the poem.

Though Lubin may be one of the most sociable solitaries in English literature, he is still a solitary. Yet the many stanzas in Clare's poem which show the influence of the oral tradition upon Lubin's developing imagination make it quite impossible for us to argue that "The Village Minstrel" may be read as a rusticated version of the Romantic narrative of alienation or that Lubin may be firmly placed within the tradition of the bardic solitary. If Lubin feels that he must separate himself from his world it is for very different reasons than those which impel the hero of Shelley's *Alastor* or the hero of Beattie's *Minstrel* to go their lonely ways. Whereas the hero of *Alastor* is disposed to solitude because he feels unbearably lonely in the company of men, Lubin is so disposed because he does not feel lonely enough. And it is upon a well-developed sense of loneliness that his whole progress depends. He pursues his solitary way not, like Shelley's hero, in order to discover some ideal companion for his imaginative life (Lubin already has the village dames with whom to share the life of the imagination), nor, like Beattie's hero, in order to indulge his penchant for melancholy states of mind (Lubin can do that within the company of the melancholic village-shepherds). He prefers the solitude of nature to the company of men because he wants to forge for himself a unique and separate identity which he cannot find within his community. Lubin knows who he is ("an humble rustic") and where he is meant to belong ("Far in the swale where poverty retires"). What he must find out is who he can become.

The only important thing he cannot share with his community is also the end towards which his whole progress is directed: the experience of writing and of being a writer. Lubin cannot share this experience not only because the culture of his village is an oral and not a literate one but because that culture is in every sense collective and not individualistic. The whole concept of individual authorship upon which modern literary theory and practice are predicated is quite foreign to the village culture which Clare describes. The stories which the village women recite and the legends the shepherds narrate are not literary properties which have been written, signed, and copyrighted by this one housewife or that particular shepherd. They do not originate in the isolated imagination or the subjective experience of their tellers, but come from a past which belongs to no one into a present which belongs to everyone in the village. They do not express the discrete and autonomous character of their tellers but the imaginative character of the collective village, the shared perceptions, beliefs, and superstitions

> That e'er in rural manners will survive,
> As long as wild rusticity has birth
> To spread their wonders round the cottage-hearth.   (*I*, 135)

Just as Lubin is not free to choose the circumstances or the community into which he is born, so he cannot choose the particular tradition he inherits. But he does decide for himself the terms of his relationship to these collective categories of his experience. Indeed, though Lubin is in so many ways a passive and a vulnerable character, apparently incapable of taking responsibility for his talents or aspirations, when he confronts the collective ways of the village he is remarkably decisive and determinedly selective. His personal autonomy is neither chastened nor swallowed up by the collective consciousness; his individual imagination is shaped within the imaginative life of communal tradition. Even so, this tradition can only take him so far: it leads him into an inheritance of language and imaginative form, even into a part of his own mind; but it cannot take him outside its boundaries into a different tradition and towards an entirely new notion of his own cultural identity. Putting his language on a page, breaking into print, thinking in proprietary terms of his creativity, his poems, his volumes: this he has to do on his own. His espousal of creative solitude is a way of serving his apprenticeship to these individualistic skills, just as his participation in the culture of "wild rusticity" is an apprenticeship to communal forms of understanding.

For Clare, both forms of knowledge were equally precious. In "The Village Minstrel" there is some wavering and flight and much pushing and pulling between the values of solitude and of community. There are countless tensions and paradoxes in the depiction of Lubin's character and situation. He is a peasant-poet and a sociable solitary, an "uncouthly lout" with a delicate sensibility. He is a determined creature of circumstance who chooses freely the nature of his response to his circumstance. He does not always participate in the customs of his native village, but these customs are an essential part of his experience. He is not always at one with the villagers, but he is always one of them. He is an impoverished child, rich in natural experience, uneducated, but tutored in many kinds of knowledge. He is caught between what he is and what he might become. He is nothing in himself, but is important because he has been claimed by nature, beauty, poetry. These paradoxes and tensions remind us how conscious Clare was of writing to an audience that was at once ignorant of and hostile to the values and the habits of mind and conduct of the rural labouring poor. His problematical relations to this putative audience profoundly affected the way he wrote about Lubin and his vocational aspirations. But this is not to say that Clare's relations to his social peers were not also problematical. Lubin's community helps and hinders his poetical progress, nourishes his imaginative life and mocks the imaginative solitary it has nourished, give him its knowledge and distrusts the knowledge it cannot give him. But despite all the problems, contradictions, and uncertainties haunting this poem, there was one article of belief Clare did not choose to doubt or to question: that his future would continue to be bound up with the rustic community within which and against which his identity as man and poet were defined. The self-portrait he offered through his characterization of Lubin was itself a guarantee of this belief.

CHAPTER FIVE

Language and Learning

Clare considered himself something of an authority on the ignorance of his class, because, as he wrote, from this dark state he had himself "struggled upward as one struggling from the nightmare in his sleep."[1] As "The Village Minstrel" shows, he did not always write with sympathy or respect about those lost in the all-too-common condition from which he had escaped. "I live here," he confessed to Taylor, "among the ignorant like a lost man in fact like one whom the rest seems careless of having anything to do with – they hardly dare talk in my company for fear I should mention them in my writings & I find more pleasure in wandering the fields then in mixing among my silent neighbours who are insensible of everything but toiling & talking of it & that to no purpose" (*Letters*, 132). However, as he revealed in his comments upon merchants, farmers, parsons, and literary critics, Clare did not believe that the working class had a monopoly on ignorance.[2] Nor did he believe that the inability to read or write was a sign of stupidity or insensitivity or moral stupor. How could he? His own mother, after all, could neither read nor write. He felt that no one should be deprived of the basic rudiments of literacy and wrote of the appalling effects of ignorance upon the poorest members of his society.[3] But the dignity of his family and his class was clearly involved in this question, and he challenged those who thought it was possible to draw an easy equation between the character and educational status of an individual. "The lower orders of England," he observed, "from their almost total disregard of Poesy have been judged rather too harshly as destitute of the finer feelings of humanity & taste" (*Prose*, 221). It was to counter just this kind of harsh judgment that Clare wrote so often about the aesthetic and emotional experience of his peers, and still more often about his own "taste" and "finer feelings."

One of his clearest statements against the felt condition of ignorance, and the waste of potential it caused, can be found in a very early lyric, "Dawnings of Genius." Though this poem is not, in the strictest sense, autobiographical, Clare was obviously drawing upon his own past in portraying the experience of a rural labourer capable of looking at nature with a poet's eye yet unable to express what he sees or feels.[4] He was also drawing upon his reading in the tradition of pastoral dissent in conveying the significance of that experience. The explicit argument of the poem – that genius is not confined to those with learning but "Glows in each breast, flutters in every vein, / From art's refinement to th' uncultur'd swain" – recalls the humanitarian argument of Gray's *Elegy*. And the aura of pathos which surrounds Clare's poem, his definition of genius, even his imagery of fire and warmth, owe a great deal to these famous stanzas:

> Perhaps in this neglected spot is laid
> Some heart once pregnant with celestial fire,
> Hands, that the rod of empire might have swayed,
> Or waked to extasy the living lyre.

> But knowledge to their eyes her ample page
> Rich with the spoils of time did ne'er unroll;
> Chill Penury repressed their noble rage,
> And froze the genial current of the soul.

> Full many a gem of purest ray serene,
> The dark unfathomed caves of ocean bear:
> Full many a flower is born to blush unseen,
> And waste its sweetness on the desert air.

> Some village-Hampden, that with dauntless breast
> The little Tyrant of his fields withstood;
> Some mute inglorious Milton here may rest,
> Some Cromwell guiltless of his country's blood.[5]

It would be cruel to compare the formal perfection of these polished lines to Clare's awkward piece of apprentice-work. "Dawnings of Genius" is not well crafted; its transitions are awkward, and it strains a little too hard for its sublime effects. But in spite of its faults it is a moving poem that almost pays back its debts to the *Elegy* by describing from the viewpoint of a "rough rude plough-man" just how it feels to have the "genial current of the soul" stopped by the barriers of ignorance:

> In those low paths which poverty surrounds,
> The rough rude ploughman, off his fallow-grounds
> (That necessary tool of wealth and pride),
> While moil'd and sweating by some pasture's side,
> Will often stoop inquisitive to trace
> The opening beauties of a daisy's face;
> Oft will he witness, with admiring eyes,
> The brook's sweet dimples o'er the pebbles rise;
> And often, bent as o'er some magic spell,
> He'll pause, and pick his shaped stone and shell:
> Raptures the while his inward powers inflame,
> And joys delight him which he cannot name;
> Ideas picture pleasing views to mind,
> For which his language can no utterance find;
> Increasing beauties, fresh'ning on his sight,
> Unfold new charms, and witness more delight;
> So while the present please, the past decay,
> And in each other, losing, melt away.
> Thus pausing wild on all he saunters by,
> He feels enraptur'd though he knows not why,
> And hums and mutters o'er his joys in vain,
> And dwells on something which he can't explain.
> The bursts of thought with which his soul's perplex'd,
> Are bred one moment, and are gone the next;
> Yet still the heart will kindling sparks retain,
> And thoughts will rise, and fancy strive again.   (*I*, 69)

The image of the ploughman stooping over the daisy is the homeliest and most touching one in the poem. By contrast, the evocation of rustic emotionality seems a little too grand and unnecessarily obscure. The ploughman sighs and mutters, has a burning soul and a throbbing heart. But one cannot be sure what he is sighing and burning about. Nor is it clear what might be achieved if he were not ignorant, if he were in fact able to explain his feelings and express his "bursts of thought." But this is, per-haps, the whole point of the poem: that we cannot be certain about what is lost in a condition of ignorance since rustic capabilities in that condition can never be expressed or measured. When potential is not realized it is lost, and the loss is always incalculable, not only to the one who possesses the potential but also to society at large. What the "rough rude ploughman" in "Dawnings of Genius" might contribute to English culture if he could only unburden himself of his perplexing thoughts and break past the barriers of his own obscurity and silence, we cannot know. Nor can the ploughman himself: he is not even aware that this culture exists. But Clare's poem encourages us to imagine what this character might have achieved. Clare does not say anything more for his silent and troubled ploughman than that he possesses feelings, taste, and curiosity. But by implication he claims a good deal more. His image of the ploughman fervently longing to hold and make permanent the "kindling sparks" of his imagination recalls most vividly Gray's "mute inglorious Milton": the figure of a poor and ignorant man who might be capable of extraordinary creative work, might follow in Milton's footsteps, if only he knew who Milton was.

"Dawnings of Genius" is about people who will never have the chance to follow the poet's vocation, and it would be wrong to identify Clare too closely with the poor ploughman he wrote about: the poem itself exists as proof that Clare was not lost in mute obscurity. Nevertheless, it sheds light upon his personal struggle against those who judged a man's sensibility and moral and intellectual capabilities solely by his educational credentials. We have seen in his comments upon Southey's essay and in the tributes he paid to Bloomfield and Burns that Clare had a principled distaste for double standards. He believed that uneducated working-class poets should be judged not for what they could not offer (an easy way with classical allusion, a knowledge of genteel life, first-hand responses to continental sights and vistas, an urbane detachment from the realities of work and economic necessity), but rather for what they did offer (in Clare's round terms: beauty, truth, nature, and feelings "to which all hearts reply"). Yet from his other writings on the question of education it would appear that, in more ways than one, Clare wanted it two ways. On the one hand, he argued that formal education, or the lack of it, had no bearing upon a person's capacity for creative achievement; on the other, he expended much energy both in apologizing for his lack of education and in boasting about it. He would claim that because he had so little learning he was, like Bloomfield, "nature's favoured choice," he would also speak of the burden of creative doubt he had to carry because he lacked the "necessary qualities for commencing Poet by rule." Apparently he couldn't even resolve whether he was an educated or uneducated man: in the *Autobiog-raphy* he described himself as a *naif* and a stranger to the world of learning; in the *Natural History Letters* he identified entirely with the poise of the well-read, cultivated "man of taste" (*Prose*, 175).

Yet such contradictory statements about his educational status cannot in any sense be adduced as evidence of his duplicity. Rather, they should be taken as proof that Clare was himself not always certain about where in the hierarchy of status he was meant to fit. He was confused by the relativity of standards. In his own village he was seen as a young man in whom great hopes had been invested, simply because his parents had contrived to send him to school for a few years. He was to observe that some of his fellow-villagers even spoke of him as a man who had been spoiled by so much learning. And this would certainly have contributed to his sense of himself as an educated man. But the reviews, the letters from his patrons, the dinners with the "Londoners" gave Clare a very different sense of himself. In the *Autobiography* he recorded his delight in the conversational abilities of the various "Londoners" he met at Taylor's table. Lamb, Hazlitt, Coleridge most of all, astonished him with their eloquence and fluency. And one wonders, when reading this record, how often Coleridge turned the dinner conversation to Plato, or Spinoza, or Boehme, or Berkeley, how often Clare among the "Londoners" was forced to smile, nod, and keep silent. He was most assuredly no scholar. But nor was he the unskilled and unknowing character he often described himself as being. No doubt he knew that, as an autodidact who had briefly attended a small village school, he would always be labelled as an uneducated man. (We need only recall the malicious class-prejudice – conveyed in the nice rhetoric of "we have our standards to uphold" – with which *Blackwood's* attacked the "Cockney school" of Keats, Leigh Hunt, and the Surrey Institution to remember how narrowly "education" was defined in the nineteenth century: as attendance at the right schools and the universities.[6] But standards change, and today "uneducated" does not appear to be an adequate term to apply to a man who was a professional writer, a knowledgeable naturalist, a hobbyist in mathematics, something of an antiquarian, and, by any standards, a well-read student of English pastoral and descriptive poetry.

What most troubled Clare about his reputation as an uneducated poet was the tendency of some of his contemporaries to argue, in loud and hostile voices, that because he had not gone to a proper school he was simply incapable of creative and intellectual work. The very authorship of his poems was questioned on the grounds that an uneducated man could not possibly have written them:

some said that I never wrote the poems & that Drury gave me money to father them with my name / others said that I had stole them out of books & that Parson this & Squire tother knew the books from which they were stolen / Pretending scholars said that I had never been to a grammer school & therefore it was impossible for me to write anything / our parson industriously found out the wonderful discovery that I coud not spell & of course his opinion was busily distributed.   (*Prose*, 78)

But rather than answering these challenges to his credibility by mustering whatever self-directed, self-created educational credentials he did possess, Clare often appears to have taken an almost perverse delight in emphasizing not only how scanty his education had been but also how little he cared about learning in general. In his autobiography he portrayed himself as a man who read on his own but had not desire to follow a basic course of study or to achieve specific educational standards prescribed by somebody else: "I never coud plod through every book in a regular mecanical way as I met it / I dip into it here & there & if it does not suit I lay it down & seldom take it up again" (*Prose*, 78). Even the Bible, he claimed, was approached in this same cavalier spirit: "tho I read it with the customary reverence instilled into my mind by my parents I read it with a lack of reflection & rather more for amusement than profit" (*Letters*, 250). The wide range of literary allusion in his poetry and letters would suggest that Clare was a more serious student than he confessed to being. But there can be no doubt that the idea of diligently working his way through a required-reading list held few attractions for him. The prospect of assailing the "pedantic garrison" of "the castle hunting grammarians" was even less appealing: "grammer in learning is like tyranny in government – confound the bitch I'll never be her slave" (*Letters*, 133). So much for the rules of grammar and for the conventions of style: "I shall never get that polish which some recomend to me / I cant abide it" (*Letters*, 41). As for the rules of punctuation, they were not worth worrying about:

I am generally understood tho I do not use that awkward squad of pointings called commas colons semicolons etc and for the very reason that altho they are drilled hourly daily and weekly by every boarding school Miss who pretends to gossip in correspondence they do not know their proper exercise for they even set gramarians at loggerheads and no one can assign them the proper places for give each a sentence to point and both shall differ. (*SPP*, xxii)

The only grammarian Clare appears to have admired was Cobbett because "he plainly comes to this conclusion – that whatever is intelligible to others is grammar & whatever is common sense is not far from a carrectness" (*Prose*, 222). But this, in fact, was not at all the conclusion that Cobbett came to. It is true that Cobbett brought to the task of writing about language a refreshing contempt for the niceties of genteel discourse and Received Pronunciation.[7] But he was equally contemptuous of the aristocrat or the labouring man who refused to submit to the authority of grammatical rule. He would not have approved of a poet who thought that being "not far from carrectness" was all that was required, since he believed that a sound knowledge of grammar was essential for any man who wanted to contribute to the literary or political life of the nation. "I press this matter with such earnestness," he wrote, "because without this knowledge opportunities for writing and speaking are only occasions for men to display their unfitness to write and speak. How many false pretenders to erudition have I exposed to shame merely by my knowledge of grammar! How many of the insolent and ignorant, great and powerful have I pulled down and made little and despicable!"[8] But it was all too dry and too intricate a business for Clare to bother himself about. And so he never learned to spell properly, to punctuate his poetry or his prose, or to follow the standard rules of usage and grammatical agreement. "I may alter but I cannot mend," he wrote to the man to whom he gave the task of making his poetry presentable to the public.

In performing this task, John Taylor found it necessary not only to correct Clare's spelling, punctuation, and grammatical forms, but also to alter many of Clare's dialect words. And for this he has earned his share of revisionist scorn. Donald Davie and Eric Robinson and Geoffrey Summerfield, in particular, have commented upon Taylor's officious, unimaginative, and emasculating editorial procedures.[9] Of those who have had cause to discuss the relationship between the poet and his editor, only Tim Chilcott has argued that within the pressures of his time and place Taylor acted responsibly, tactfully, and in Clare's best interests.[10] And this is an argument with which I find myself in complete agreement. For if Taylor believed that it was necessary to tidy up the grammar and delete many (though by no means all) of Clare's dialect and coined-words, it was not because he was unappreciative of Clare's particular stylistic qualities. In the Introduction to Clare's first volume, and then again in an essay he published in *London Magazine*, he offered a spirited defence of the various provincial expressions and stylistic "peculiarities" that he did not alter in or delete from the manuscripts Clare sent to him.[11] Though it would have made his own work much easier, he did not insist that Clare submit himself to a long and heavy course in grammatical self-improvement. "Keep as you are," he wrote to Clare, "your Education has better fitted you for a Poet then all [the] School Learning in the world would be able to do."[12] His were not the instincts of a *précieux* but those of a fine editor who believed that his first responsibility was to present the best of his author, in the best possible way, to a public that was unused to unpunctuated lines, misspelled words, ungrammatical clauses, and "peculiarities" of diction.

In his letters to Taylor Clare expressed irritation over the fact that many of his dialect-words were altered, and from his reaction to these alterations we can conclude that at an early stage in his writing career Clare understood that his use of dialect was in some sense integral to the fabric of his poetry. He was committed to his dialect-words even though he was forced to recognize that without these words his first volumes might have had smoother passage into the literary scene of the early nineteenth century. We have no evidence of such a commitment to the solecisms in his poetry or to the unpunctuated state of the manuscripts he submitted to Taylor. He voiced no dissatisfactions or resentment over the fact that Taylor corrected his grammar, spelling, and punctuation. On the contrary, he appears to have been delighted that he could leave these tiresome matters in the hands of a man whose literary taste he never questioned.[13] For this reason I am not at all convinced by the arguments which have been proposed by recent critics that Clare's lack of punctuation, grammatical agreement, or correct spelling are essential or intentional elements in his poetic style. We have heard about the sense of place conveyed by Clare's misspellings, of the freer, open style he espoused through his failure to punctuate his writing, of his attempt to marry the grammar of his locality with the grammar of his public by failing to marry plural subjects and plural verbs.[14] Such arguments may be accepted as exercises in critical ingenuity – as long as the question of intentionality is not raised. Clare's refusal to learn the correct forms seems to have been wilful enough. And because his refusal was expressed in military and political metaphors (punctuation as a drill-master, grammar as tyranny), it is inviting to suppose that his grammatical errors represented a gesture of solidarity with the uneducated, disenfranchised, working class and an act of resistance to the grammatical standards and cultural hegemony of the "genteel race." But the wilfulness of Clare's refusal was the wilfulness not of principle but of indifference. He intended nothing by his grammatical errors. He simply made them because he had not bothered to follow the sort of regimen in grammatical self-improvement which Cobbett had advised. In discussing Clare's use of dialect-words, we can speak, albeit with a shadowed confidence, of their intended affective qualities. But in discussing his grammatical errors, we must fall back to the critically uninteresting question of what he would not and could not bring to the art of writing.

The importance of Clare's dialect-words to the style and content of his poetry has, at least recently, been well recognized, though nowhere quite so forcefully as in John Barrell's *The Idea of Landscape and Sense of Place.* Proceeding through close textual analysis of selected poems, Barrell has argued that Clare's dialect-words together with his unusual syntax are the distinguishing features of his language, that this language was essential to the sense of place that he sought to convey, and that this sense of place was in turn essential to the whole nature of his poetic enterprise, which was "to write 'locally,' to make the individuality of Helpston the content of his poems."[15] In his knowledge of the place in which he lived and in his single-minded commitment to record that concrete and particular body of knowledge, Barrell has found both what is original in Clare's vision and the reason for his "simple and irresoluble opposition" to the poets who preceded him: "The eighteenth-century poets, compared with Clare, moved as tourists through the places they wrote about – but we are all tourists now, so that insofar as Clare was successful in expressing his own sense of place, he was writing himself out of the main stream of European literature."[16] I am not convinced that we are all tourists now, nor that the detached, abstracting, and comparing stance of the tourist is all that one meets with in the mainstream of European literature of place. But I am not qualified to discuss the general tendencies of European literature, and I do not wish to engage in extended debate with a critic who has offered some of the most perceptive observations on Clare that have appeared in print. If we are now in a position to argue about the complexities in Clare's work, it is at least partly because Barrell has mapped out several of those complexities for us. But his is by no means a complete account of Clare's form or style or content, and his argument appears to carry more authority once these limits are acknowledged: the particular individuality of Helpston is not the only thing that Clare sought to convey and the total form of his poetry involves more than the sum of its local aspects. Perhaps the least convincing part of Barrell's study is his assertion that his knowledge of Helpston is all that Clare was capable of expressing:

The idea that Clare entertained of his 'knowledge', at once the place he knew and everything he knew, means that the sense of place he communicates in his poems becomes their entire content, from which no other more abstract knowledge could be deduced. [17]

For Barrell Clare's poetic preoccupations, his identity, even his knowledge are only local, and his language is

purely local – a vocabulary of the names he and his neighbours use for what things are and what they do. It names things precisely, but as it does so it reminds us that this precision, the rightness of this or that word, is completely dependent on its being used of the things and actions in the place to which that language belongs. [18]

To these statements one has first to answer that if Clare's language "belongs" in any place (in the prescriptive or descriptive sense) it is not in the village he happened to inhabit but in the poems he chose to write. Only within the context of his poems can "the rightness of this or that word" finally be assessed. Our central concern as critics of the text should not be with the *langue* of the community to which Clare belonged but with his own *paroles*, with the region of linguistic activity in which his will, intelligence, and creativity were exercised. To confuse these Saussurian categories, to suggest that Clare's language was nothing more than the language of his Helpstonian neighbours, is to reduce Clare to the role of an amanuensis, the passive reflector of the village language he heard and inherited. One is especially troubled by the tendency exhibited by Barrell to assume that whereas the language of Clare's locality was "*his* language," the language of the English tradition was alien to him. [19] There is a kind of unintended insolence in the idea that the vocabulary which this practising writer acquired from the great texts of the tradition was somehow alien or less real to him than the vocabulary he learned from his neighbours and family. I have already discussed the problematical nature of Clare's relationship to "the glorious host of poets to my country born," and as we shall see, his heightened awareness of "the wider space / Between the genteel and the vulgar race" was to make certain theoretical questions about language and many practical questions of usage no less problematical for him. But this does not mean that Clare approached the "language of the centre" as though he were a *métèque*. Since he brought into his poems both the words and phrases he culled from his reading in Thomson, Collins, Cowper, and Gray and the dialect-words spoken in Helpston, clearly the language of the tradition and the language of the community were both "his." Within the unity of his experience as a speaking, listening, reading, writing man, Clare had many linguistic resources and many choices to make.

He does not appear to have chosen his words with great care or deliberation. Indeed, he was quite proud of the fact that he wrote quickly and spontaneously and rarely revised his first drafts: "I found the poems in the fields, / And only wrote them down" (*LPJC*, 19). But however spontaneously, even carelessly, he "wrote them down," Clare chose the words and phrases that made up his poems, and in choosing his dialect-words he was no more and no less careful than he was in choosing words from the standard vocabulary of the tradition. This is not to say that we have no reason to distinguish between his two more important linguistic resources. His provincialisms and his conventional poetic diction affect us very differently, and Clare himself must have been aware that his reading and his oral communication with his fellow-Helpstonians helped him in very different ways. From the one he would have learned to think of the night wind as "the loud glabber round the flaze"; from the other, he may have learned to describe the night wind in terms of a "thickening darkness" which "from the sobbing woods / Clamours with dismal tidings of the rain" (*II*, 315). We cannot ignore the peculiarities in Clare's diction and we should not underestimate the differences between the language of his community and the language of literary tradition. In an essay on "The Consequences of Literacy," Jack Goody and Ian Watt have written that,

in so far as an individual participates in the literate, as distinct from the oral, culture, such coherence as a person achieves is very largely the result of his personal selection, adjustment and elimination of items from a highly differentiated cultural repertoire; he is, of course, influenced by all the various social pressures, but they are so numerous that the pattern finally comes out as an individual one. [20]

In contrast, the linguistic experience of the person who communicates in an oral culture is less individualized and, as Barrell might have said, the meanings of his words are less capable of being abstracted from the context in which they are uttered. Goody and Watt explain that

the intrinsic nature of oral communication has a considerable effect upon both the content and the transmission of the cultural repertoire. In the first place, it makes for a directness of relationship between symbol and referent. There can be no reference to 'dictionary definitions', nor can words accumulate the successive layers of historically validated meanings which they acquire in a literate culture. Instead, the meaning of each word is ratified in a succession of concrete situations, accompanied by vocal inflections and physical gestures, all of which combine to particularize both its specific denotation and its accepted connotative usages ... The totality of symbol-referent relationships is more immediately experienced by the individual in an exclusively oral culture, and is thus more deeply socialized. [21]

The difference between the oral culture in which Clare learned his dialect-words and the textual culture from which he acquired so much of his conventional vocabulary is, then, considerable. But the point we must recognize is that, in writing his dialect-words into his poems, Clare was moving outside the concrete and "deeply socialized" context in which those dialect-words were used and ratified. He was transferring the cultural repertoire of oral communication into the territory of the written text where the pattern of usage was individual rather than collective, and where the relationship between author and reader supplanted the immediate relationship between neighbour and neighbour.

We can never be certain about just how self-conscious Clare was in effecting this transference. But it seems unlikely that he was not in some sense conscious of what he was doing in drawing upon the dialect-words of his speech-community, if for no other reason than that he was writing down words that he had never seen in print. He had not only to select the words but to decide how to spell them. To argue, as Barrell had done, that Clare used provincialisms because "he had no choice but to use them" is to skate blithely past the actual difficulties and moments of decision involved in translating the repertoire of an oral medium into a literate and, more crucially, a poetic medium. To support his argument, Barrell has quoted from a letter Clare wrote to James Hessey in which he said, "I think vulgar names to the flowers best as I know no others." [22] But this statement seems to me to be proof not of Clare's incapacity to write in anything except a local language, but rather proof of his capacity to find even in the most disingenuous claims some way to justify his diction: he had linguistic choices to make and when those choices were criticized, he justified them by saying he had no choice. It is hard to believe that a man who included among his friends an accomplished botanist, who had read Linnaeus, Gilbert White, and Erasmus Darwin, and who also possessed such volumes as *Natural Philosophy*, *The Florist's Directory*, and *The Culture and Management of the Auricula, Polyanthus, Carnation, Pink, and the Ranunculus*, was not familar with more than "the vulgar names to the flowers." It is, of course, dangerous to speculate about what a poet may have known. But it is even more dangerous and, in the most obvious way, insolent to speculate about what a poet did not know. One needn't suppose that Clare thought long and hard when he used the term "princifeather" rather than lilac, "water-blob" rather than marsh-marigold, "cowslap peeps" rather than cowslip eyes, "jenny-burnt-arse" rather than will o' the wisp. Quite probably he used dialect-words because they were the first ones that came to mind. But one need not suppose that Clare was a deliberate and self-conscious experimenter in language to claim that he knew what he was doing. He not only had choices; he had reasons for his choices.[23]

One other question which bears closely upon Clare's social and creative situation may be posed here: whether his dialect-words do not convey something at once more obvious to the reader and more problematic to the poet himself than his sense of place, whether it is not in his sense of self rather than in his sense of place that the main qualifying significance of his dialect-words is to be found. In raising this question, I do not mean to suggest that Clare's locality was not important to him and to his poetry. One has no cause to quarrel with Barrell's observation that Clare's dialect-words help to express the particularly local quality of his experience, and certainly this local experience was one of the defining aspects of both his social and creative situation. But surely the first and most important thing that is conveyed by Clare's dialect-words is not "the individuality of Helpston" but rather the individual character and identity of the poet. Wallace Stevens wrote that

> The man in Georgia walking among pines,
> Should be pine-spokesman.[24]

And if this is a prescription for the poet, then it is one that Clare filled perfectly. When he wrote of the wild and working landscapes of his locality he was, as it were, a heath-and-fen spokesman. He wrote of the "drowking meadow-sweet," the "pudgy paths," the "ramping sallows," the "popples tapering to their tops."[25] He watched the "oddling crow," the "pranking" bats, the "cading calves," and the pewits who "strime their clock like shadows."[26] He observed

> on hedgerow baulks in moisture sprent
> The jetty snail creep from the mossy thorn
> In earnest heed and tremolous intent
> Frail brother of the morn
> That from the tiney bents and misted leaves
> Withdraws his timid horn
> And fearful vision weaves   (*JCOA*, 127)

In winter he waited as the cold weather "in crispy rime / Comes hirpling on."[27] In summer he listened to the "chickering cricket tremolous and long" while he watched "the evening curdle dank and grey / Changing her watchet hue."[28] As a child, he left his friends, their games and "taws," to stand beside a "pingle" and listen to the birds.[29] He watched "the old heaths withered brake / Mingle its crimpled leaves with furze and ling."[30] He tracked the "uncheckt shadows" of moors that were "smooth and blea."[31] He lay beneath "the curdled arms of this stunt tree."[32] He hid where "these crimping fern leaves ramp among / The hazel under boughs."[33] He observed the "younkers" in the village, the "sawning boys" set to watch for crows, the cowboys who would walk the fields "with plashy step and clouted shoe," the herdboys who would "fish for struttles in the brooks."[34] He watched a weary woodman – "croodling and thin to view" – who crossed the winter fields with "wetshod feet and hacking cough / That keeps him waken till the peep of day."[35] He wrote of the village gossip who was always "chelping bout the town," of a housewife who would "shool her nitting out at night," of harvesters who "enjoy'd the bevering hour," of shepherds who would in the heat of the day "with their panting sheep / In the swaliest corner creep."[36]

Certainly all the dialect-words I have quoted here convey a sense of place. But what place exactly? Helpston? the Soke of Peterborough? the whole county? the entire fenland? Or could it be that the speech-community to which Clare's dialect-words belong was yet broader still? Could the word "oddling" have been understood by a solitary who lived far away from Clare's locality? Could a gossip in Somerset have understood that she "chelped" too much? Could a rheumatic woodman from Yorkshire have known that he "hirpled"? Were children in Devon called "younkers"? Were they as "sawning" as the lazy herdboys of Helpston? I raise these questions because I wish to draw attention to a rather obvious but critically significant fact: that those of us who are not dialectologists cannot tell by Clare's dialect-words alone to what particular region he belonged. Indeed, without the assistance of Baker's *Glossary of Northamptonshire Words and Phrases*, one might almost suppose that such words as "crimpled," "drowking," "croodling," and "plashy" were not dialect-words but portmanteaux of the poet's own invention. [37] Thus: crimpled leaves are crimped and crumpled; drowking meadows are drowning and sunk in drought; a croodling man is one who cringes and huddles against the cold; a plashy step describes the splash created when one plunges into muddy fields.

But of course even those of us who are not philologically-minded but have dipped here and there into the writings of Burns, Barnes, Scott, Charlotte and Emily Brontë, George Eliot, and Hardy will suspect that these are not portmanteau-words, not merely witty elements in a poet's idiolect, but are dialect-words which gesture to their place in the pretextual discourse of a particular historical and regional community.

With the most famous regionalists in the mainstream of the English tradition, as with Clare himself, a good deal of the evidence we might adduce as proof of their religionalism could be found in their use of dialect-words to characterize the inhabitants of the regions they have chosen to describe. But perhaps the first and most important thing we learn from the regional texts of the nineteenth century is that dialect-words tend to be used only when the subject is humble and rustic life. [38] The local differences and the regional expressiveness of language tend to be registered only in lower-class characters: Squire Donnithorne of *Adam Bede* and Edgar Linton of *Wuthering Heights* share the same way of speaking for they are both gentlemen; Lisbeth Bede from the one novel and Joseph, the servant from the other, do not. That characters possessed of property, genteel status, and formal education do not normally employ dialect-words is made very clear in the first chapter of *Adam Bede*, in the colloquy of a passing traveller and an inhabitant of Hayslope, the novel's main setting. The local inhabitant offers this piece of information to the stranger passing through his community:

They're cur'ous talkers i' this country, sir; the gentry's hard work to hunderstand 'em. I was brought hup among the gentry, sir, an' got the turn o' their tongue when I was a bye. Why, what do you think the folks here says for 'hevn't you?' – the gentry, you know, says, 'hevn't you' – well, the people about here says 'hanna yey.' It's what they call the dileck as is spoke hereabout, sir. [39]

To remark that the "cur'ous talkers" who employ "dileck" happen to be from the lower orders is to offer an observation so obvious to readers of George Eliot, or Hardy, or the Brontës, that it hardly needs to be substantiated by specific quotation. We do not need the dialectologists to tell us that in literature, as in life, there is "a high degree of correlation between working-class status and use of a localized variety of English."[40]

But this most obvious point – that dialect-words tend to express the class-identity of their speakers as much as they place them in a specific region – is one that we must bear in mind if we are to understand not only why Clare's language was attacked but also the nature of his defence of his dialect-words. Barrell has suggested that the "simple and irresoluble opposition" to Clare's language was due to the fact that his language conveyed a sense of place which countered the prevailing tendency of eighteenth- and nineteenth-century writers to approach rural scenes and rural communities with the abstracting, generalizing, uniformitarian attitudes of those who travelled through the landscape but were never "irrevocably bound up in a particular locality which they had no time, money, or reason, ever to leave."[41] No one who has had cause to examine the rural literature of the eighteenth and nineteenth centuries would dispute that the experience of travelling and the detached, analytically comparing modes of observation it engendered were of determining significance to that literature. But it has also not gone unobserved that in a period in which the prestige of Burns, Cowper, Crabbe, Wordsworth, and Mary Mitford were readily acknowledged, the influence of what Carlyle was to call an "attenuated cosmopolitanism" was matched and balanced by the compelling reasons of "local attachment."[42] Burns in Ayrshire, Cowper in Olney, Wordsworth in Grasmere, and Mary Mitford in Three Mile Cross had all testified to the rich literary possibilities offered by life in a "confined locality."[43] Thus, if Clare's dialect-words gave offence to many of his critics it was not because they bespoke a sensibility that was too decidedly local or provincial, but because they conveyed the character, attitude, and situation of a poet who was too obviously, too unabashedly working-class.

His critics considered his language coarse, vulgar, "radically low and insignificant."[44] It was characterized by an unfortunate "*grossièreté*" which, as one peevish critic was to say, "cannot fail to offend every reader."[45] It was evidence that Clare was either incapable of understanding or, worse still, was deliberately refusing to accept the principle that the language of "the *canaille*" had no business appearing in the literature of the nation. Many of his expressions, another critic was to say, "are mere vulgarisms, and may as well be excluded from the poetical lexicon, as they have long since been banished from the dictionary of polite conversation."[46] The "poverty of his vocabulary," yet another was to say, "obliged him frequently to coin words and to use provincialisms."[47] But surely this last statement is a contradiction in terms? Surely a man who can draw upon the linguistic resource of "provincialisms" and has the linguistic resourcefulness to "coin words" is not a man who suffers from poverty of vocabulary? But then none of the objections to Clare's dialect-words have worn well; now they all seem absurdly narrow, elitist, and unimaginative. One has sympathy only for the critic of the *London Weekly* who did not complain about the dialect-words *per se*, but objected to the fact that Clare's third volume was without a glossary. However, even his objection was expressed in an unnecessarily harsh way: "There was nothing, perhaps, which more provoked our spleen ... for, without such an assistance, how could we perceive the fitness and beauty of such words as - *crizzling* - *sliveth* - *whinneys* - *greening* - *tootles* - *croodling* - *hings* - *progged* - *spindling* - *siling* - *struttles*, &c. &c."[48] We can add to this list references Clare was to make to "moozy" days, "rawky" smoke, "blathering" calves, "proggling" sticks, "chumbling" mice. Translations would be helpful, but are they absolutely necessary? Surely to those of us who can perceive - without a glossary - the fitness and beauty of Hopkins's "stippling" trout and Lewis Carroll's "slithey toves," Clare's witty and evocative dialect-words can be sounded (in both senses of the word) without the aid of a lexicographer. They are possessed of "raciness," that quality which, as F.R. Leavis was to suggest, allows us a point of entry into the speech-rhythms and the rich idiomatic life of a particular kind of community.[49]

The terms with which Clare's dialect-words were attacked suggest that his critics saw little reason to deviate from Dryden's strictures that the language of the poet should be the language of the gentleman, and that "village words" were to be avoided because they "give us a mean idea of the thing."[50] This was certainly the tenor of Lamb's expressed objection to Clare's diction:

In some of your story telling Ballads the provincial phrases sometimes startle me. I think you are too profuse with them. In poetry *slang* of every kind is to be avoided. There is a rustick Cockneyism as little pleasing as ours of London. Transplant Arcadia to Helpstone. The true rustic style, the Arcadian English, I think is to be found in Shenstone. Would his Schoolmistress, the prettiest of poems, have been better, if he had used quite the Goody's own language? Now and then a home rusticism is fresh and startling, but where nothing is gained in expression, it is out of tenor. It may make folks smile and stare, but the ungenial coalition of barbarous with *refined* phrases will prevent you in the end from being so generally tasted, as you deserve to be.[51]

Lamb's advice was offered in a kindly spirit, but Clare never felt impelled to follow it, and not only because he was not interested in composing "the prettiest of poems." Of Shenstone's pastoral poetry Clare wrote that "Putting the Correct Language of the Gentleman into the mouth of a Simple Shepherd or Vulgar Ploughman is far from Natural" (*Letters*, 25). And this statement leads one to believe that in answer to Lamb's question – would *The Schoolmistress* have been a better poem if Shenstone had used "quite the Goody's own language"? – Clare would have said yes. When he was asked to explain the "vulgar names" which he used to designate the flora and fauna he wrote about, he simply said: " 'tis what we call them & that you know is sufficient for us" (*Letters*, 103). When he was asked to justify one of his "radically low" phrases, he wrote: "whether [it is] provincial or not I cannot tell; but it is common with the vulgar, (I am of that class)."[52] And these unequivocating comments, brief as they are, suggest that Clare himself understood very well that what was at issue was not, in Barrell's word, "the localness" of his language, but rather its identification with a class of men and women who spoke, lived, and (as Coleridge was to claim) ruminated in habitual ways that were thought to be decidedly unpoetic.

In a review of Clare's second volume, the critic for the *Monthly Magazine* was to observe:

If the example of Burns, Ramsay, Ferguson, or other Scottish poets be pleaded, we answer, that they employed a dialect in general use through an entire country, and not the mere *patois* of a small district. If the peculiar phraseology of the Northamptonshire rustics is to be licensed in poetry, we see no reason why that of Lancashire, Somersetshire, and other counties should not be allowed an equal currency; and thus our language would be surprisingly enriched, by the legitimization of all the varieties of speech in use among the *canaille* throughout the kingdom.[53]

In Clare's letters and prose-fragments we can find no pithy and resounding statement which might serve us as answer to this harsh instance of class-malice. But everywhere in his poems, in his refusal to "get that polish that some recommend to me," in his wayward clinging to his dialect-words, we find evidence enough that Clare did believe that the speech of the critics could be enriched by the speech of "the *canaille*," that the language of the "glorious host" could be enriched by the language of his class. The few comments he offered about his use of dialect-words indicate that he was very aware (he was forced into the awareness) that he was using words which were considered too coarse and "too rustic for the fashionable or prevailing system of rhyme" (*Prose*, 173). But Clare did not employ these words because he thought that they were inherently coarse, nor because he believed that lowness and vulgarity were inherently defensible qualities. His dialect-words were only "*reckond* low & vulgar," and he believed that when "some bold inovating genius rises with a real love for nature ... then they will be considered as great beautys which they really are." Nature, genius, beauty, bold literary innovation, were the terms Clare used to justify his language, and these terms suggest that his refusal to give up his dialect-words was for him a primarily aesthetic decision. He continued, against the pressure of hostile and friendly criticism, to write about "drowking" meadows and "croodling" men because he wished to convey his experience in nature and in rural society as truthfully, beautifully, and naturally as he could. To describe with precision the landscapes he knew best, to evoke the exhilarations of his childhood, to express the personal value of his perceptions: this was what Clare sought to do when, in writing these lines from "Remembrances," he chose to draw upon the language of his class and community:

When jumping time away on old cross berry way
And eating awes like sugar plumbs ere they had lost the may
And skipping like a leveret before the peep of day
On the rolly polly up and downs of pleasant swordy well
When in round oaks narrow lane as the south got black again
We sought the hollow ash that was shelter from the rain
With our pockets full of peas we had stolen from the grain
How delicious was the dinner time on such a showry day
O words are poor receipts for what time hath stole away
The ancient pulpit trees and the play
When for school oer 'little field' with its brook and wooden brig
Where I swaggered like a man though I was not half so big
While I held my little plough though twas but a willow twig

And drove my team along made of nothing but a name
'Gee hep' and 'hoit' and 'woi' - O I never call to mind
These pleasant names of places but I leave a sigh behind
While I see the little mouldywharps hang sweeing to the wind
On the only aged willow that in all the field remains
And nature hides her face where theyre sweeing in their chains
And in a silent murmuring complains   (*JCOA*, 259)

And yet, in considering Clare's use of dialect, the question of his
literary intention must finally be related to the question of social
identity and principle. Clare wrote no extended defence of his
dialect-words, offered very few theoretical pronouncements upon
the relationship between the language of men and the language of
poetry, and so it is difficult to speak with any certainty about the
intentionality of his diction. This is one reason why I find myself
disagreeing with Stephen Wade who has written that when Clare
employed dialect "there was no intention to identify with a particular group or to prove himself a poet of a sub-culture and no
more - he was not an Ebenezer Eliott - he had no aspirations to be
a mouthpiece of an undertrodden populace."[54] I find this statement questionable, not so much because it is founded upon insufficient evidence, but because it ignores the evidence we possess.
From his various writings upon the great English poets we know
that Clare wished to be more than "a poet of a sub-culture." But in
his writings upon poverty, property, politics, education, and class-
prejudice he revealed himself to be a poet who did indeed identify
with a particular group, who found in his own experience a representative significance that caused him to feel that he could hardly
put pen to paper without in some sense acting as the "mouthpiece
of an undertrodden populace." I would not suggest that Clare used
dialect-words merely as a gesture of solidarity with his class. He
used them because he wished to write about those aspects of society
and nature he knew best, from the vantage-point of his own social
and creative situation, drawing upon all of the linguistic resources
available to him. But because by using dialect-words he was coun-
tering a set of literary standards which were defined by and reflexive of the cultural hegemony of the genteel class, then language
itself became for this practising writer one of the most obvious and
most radical fronts upon which he had to challenge that hegemony. And when his dialect-words took their place in poems which
cried out against the social conditions of the rural labouring poor,
then these words, however spontaneously or carelessly they may
have been chosen, became a part of the rhetoric of Clare's protest.

CHAPTER SIX

Literary Principles

"THE RIGHT TO SING"

When he thought it necessary to his survival as a professional poet, Clare could pull his forelock with energetic flourish. He would not have been pleased to be remembered by such a gesture, but one comes away from "The Effusion to Poesy," "The Village Minstrel," and even to some extent "To the Rural Muse" with a clearer sense of Clare's deference to genteel prejudice than of his active resistance to it. However, sometime during the 1820s Clare's attitude towards his audience changed, and by the early 1830s he was writing poems in which his defiance of genteel prejudice was no longer tempered – or undercut – by deference. One can trace similarities and continuities between Clare's early work and the poems and prose-fragments to be considered here, and it would be wrong to say that at a particular moment in his career Clare underwent a dramatic sea-change after which he never again evinced deferential attitudes or experienced doubts about his anomalous situation as a peasant-poet. But we can say with some confidence that during the years between the publication of his second volume (1821) and his third (1827) he began to write about himself and his poetry, not in terms of the way he assumed he was seen by gentle readers, genteel opinionists, or the gentlemanly critics of the *Gentleman's Magazine*, but in terms of the way he saw himself. And with this new way of seeing came a new set of questions to be posed: not, will you accept me as a poet? will you allow me a hearing? but rather, what kind of poet must I be? to what kind of poetry shall I commit my energies? Clare's challenge to literary values prejudicial to his particular situation and to his work, the democratic nature of his own literary principles, and his faithful practice of these principles are the subject of this chapter.

One of the most important lessons Clare learned in the 1820s was that the reading public was a capricious creature. Hot and cold by turns, it could not be relied upon for either moral or financial support. In 1820 Clare was a best-seller; a year or so later, already something of a has-been. He had been encouraged by the excellent sales of *Poems Descriptive*, and saw his success as a vindication of his talents. When *The Village Minstrel* and then *The Shepherd's Calendar* proved to be failures in the market-place, a sharp blow was struck at his self-confidence. And yet, at least at this point in his career, Clare had more resiliency of spirit than has been supposed. Though he longed to be accepted, he refused to accept the market-place as the final arbiter of literary merit: "God protect all hopes in difficulty from the patronage of Trade. When the Cow grows to old in profits in milk she is fatted & sold to the butchers & when the Horse is grown too old to work he is turned to the dogs, but an author is neither composed of the materials necessary for the profit of butchers meat or dogs meat – he is turned off & forgotten" (*Letters*, 273). His belief that within so ruthless a system the poet would always be scorned, misunderstood, and, of course, poor, did not evolve only as a reaction to his own failure; he thought that Keats, Bloomfield, and even Wordsworth had failed to win the faithful and enthusiastic following that they deserved. In 1820 when his own prospects were still very hopeful, he wrote to tell Taylor of his great admiration for Keats. He was always "Poor Keats" to Clare, always to be pitied "as a brother wanderer in the rough road of life & as one whose eye picks now & then a wild flower to cheer his solitary way who looks with his wild vain & crackd braind friend to the rude break neck hill where sits the illustrious inspirer – Fame – who looks with me – as carless of her anointed few – but who as he turns away cannot help but heave a sigh" (*Letters*, 51). Clare missed his prophetical mark here and his pity for Keats now seems pitifully misplaced, but his comment illuminates for us the belief which was his solace and inspiration, that if there was no public to support the poet's work (materially and otherwise), then he must find his community in his fellow-poets or must learn to wander alone. By 1827 Clare was of the firm opinion that a reading public which so slavishly followed the "two false prophets" of criticism and fashion, and allowed the finest poets of the age to struggle with neglect, disappointment, and poverty, was not to be trusted to judge the merits of his work or that of any true poet. It must be, he wrote to Taylor, that "the age of Taste is in dotage & grown old in its youth," for how else could one explain the failure of Wordsworth and Keats to win a large readership

(*Letters*, 200)? The poet must write then for future generations and ignore the sneers of the present age, confident in the knowledge that "public praise is not to be relied on as the creditor of the future" (*Prose*, 210).

It is one thing to counsel indifference, quite another to be indifferent to the opinions of one's contemporaries. Clare might argue that the poet should trust in the judgments of the future, but he never ceased to feel most keenly the judgment of his own time. He never stopped longing for success and "public praise," and continued to react most defensively to poor sales and unfavourable reviews. But indifference to the public was by no means a purely theoretical matter for him. His sudden success in 1820 and his disturbing failures after 1821 caused him to look more critically at the reading public and to question his precarious relations to it. His own experience and his knowledge of Keats's and Bloomfield's gave him cause to feel that the reading public was inconstant, untrustworthy, most fallible in its judgments. And so, why should he defer to such a public? Why should he apologize for his humble station in life or his lack of formal education when the genteel, educated, sophisticated readers to whom the apology was offered had proven themselves to be incapable of appreciating some of the finest poets of the age? These are the questions Clare posed in his letters and attempted to answer in the vocational poems he wrote through the 1820s and early 1830s. The tone of these poems – poised, defiant, self-assertive – suggests to us that Clare no longer respected or feared the reading public as he once had, was no longer quite so willing to place himself in the paradoxical position of complying with its genteel standards through the very act of confessing his inability to comply with those standards.

We can hear the new tone and observe the new-found creative poise to which it testifies in "The Progress of Ryhme," a poem I earlier cited as evidence of Clare's disabling self-consciousness about his social background and educational credentials. In the self-castigating language and abjectly humble tone of many of its passages one found, I argued, proof of the extent to which Clare had internalized the harshest angles of genteel perception. Certainly a poet who writes of himself as

A clownish silent haynish boy
Who even felt ashamed of joy
So dirty ragged and so low
With nought to reccomend or show
That I was worthy ...   (*JCOA*, 160)

suggests a man whose knees have been permanently bent in the rituals of deference. Yet other passages offer a very different image of Clare and of his attitudes to genteel prejudice, and to read the poem as a whole is to feel that it records the moment when Clare finally stood up, dusted off his deferential knees, and found a new way of writing about his vocational aspirations. One could say that in "The Progress of Ryhme" he sounded the depths of his own deference in order to say goodbye to it. A turning point in his career, it reflects his growing awareness of what he lost by seeing himself through the eyes of the genteel reader and of what he gained by defining his experience in his own terms. In the following passages the quality of his experience is not conveyed through the language of shame and self-abasement but through selected images of paradisal innocence, dignity, and joy which directly counter that earlier language:

> My harp tho simple was my own
> When I was in the fields alone
> With none to help and none to hear
> To bid me either hope or fear ...
> I whispered poesys spells till they
> Gleamed round me like a summer day ...
> And each old leaning shielding tree
> Were princely pallaces to me
> Where I would sit me down and chime
> My unheard rhapsodies to ryhme ...
> I felt and shunned the idle vein
> Laid down the pen and toiled again
> But spite of all thro good and ill
> It was and is my worship still
> No matter how the world approved
> Twas nature listened – I that loved
> No matter how the lyre was strung
> From my own heart the music sprung ...
> ... – and when I pluckt the blade
> Of grass upon the woodland hill
> To mock the birds with artless skill
> No music in the world beside
> Seemed half so sweet – till mine was tried
> So my boy-worship poesy
> Made een the muses pleased with me
> Untill I even danced for joy
> A happy and a lonely boy

Each object to my ear and eye
Made paradise of poesy   (*JCOA*, 156-8)

Clare portrays himself in these lines as a poetic figure basking in
the reflected glory of a natural landscape that is divine, enchanting, princely, lit with a gleaming summer light. His creativity is
associated with – indeed, is based upon – this landscape which
serves him as inspirer, teacher, and audience. Like the hero of
"The Village Minstrel," this poet-hero depends upon nature to
serve these functions because he has nothing and no one else to
depend upon:

And I with nothing to attone
Had felt myself indeed alone.   (*JCOA*, 154)

But the quality of this dependency is treated very differently in
the later poem, and this difference suggests that "The Progress of
Ryhme" represents a significant advance upon "The Village Minstrel." In "The Village Minstrel" Clare preferred to emphasize the
poetic qualities inherent in nature rather than risk the charge of
pride and presumption by affirming his own poetic capabilities.
But in "The Progress of Ryhme" his energetic celebration of nature
does not prevent or circumvent the spirited self-assertion of "My
harp tho simple was my own" and "From my own heart the music
sprung." He acknowledges that the quality of his poetry depends
upon the quality of his relationship to nature: the fields and woods
through which he wanders are, he claims, "the essence of the
song." But he recognizes that "tis I not they" who write the poems,
and that if he is to keep on writing, he must depend upon himself, must draw upon insights that are self-won, feelings that are
self-affirming, creative instincts that are self-generated.

"The Progress of Ryhme" is unlike any of Clare's earlier vocational writings if for no other reason than that it is the first work in
which Clare affirms his independence of his audience. "I felt that
I'd a right to song," he says, for

No matter how the world approved,
'Twas nature listened I that loved.   (*JCOA*, 158)

Clare's indifference to the approval of the genteel reader could not
be stated more explicitly. But indifference is not all that is suggested throughout the more positive passages. By emphasizing his
dual identity as poet and swain, by equating eloquence with simple

sincerity, by defining his creative power in terms of his social obscurity, finally by bringing the bardic language of "soul enchanting poesy" together with the plain and local language of sweat and tears, barns and ditches - by insisting in all these ways that the social circumstances of an uneducated workingman did not preclude him from creative aspiration or achievement, Clare was offering direct resistance to genteel literary and social values. Learning, sophistication, good breeding are not attacked; they are simply ignored as qualities quite inessential to the work Clare proposed to do. He was now bold enough to venture to say that he would "sing as well as greater men" not in spite of, but because of his circumstances. For "the essence of the song" depended upon only three things: a feeling heart, an adverting mind, and a landscape in which he could find "Real teachers that are all divine" - by which Clare meant not Horace or Pindar, not even Thomson or Gray, but rather woods, fields, birds, and flowers. He appears to have meant this almost literally; it was not entirely a conceit. One may say, with full awareness of the paradox, that "The Progress of Ryhme" is perhaps the most radical enactment of the dictum "first follow nature" to be found in the language, for the "soul enchanting poesy" that is celebrated throughout is not defined in terms of a palpable body of written texts, but as an "essence," a "spell," a "vision," a "dream song," a "magic strain" which the poet sees and hears, not by reading the monumental texts of literary tradition, but by gazing at weeds and listening to blackbirds.

The argument of "The Progress of Ryhme," which was to be renewed and developed in the poems which followed it, carried within its very terms the standards by which Clare wanted his poetry to be judged: by its "truth to nature," by its ability to evoke the spirit of nature and to describe its visible manifestations in a local landscape, and finally by its capacity to speak of and to natural human feeling. To these standards Clare rallied his resistance to those critics who believed that a poet must have the experience of a gentleman and could only be as good as the formal education he had received. But there is a sense in which these standards forced Clare into argument not only with genteel readers and critics but with particular kinds of poetry. Certain elements and phases within the tradition itself were inevitably set up for interrogation, not by the belief that the poet must be true to nature, but by the radically mimetic way this belief was defined in Clare's vocational poems and enacted in his nature poetry. Throughout the 1820s and 1830s Clare wrote a vast number of poems about the plainest, most common, least praised objects of nature: wrens, blackbirds, weeds, common grass, mice, hedge-hogs and badgers. In "The Progress of Ryhme" he offered an explicit defence of this chosen subject-matter, arguing that every-thing in nature and anything in human experience was worthy of a poet's interest:

> For every thing I felt a love
> The weeds below the birds above
> And weeds that bloomed in summer hours
> I thought they should be reckoned flowers
> They made a garden free for all
> And so I loved them great and small
> And sung of some that pleased my eye
> Nor could I pass the thistle bye
> But paused and thought it could not be
> A weed in natures poesy
> No matter for protecting wall
> No matter tho they chance to fall
> Where sheep and cows and oxen lie
> The kindly shower when theyre a dry
> Falls upon them with cheering powers
> As when it waters garden flowers
> They look up with a blushing eye
> Upon a tender watching sky
> And still enjoy the kindling smile
> Of sunshine tho they live with toil
> As garden flowers with all their care
> For natures love is even there
> And so it cheered me while I lay
> Among their beautiful array
> To think that I in humble dress
> Might have a right to happiness
> And sing as well as greater men   (*JCOA*, 155)

The poet insinuates his own social identity into his Franciscan argument, and in this way offers a challenge to those who would restrict literary aspiration and achievement to the hothouse culture of polite and educated people. The poems and the poets of this rich culture live and prosper in "their beautiful array" like garden flowers within a "protecting wall." But the poems of an unculti-vated rustic were not necessarily any less beautiful because like common weeds they "chance to fall / Where sheep and cows and oxen lie." The fact that the rain fell on the rich and the poor, on the garden flower and the wild one, that a robin sang as sweetly as the more celebrated nightingale, that a rustic felt as deeply as a gentleman, was proof, in Clare's terms, of the universal principle of "natures love." Poetry ought to reflect that principle, ought to be "a garden free for all," open to all aspects of nature, accessible to any man with taste and feeling. In a reversal of his own early compliance with genteel values, Clare was now willing to imply that any one who, in deference to the status-hierarchies of society or in service to the priorities of a particular aesthetic theory, included the rose, the nightingale, the aristocrat's park in the golden world of his poetry, but left the weed, the sparrow, the ploughman's field in the brazen world of unrecorded experience was committing himself to a poetry that was impoverished, partial, false.

"NATURES TRUTH"

William Empson has well observed that in England after the Restoration, "the arts, even music, came to depend more than before on knowing about foreign culture, and Puritanism, suspicious of the arts, was only not strong among the aristocracy. A feeling gradually got about that anyone below the upper middles was making himself ridiculous, being above himself, if he showed any signs of keeping a sense of beauty at all, and this feeling was common to all classes."[1] But Clare's early poems prove (if proof were needed) that this climate of harsh and unreal belief was still very much a part of the cultural scenery in the nineteenth century. Within such a climate, Clare's assertion of his "right to sing as well as greater men," to compose poetry which was "free for all," assumes a significance that is more than merely personal, or purely aesthetic. Even his most casual and impressionistic pronouncements may be related to his argument on behalf of a kind of poetry that must be as accessible as nature to the mind of any man of feeling and taste. And this argument in turn may be related to Clare's desire to enter, without apology or hesitation, into the mainstream of English cultural life – and by passing in, to bring his class with him. His declared preference for "Tam O'Shanter" over the *Iliad* and *Odyssey*, his dislike of Keats's dryads and naiads, his criticism of the classical motifs in academic landscape art, his commendation of the "English truth" in the paintings of Hilton, Rippingille, and de Wint: all these were statements not of merely personal taste, but of principle, consistent claims for a British idiom in literature and art in which all Englishmen could participate, whether as authors or readers, artists or observers.

Clare's belief that English landscape art - whether painting or poetry - ought to be informed by English experience and to reflect faithfully the real English countryside is vigorously asserted in his "Essay on Landscape." In this informal and unfinished piece of work the argument for an aesthetic based upon common experience rather than upon "fashionable accomplishment" is renewed and extended within a polemic launched against the incongruous "drapery" of classical allusion, against any art which carried unjustifiable pretensions of sublimity, and finally against "the taste and the fashion of the day." One might have supposed that the scornful attitude Clare expressed in this essay towards classical elements in English art would force him to recognize that he was challenging some of the great classicists of the eighteenth-century literary tradition. But Clare was loathe to criticize any of the great poets of the tradition to which he wanted to belong. He was willing to meet the challenge which a learned tradition posed to an uneducated poet wanting to be at once himself and a part of the "glorious pride / That England from her bards hath won." He was unwilling to appear critical of that tradition, and this explains some of Clare's more curious silences and evasions, of which we can take as one example his entirely unfounded belief that classical forms and themes were not integral and longstanding elements within the tradition, but merely ephemeral and superfluous elements which some poets dragged into their lines, some artists threw into their paintings, because they didn't know enough about what mattered most: English experience, English landscapes, English ways of speaking and seeing. This is the way classical motifs are seen in his "Essay on Landscape." The original English artist, Clare argues, who eschews "the Grecian style" and "excells others in his simplicity of merit or in the naked excellence of his power," does not have to fight tradition, for traditions are founded upon excellence and originality. But he must fight against a public which meekly submits to being ruled by "the two Gadflyes," criticism and fashion. He must challenge public taste in order to transform it and so establish the standards which will allow his work to be appreciated as it should be: "real excellence must be its own creation / it must be the overflowings of its own mind & must *make* its admirers willing converts from its own powerful conceptions & not yield to win them by giving way to their opinions of excellence" (*Prose*, 213).

Clare was under no illusion that the painter's struggle in the market-place was any easier than the poet's. He knew that the tides of fashion could sweep up even the most determinedly original artists: "even Hilton & Etty & Rippingille & DeWint powerful as their pencils are must sacrifice something of their own taste to the taste of the public." It is, however, the degree to which these English painters resisted the urge to cater to public taste that concerns Clare in his essay, and he maintains that their integrity is remarkable in comparison to other painters who trade in "extravagances of false effects," in "ridiculous situations," in trickery, mannerisms, and "taste trimming," and "worn & mossy claptrap." Rippingille, Clare writes, is the "Theocritus of English painting" and de Wint is the "only artist that produces real English scenery in which British landscapes are seen & felt upon paper with all their poverty & exillerating experience of beauty about them." It was wrong, Clare argued, that these men, who "honoured a country with their labours & their truth," should be repaid "with passing notice & no praise," while others should win praise and profit from the public. The artists who did succeed were nothing but classical transvestites in whose paintings

we see the most natural reflection of scenery crowded with groups of satyrs & fawns & naiads & dryads & a whole catalogue of the vampire unaccountables dancing about in ridiculous situations round modern fishponds and immence temples in the Grecian style ... & mown pleasure grounds kept as smooth & as orderly as a turkey carpet / but are these the proper place for the introduction of ancient mythology ... the very clouds were not out of the reach of these patronizing deformers – so they are loaded with fiddling Gods & gossiping Goddesses holding their starry conversations. (*Prose*, 214)

Such paintings were "all trick and effect" and the artists who painted them failed to live up to the responsibilities of their profession. The greatest artists, Clare believed, saw nature as she was and rendered their perceptions faithfully so that their paintings were "her autographs & not a painters studys [*sic*] from the antique." Thus some of the finest landscapes were those of de Wint in which "nature is always herself in her wildest moods of extravagance." "Look at them," Clare demands, "they are the very copys of nature – & she rewards the faith of her worshippers by revealing such beautys in her settings that the fanciful never meet with" (*Prose*, 211).

The fact that these comments are based upon the assumption that there exists an exact correspondence between perception and representation does not vitiate the significance of Clare's resistance to the studio-landscapes which delivered only the old motifs of an ancient way of seeing. E.H. Gombrich has suggested that the notion of an artist painting what he "really" sees is naive and untenable, and so to offer as the criterion of a painting's merit its "truth to nature" is to be guilty of critical vulgarity.[2] But if this is so, Clare's vulgarity is that of the democrat and not of the philistine, for by resisting the fanciful sophistications of a classical idiom in which he could have no share ("for I have no latin"), he was asserting the value of an art based, not upon the gentleman's easy way with classical conventions, but upon the instruments and objects of perception which are accessible to anyone with eyes to see. In this respect, Clare reminds us of Constable, his contemporary and fellow-countryman. We know that Constable worked in his studio, painting from models made of broccoli spears and pieces of broken mirror. But there is also the Constable of the notebooks who, like Clare and in remarkably similar terms, made this crucial distinction between two kinds of landscape art:

In the one the Artist by careful application to what others have accomplished, imitates their works, or selects and combines their various beauties; in the other he seeks excellence at its primitive source NATURE. The one forms a style upon the study of pictures, and produces either imitative or eclectic art, as it has been termed; the other by a close observation of nature discovers qualities existing in her, which have never been portrayed before, and thus forms a style which is original.[3]

The "Essay on Landscape" is written in strong language, and it is most telling that Clare reserved this strong language for the classical elements in painting rather than poetry. The poetry of Milton, Pope, Collins, Gray was sacrosanct, and if there were classical meanings and forms in their poetry which Clare could not follow, well, he kept quiet about it. He did not keep quiet, however, about the Hellenist aspects of Keats's poetry and his comments upon Keats's fanciful visions indicate how strongly Clare believed that any poetry which pretended to be about nature must be descriptive, based upon a mode of seeing which is informed by experience. Keats is reported to have said that in Clare's poetry "the Description too much prevailed over the Sentiment."[4] The following may have been written in answer to that charge. Keats, Clare writes,

keeps up a constant alusion or illusion to the grecian mythology & there I cannot follow - yet when he speaks of woods Dryads & Fawns are sure to follow & the brook looks alone without her naiads to his mind / yet the frequency of such classical accompaniment make it wearisome to the reader where behind every rose bush he looks for a Venus & under every laurel a thrumming Appollo – In spite of all this his descriptions of scenery are often very fine but as it is the case with other inhabitants of great cities he often described nature as she appeared to his fancies & not as he would have described her had he witnessed the things he describes – Thus it is he has often undergone the stigma of Cockneyism & what appears as beautys in the eyes of a pent-up citizen are looked upon as consciets by those who live in the country.   (*Prose*, 223)

This passage could be adduced as evidence of the distance between Clare's aesthetic and that of his Romantic contemporaries, for he appears to repudiate here one of the fundamental Romantic premises: that nature must be rendered not as it is, but as it appears to the mind of a poet, coloured by his imagination and modified by his passions. But Clare is arguing not only for descriptive versus expressive modes and for an English versus a classical idiom, but also for the countryman's versus the city-dweller's version of nature. And he seems to have remarkable confidence here in the superior merit of the countryman's version. Nowhere else in his writings is his rural bias quite so brashly asserted. It is as though Clare, believing that Keats's criticism of his poetry had been determined by his limitations as an urban man, had seized the opportunity which Keats's own poetry provided to register his standards of judgment as a countryman on the fanciful "consciets" of a "pent-up citizen." His standards were nobler than others. In contrast to *Blackwood's* derogation of Keats's immeasurable talents, Clare's criticism of Keats seems like a piece of brotherly advice offered to a poet who had to suffer the "stigma of Cockneyism" from one who had to endure the stigma of "wild rusticity."[5]

Obviously, Clare's social and creative situation fuelled his commitment to the idea that poetry must be based upon seeing rather than learning, upon English experience rather than classical borrowings. But his ideas were formulated not only in response to the limitations of his own education and experience. Clare was of the opinion that he was defending not merely his own creative practice and the literary potential of other working-class men and women but the future of all poets and all poetry. Poetry itself, he felt, must necessarily suffer a loss of prestige if the limited and transitory values of a particular social order rigidly determined a poet's style or subject-matter. Poetry accessible only to a small elite, reflecting only the conventions and experiences of that elite, threatened the prestige of literature, which was founded, he believed, upon its capacity to speak of things "universal as the light of heaven / And common as the grass upon the plain (*II*, 40). Such beliefs were behind these sharp questions:

> Is poesy dwelling in a nice-culled sound,
> Or soft smooth words that trifle on the ear
> Unmeaning music? Is it to be found
> In rhymes run mad, that paint to startled fear
> Monsters that are not and that never were?
> Is it in declamations frothing high,
> Worked like machinery to its mad career?   (*I*, 453)

For Clare, the only answer was:

> No, poetry lives in its simplicity,
> And speaks from its own heart, to which all hearts reply.

If notions of sublimity or nobility were to be class-bound, if poetic diction was to be nothing more than the dialect of a literary caste, if "soft smooth words" were to amuse the gentleman and leave the common man perplexed and unmoved, if this was all that poetry had become, then, Clare argued, it had lost not only its prestige but its power to convey any truth of enduring values. For social elites, social values, critical fashions, and literary styles, were always coming and going; all would eventually decline and perish and take with them the poetry they had bred.[6] If poetry was to transcend the rule of historical change, it must reflect the truth of nature since only nature was constant, was capable of perennially renewing itself. Poetry must be brought down to earth, pared down to its universals, freed from the stigma of class.

Sometimes Clare's advocacy of these ideas led him to speak rather ungenerously of alternative poetic modes. One can see this in "The Flitting," for example, which he wrote in 1832 after he had left Helpston to live in Northborough. As its title suggests, the poem is about this move, a dislocation which (as the title again suggests) Clare associated with the loss of his creative power. Loss, exile, mutability, and death constitute the central subjects of "The Flitting," but it ends, if not optimistically, then at least on a note of muted consolation found in the idea that man's life in nature will endure even if his achievements die and are forgotten. This is an important though sweetly erratic work and to do it justice one ought to attend closely to its imagery of exile and belonging, nest and flight. But I want to discuss here only those aspects of the poem which reveal Clare's tendency to speak for a poetry that is palpable, specific, and common by putting down its opposite. "The Flitting" asks us to consider the possibility that heroic verse can sometimes be nothing more than "pomp in marching chime," that hieratic imagery deflects our attention from the sublimity of "plain and simpler things," that visionary poets would do well to look around them rather than strain for lofty effects. That Clare could speak critically of the visionary mode will seem, no doubt, surprising to readers who know him only as the author of the visionary asylum lyrics. But before the break into insanity he was to describe his own visionary capacity as a force which fills

> the restless mind,
>   At once to cheat and cheer
> With thought and semblance undefined,
>   Nowhere and everywhere. (*II*, 274)

His distrust of "Fancy's straining eye" is conveyed persuasively in "The Flitting," and in a way that anticipates Yeats's fear that the heart that feeds on fantasy grows "brutal from the fare."[7]

> Some sing the pomps of chivalry
> As legends of the ancient time
> Where gold and pearls and my[s]tery
> Are shadows painted for sublime
> But passions of sublimity
> Belong to plain and simpler things
> And David underneath a tree
> Sought when a shepherd Salems springs
>
> Where moss did unto cushions spring
> Forming a seat of velvet hue
> A small unnoticed trifling thing
> To all but heavens daily dew
> And Davids crown hath passed away
> Yet poesy breaths his shepherd-skill
> His palace lost - and to this day
> The little moss is blooming still
> ...
> Give me no high flown fangled things
> No haughty pomp in marching chime
> Where muses play on golden strings
> And splendour passes for sublime

Where citys stretch as far as fame
And fancys straining eye can go
And piled untill the sky for shame
Is stooping far away below

I love the verse that mild and bland
Breaths of green fields and open sky
I love the muse that in her hand
Bears wreaths of native poesy
Who walks nor skips the pasture brook
In scorn - but by the drinking horse
Leans oer its little brig to look
How far the swallows lean across
. . .
I love the muse who sits her down
Upon the molehills little lap
Who feels no fear to stain her gown
And pauses by the hedgerow gap
Not with that affectation praise
Of song to sing and never see
A field flower grow in all her days
Or e'en a forests aged tree
. . .
Time looks on pomp with careless moods
Or killing apathys disdain
- So where old marble citys stood
Poor persecuted weeds remain
She feels a love for little things
That very few can feel beside
And still the grass eternal springs
Where castles stood and grandeur died   (*JCOA*, 252-6)

There is a sly ideological bias to the imagery of these stanzas.
One notes, for instance, that the things associated with a merely
superficial and ephemeral grandeur - the "pomp of chivalry,"
marble cities, castles, crowns, gold, and pearls - are emblems of
social privilege and power. In contrast those "plain and simpler
things" associated with the true and enduring sublimity of life - the
field flowers, the obscure moss, the "poor, persecuted weeds," and
the "shepherd-skill" of the unroyal David - suggest the humble
and rustic class. I doubt, however, that ideological considerations
were uppermost in Clare's mind when he wrote "The Flitting." It
was not the conflicts and disparities between social classes that con-

cerned him here, but rather the contrast between the enduring power of nature and the mutability and inevitable decay of most human achievements. The grass always returns, but men die and what they have created – castles, regimes, "high flown fangled" artifacts – die too and are forgotten: one normally thinks of this as a tragic and unsettling recognition. But for Clare, whose poems had nothing to do with decaying castles and everything to do with the eternal grass, the mutability of merely human achievement was cause, certainly, not for great exultation, but, perhaps, for some small measure of personal satisfaction. There was reason to hope that by celebrating "in living character and breathing words" the permanent forms of nature and man's life in nature, he was writing poems which would ultimately prove as "lasting as truth and the eternal sky."

The idea of human mutability and its particular relevance to Clare's aesthetic is explored again in "The Eternity of Nature." Though it was written during the period when Clare was writing some of his finest enclosure elegies, this poem challenges the very premise and function of the elegiac mode. Its subject (named in its title) is celebrated at the expense of man's attempt to create enduring monuments and serves as a satiric foil to the pride and folly of our longings to be remembered. It is only possible to believe that an elegy, or an epitaph, or an inscription guarantees that what is past or passing away – whether it be a social order or an individual life, a structure of feeling or a fleeting perception – will be transfixed in the memory and never forgotten if one believes that the epitaph one writes or builds will never be forgotten. But in "The Eternity of Nature," Clare claims that no epitaphs, gravestones, pyramids, or poems, nothing made by the "proud skill" of the human mind, can last through time or outlast nature. The grandest memorials, Clare writes, will eventually and inevitably, like "kings and empires," fade and die. Only nature will endure:

> Leaves from eternity are simple things
> To the worlds gaze where to a spirit clings
> Sublime and lasting – trampled underfoot
> The daisey lives and strikes its little root
> Into the lap of time – centurys may come
> And pass away into the silent tomb
> And still the child hid in the womb of time
> Shall smile and pluck them when this simple ryhme
> Shall be forgotten like a church yard stone
> Or lingering lye unnotised and alone …

The little Robin in the quiet glen
Hidden from fame and all the strife of men
Sings unto time a pastoral and gives
A music that lives on and ever lives
Both spring and autumn years rich bloom and fade
Longer then songs that poets ever made   (*JCOA*, 165-6)

The poet can hope to escape the general condition of mutability only by acting, not as nature's competitor in a race he can never hope to win, but as a most humble mediator between nature and humanity. He must imagine himself a creature of nature rather than of human history, must be at one with the obscure robin and simple daisy in order to become one of "times partners":

Time loves them like a child and ever will
And so I worship them in bushy spots
And sing with them when all else notice not
And feel the music of their mirth agree
With that sooth quiet that bestirreth me
And if I touch aright that quiet tone
That soothing truth that shadows forth their own
Then many a year shall grow in after days
And still find hearts to love my quiet lays   (*JCOA*, 166)

That Clare could conclude this poem by offering himself as a paradigm of the true poet, who seeks to understand the secrets of nature's eternity and appreciates its subtler forms "when all else notice not," suggests how far he had travelled away from the self-effacing "lowly clown" who had, in his earlier poems, asked his readers to pardon his presumption in daring to write anything at all. We ought to applaud the confidence and creative poise (they did not come easily) that allowed Clare to present himself in such a way. Yet some readers may feel that the extended claims Clare made for himself as a true and original poet coincide with rather attenuated claims for cultural achievement in general. It may be felt that he challenged the uniqueness and authority of human art much too readily, that by recording his belief that the poet's noblest function is to act as nature's echo or shadow, he proved himself blind to humanity's capacity to generate enduring truths of its own. Certainly Clare, so avowedly dependent upon and "emulous" of nature, had little patience for those who thought that great art was created only by transcending nature, or transforming it, drawing moral analogies or objective correlations from it, projecting upon it, or forcing it to conform to our small and shifting purposes. In the centuries-old conflict between nature and art, he stood firmly on the side of nature. He thought that art should aspire to the condition of nature, that human creativity should work in concert with creation, and these beliefs encouraged him to hold to mimetic standards which were in some ways limiting and impractical – nature will always be more "natural" than art. But we must recognize that Clare was responding to standards which he believed were themselves rigid, limiting, and not simply unnatural, but inhuman. When he wrote that "arts strong impulse mars the truth of taste" (*JCOA*, 174) he was not attacking art in general but only that kind of art which he thought was reflexive of the exclusive, arrogant, egocentric, and order-obsessed ideology of a very small minority of humanity. He was particularly incensed by practitioners of landscape art – gardeners, poets, painters – who shared the arrogance of enclosers and improvers towards the luxuriant and wild disorder of nature:

> With them disorder is an ugly weed
> And wood and heath a wilderness of thorns   (*JCOA*, 174)

He was not advocating disorder for its own sake; he was challenging the "spruce and delicate ideas" of those who failed to recognize that "wild nature," like "wild rusticity," possessed a formal perfection of its own.

To catch Clare quarrelling with this convention or that attitude is to see him coming into his own. The quarrels, as we have seen, were numerous, the agenda of "thou shalt not's" a long and idiosyncratic one: learning and gentility must not be considered prerequisites for the poet's vocation; the taste and objectivity of the gentle reader was not to be trusted; the poet should not follow the "two false prophets" of criticism and fashion; Greek goddesses had no business appearing in English poems or paintings; a poet must not lose touch with the democratic principles of "natures love"; he must not impose his notions of aesthetic order upon the wild disorder and variety of nature. But the pressure of a single feeling sustains and gives coherence to all of these quarrels: a longing for a poetic tradition which was open to everything in nature and human life, which did not exclude the ordinary sparrow because it was lack-lustre, or a clump of wild fern because of its recalcitrant disorder, or the common experience of labouring people because the harsh particulars of their experience did not seem to fit smoothly into the golden world of the conventional pastoralist. The critical, dissentient, almost combative stance Clare assumed towards some aesthetic pieties – in particular, the equation of beauty and order, sublimity and a high, earth-disdaining style – were not the product of his indifference to the responsibilities of humanist assertion but of his belief that those responsibilities had to be extended and redefined. In the twentieth century, Wallace Stevens was the poet who wrote most eloquently of the need to "see the earth again / Cleared of its stiff and stubborn, man-locked set."[8] And it is, perhaps, within the terms of this, no doubt, inappropriately modern idea that the significance of Clare's commitment to the "truth of nature" can best be assessed, though in his case one might say that he was writing not only against a "man-locked set," but against a stiff and cruelly stubborn gentleman-locked set of attitudes. If in such poems as "The Flitting" and "The Eternity of Nature" he appears to give nature the monopoly on generous, creative, and permanent achievement, it may have been because this was the best way he knew how to challenge a different kind of monopoly – the monopoly which the genteel classes held upon the literary life of the nation. And this is a challenge in which I think it is impossible to disentangle his social and aesthetic motives, his commitment to his class and to his vocation. The work of extending the mandate, the provenance, and so the prestige of poetry was synonymous for Clare with the work of purchasing a literary franchise for the uneducated working-class men and women whom he represented.

THE "UNIVERSAL LANGUAGE" OF THE IMAGE

Clare's challenge to the excluding literary ideas of an exclusive minority links him closely to Wordsworth's revolt against literary convention and poetic diction, a revolt which, as Hazlitt was to argue, could be related (though perhaps more indirectly than Hazlitt would have it) to the levelling and democratizing ideals of the French Revolution. That Clare himself seems not to have considered these connections does not preclude us from recognizing them today. And no Romantic document maps out these connections quite so clearly, though inadvertently, as William Hazlitt's "On the Living Poets." In this lecture (written in 1818, two years before Clare's first volume was published), Hazlitt presents an analysis of Wordsworth's literary principles and practice which might be applied just as easily to Clare. Indeed, I think that at least in some of its particulars, Hazlitt's analysis could be applied more suitably to the author of "The Flitting" and the "Essay on Landscape" than to the author of the *Lyrical Ballads* and the Prefaces. The school of poetry which Wordsworth founded, Hazlitt wrote,

had its origin in the French Revolution, or rather in those sentiments and opinions which produced that revolution; ... The change in the Belles-lettres was as complete, and to many persons as startling, as the change in politics, with which it went hand in hand. There was a mighty ferment in the heads of statesmen and poets, kings and people. According to the prevailing notions, all was to be natural and new. Nothing that was established was to be tolerated. All the commonplace figures of poetry, tropes, allegories, personifications, with the whole heathen mythology were instantly discarded; a classical allusion was considered as a piece of antiquated foppery ... Authority and fashion, elegance or arrangement, were hooted out of countenance, as pedantry and prejudice. Everyone did that which was good in his own eyes. The object was to reduce all things to an absolute level; ... our native writers adopted a wonderful simplicity of style and matter. The paradox they set out with was, that all things are by nature equally fit subjects for poetry; or that if there is any preference to be given, those that are the meanest and most unpromising are the best ... Their poetry has 'no figures nor no fantasies,' which the prejudices of superstition or the customs of the world draw in the brains of men; 'no trivial fond records' of all that has existed in the history of past ages; it has no adventitious pride, pomp, or circumstance to set it off. [9]

In emphasizing Wordsworth's "revolutionary and renegado extravagances," Hazlitt demonstrated a devious and ironically levelling attitude of his own towards the very leveller he was describing. But whether his outline of Wordsworth's principles and practice is accurate or fair is a question we may leave to Wordsworthians; we are concerned here not with Hazlitt's critical virtuosity, but with the fact that the values he believed central to Wordsworth's poetry (the resistance to authority, fashion, pedantry, and prejudice; the espousal of the common, the simple, the natural, the democratic) were the same values which, as we have seen, were of central importance to Clare. That one of the greatest critics of the Romantic period should write about the greatest poet of the age in terms that may be applied quite as judiciously to Clare prompts one to challenge such critics as Robinson and Summerfield when they claim that "as a poet, Clare was out of his time" and "belongs to the worlds before the French Revolution."[10] On the contrary, to set Clare's vocational writings against selected passages from Hazlitt's lecture "On the Living Poets" is to recognize that Clare was very much a poet of his time, Wordsworth's comrade though he did not know it.

But I do not wish to labour these Romantic connections. We should not be too eager to place the project of Clare's vocational poems or of his nature poetry within the brackets of the Wordsworthian project, not because the connections between Clare's challenge and Wordsworth's revolt are necessarily spurious, but because what is peculiar to Clare, what is assumed and what is most urgently and thoughtfully articulated in his poetry is obscured if we try to read Clare into Wordsworth. It is certainly inviting to consider what these two poets, so different in so many obvious ways, had in common, especially within the area of linguistic principle. Wordsworth argued against the "false refinements," "the gaudiness and inane phraseology" of poetic diction, and argued for the language of "humble and rustic life" because he believed that it was "a more permanent, and a far more philosophical language, than that which is frequently substituted for it by Poets."[11] Clare opposed "the old threadbare epithets," and "soft smooth words" of conventional pastoral verse, and proposed the "bold inovating" inclusion of themes and words which were thought of as "low and vulgar" but which, he believed, were truly expressive of a "real love for nature" (*Prose*, 173). But what the greatest poet of the Romantic tradition and the self-proclaimed "meanest of the throng" did not and could never share is much more important than what they happened to have in common. Indeed, linguistic principle, an issue which might encourage us to cement the link between a humble and rustic poet and the poet of humble and rustic life, proves to be one of the most obvious issues upon which Wordsworth and Clare radically differed. In the first place, Clare, who dispensed with Wordsworth's poetic experiments in the language of humble and rustic life as "affectations of simplicity," does not appear to have known or understood what Wordsworth was attempting to do in *Lyrical Ballads*. In the second place, one can hardly suppose that Wordsworth would have approved of a poet who employed dialect words and defended a vocabulary that was "low and vulgar." Wordsworth made very clear in the Preface to the *Lyrical Ballads* that the bald "vulgarity and meanness of ordinary life" was not what the poet was meant to convey. [12] He also made clear that in his own poems the language of humble and rustic men had not been faithfully reproduced, but had only been "adopted (purified indeed from what appeared to be its real defects, from all lasting and rational causes of dislike or disgust)." [13] Wordsworth had then his own "rational causes" for disliking the "real defects" in the "very language of men." In the third place, Clare did not share Wordsworth's profound theoretical interest in language, for his defence of his dialect-words can hardly be said to constitute a theory of language. Finally, even in the very few poems in which we do find Clare offering cryptic theoretical pronouncements upon language, we find no evidence that he shared Wordsworth's confidence in the mediating and memorializing capacities of language.

We have no concrete evidence that Clare ever read Wordsworth's Preface to the *Lyrical Ballads* or the "Prospectus" of *The Recluse*. Had he read the Preface, he would, no doubt, have been encouraged and lifted up by the democratic elements in Wordsworth's argument. But, however delighted he might have been, there is good reason to suppose that Clare would not have agreed with Wordsworth's idea that in the language of humble and rustic life the poet could find and express the permanent and primary laws of our nature. He would not, needless to say, have disagreed with the idea that humble rustics are fitting exemplars of humanity. But Clare, who said in "Remembrances" that "words are poor receipts for what time hath stole away," who wrote in "To a Fallen Elm" of the way the meaning of so crucial a word as "freedom" could be preempted, falsified, put to the service of a deceitful political rhetoric, was much more sceptical than Wordsworth about the epitaphic or universalizing functions of language. In the "Prospectus" of *The Recluse* Wordsworth wrote with characteristic confidence:

>   by words
> Which speak of nothing more than what we are,
> Would I arouse the sensual from their sleep
> Of Death, and win the vacant and the vain
> To noble raptures; while my voice proclaims
> How exquisitely the individual Mind
> (And the progressive powers perhaps no less
> Of the whole species) to the external world
> Is fitted. [14]

The "spousal verse / Of this great consummation" depended for Wordsworth upon his belief that he had found his way to "a strain of words / That shall be life, the acknowledged voice of life."[15] But, at least in principle, this was a search and discovery in which Clare could not share. For him language was always to some extent a false mediation, an all-too-human intervention which could unite the poet and his subject, man and nature, only by tipping the balance of the relationship in our favour.

His scepticism, distrust, and problematical relationship to language can, I believe, be related very directly to the fact that he was writing, and was profoundly conscious of the fact that he was writing, within a class-divided society. As we noted earlier in considering his relationship to the vocabulary of his community and of the English literary tradition, Clare resisted the idea that words or word-systems were private property. But he also knew that within the public territory of language private appropriations by select classes and groups were always taking place. He knew that the way a man spoke or wrote – in his time, whether or not a man could write at all – was profoundly affected by the situation and expectations of the class into which he was born. He learned the hard way that whether a man spoke of the "will o' the wisp" or (as Clare did) of the "jenny-burnt-arse" was a question normally determined by the geographical and social place he was fated to inhabit. Thus, while Wordsworth could write with calm assurance of the "words / Which speak of nothing more than what we are," for Clare the words that spoke of what he was also spoke of what society had made of him:

> An humble rustic hums in lowly dreams
> Far in the swale where poverty retires   (*I*, 133)

For Clare, language could not effect more than a frail and tentative reconciliation between the gentleman and the workingman, because it was itself all-too-social, too tainted by the radical disharmonies of social caste. Thus, though the poems examined in this chapter suggest that he was as interested as the author of the *Lyrical Ballads* in revitalizing poetry by breaking down the barriers between man and nature, gentleman and rustic, we cannot say of Clare as we can of Wordsworth that language was the "central weapon" in his revolutionary project.[16] Far from being the solution to the problem of writing within a class-divided society, language was for Clare part of the problem.

Nothing could be more paradoxical than the situation of a poet who declared his distrust of language – and kept on writing poem after poem, year after year. Clare was aware of this paradox, this contradiction of principle and practice, and he wrote about it with brilliant economy in "Songs Eternity," a poem which I want to examine rather closely. I should say now, before quoting from the poem, that it does not seem at first glance to warrant close critical attention, nor does it seem to deserve to be called profound, paradoxical, or brilliant. On first reading it appears to be nothing more than a bagatelle, a naive and easy bit of rhyme, less a piece of work than a piece of play. It seems not only trivial but trivializing in the way it dispenses so easily with such weighty matters as life and death, time and eternity, man and nature. But a second reading of the poem reveals it to be a technically remarkable piece of work, a disturbing and ironic treatment of certain humanist pieties but one which does not then preclude the poet from celebrating his own peculiar brand of natural humanism. Like "The Eternity of Nature" and "The Flitting," this deceptively simple poem describes the literary and social achievements of mankind in reductive and circumscribing phrases ("pride and fame," "noise and bustle," "crowds and citys"), phrases which convey the quality of insignificant and transitory business which rules human life. The language of the poem and, indeed, all its formal elements are, in the Brechtian sense, alienating in their effect. "Songs Eternity" is constructed from short, compacted lines, words which are simple, but semantically dense, short disturbing questions and callously simple answers, an exacting pattern of internal and end-rhymes, and finally a sing-song rhythm which allows the reader no time to catch his breath or to meditate upon the sound and semantic relationships of the poem's rhyme-pairings. These formal elements create a mood which is at once sweet and ruthless, innocent and too-knowing. It is as though "Songs Eternity" were written with the cruelty of a child grown old before his time.

The mood and tone correspond perfectly to the theme. In fact, they carry the burden of Clare's argument that since in the long run time will treat human achievement with a callous indifference, it is best that men relinquish their longings to create anything of permanence. Humanity is relegated to the role of a listener ("adams ears"), an appreciator of "creations music," but not the creator of a music or a universal language of its own. And, at least at the level of explicit statement, Clare relegates to himself the same role by speaking of his poetic experience, not in terms of the poems he has written, but in terms of the "songs Ive heard and felt and seen":

What is songs eternity
Come and see
Can it noise and bustle be
Come and see
Praises sung or praises said
Can it be
Wait awhile and these are dead
Sigh sigh
Be they high or lowly bred
They die
...
Mighty songs that miss decay
What are they
Crowds and citys pass away
Like a day
Books are writ and books are read
What are they
Years will lay them with the dead
Sigh sigh
Trifles unto nothing wed
They die
...
Tootle tootle tootle tee
Can it be
Pride and fame must shadows be
Come and see
Every season own her own
Bird and be[e]
Sing creations music on
Natures glee
Is in every mood and tone
Eternity

The eternity of song
Liveth here
Natures universal tongue
Singeth here
Songs Ive heard and felt and seen
Everywhere
Songs like the grass are evergreen
The giver
Said live and be and they have been
For ever   (*JCOA*, 122-4)

The poet hears the eternity of song not in the "praises sung" by men but in the song of the bluecap, and so it is the quality of the birdsong which he seeks to convey in his poem. As the Tibbles were the first to observe, "Songs Eternity" is a sustained and beautifully realized exercise in onomatopoeia, not in the narrow sense that it is merely a verbal mimicry of nonverbal sounds, but in the richer sense of the word: the poem is onomatopoeic because its language and form correspond to its central image.[17] With its abrupt but regular metric shifts, its short lines and simple words, its assonant and alliterative sounds, "Songs Eternity" reflects and echoes the thin cry, the quick turn and return, of the bluecap's song. The poem is not metrically flawless. Extra syllables are added to some of the lines of the last three verses, stresses are displaced, and the syntax obtrudes upon the metre and fights against the line integrity and rhythmic expectations established in the first half of the poem. But the metrical errors are structurally logical. In the last three verses the lines are extended, the rhythm slower and more complicated, because these verses carry the weight of the answer to Clare's initial question, "What is songs eternity." His response appears to give little credit to human creativity or language. "The eternity of song," he claims, is identical with "Natures universal tongue" and with "creations music" and can be found everywhere in nature, but nowhere, it would seem, in the places where crowds and cities, books and poems, come and go. This is an answer which might encourage the reader to feel that Clare held to a limited and literally inhuman vision of what poetry ought to be: as simple, musical, and wordless as the bluecap's "tootle tee."

But, as with the crisis-lyrics of Coleridge and Wordsworth and the nature-lyrics of Shelley, so with Clare's "Songs Eternity," the very existence of the poem serves as an ironic commentary upon its initial premise. The premise of Coleridge's famous ode – that in the state of dejection the poet can find "no natural outlet, no relief, / In word, or sight, or tear" – is unravelled by the poem itself.[18] The same can be said of Shelley's "To a Skylark," which carries its burden of proof against the premise that simile, metaphor, and human language are inadequate to catch the sound or meaning of the skylark's song. In "Songs Eternity" the reductive way Clare describes literature and literary aspirations is subverted by the very fact of the poem and by the total coherence of its meaning and form. The very fact that Clare wrote his poem represents, one might say, the triumph of the human perspective over the inhuman perspective of the bluecap's eternity. And the poem that he wrote suggests that Clare did not wish to prove his premise that literary works are "trifles unto nothing wed," but quite to the contrary had written to prove that men should not relinquish their creative aspirations nor become merely appreciators of "creations music." The total form of "Songs Eternity" expresses what the poet will not explicitly say: that poetry has the capacity to unite the ancient "melodies of earth and sky" with the language of men. For it is not through verbal mimicry of the bluecap's cry that Clare conveys the sound and sense of "songs eternity," but rather through poetic devices, metrical decisions, human language, and images which convey an all-too-human understanding of futility and aspiration. The sum of these elements is a piece of work which represents both an act of praise for poetry as a uniquely human achievement, and a celebration of language because it can express what the bluecap can say and what it cannot say.

Nevertheless, even though Clare's practice contradicted his stated principles, even though his poetic fluency belied his declared distrust of language, the fact remains that at the level of explicit thematic statement, when he wrote about language it was in terms of its inadequacies, its inability to convey "that quiet tone / That soothing truth that shadows" from the song of the robin or the bluecap. We find nothing in Clare's letters or prose to suggest that he shared Wordsworth's great faith in the magisterial and transforming capacities of language.[19] Geoffrey Hartman has observed that the end towards which the Wordsworthian revolt against poetic diction was directed was "the discovery from within nature or felt experience of truly universal universals – concepts and words that could spread, like joy, 'in wildest commonality'."[20] The last two poems I want to consider in this chapter, "The Voice of Nature" and "Pastoral Poesy," make very clear that Clare believed as urgently as Wordsworth that the poet must speak of "truly universal universals" and that he must locate these universals within nature or felt experience. But these poems also indicate that it was not through his concepts and words that Clare hoped to break down the barriers between man and nature, gentleman and worker, but rather through his feelings, his perceptions, and his imagery.

In both these poems speech and language are crucial terms. But Clare's use of these terms would have been quite incomprehensible to nineteenth-century philologists, though they would, no doubt, pose no problem at all to twentieth-century semiologists who are used to finding their "langues" and "paroles," their signs and signifying systems, in images, gestures, silences, structures of perception, objects, rituals. I draw attention to the unlikely resemblance between Clare and the semiologist not because I think it useful to place him within the highly intellectualized project of semiotics, but because I want to emphasize the fact that Clare's "green language" in "Pastoral Poesy" is not, in the strictest sense, a language at all. For Clare, the universal language "to which all hearts reply" was founded, not as Wordsworth would have it, upon "words / That speak of nothing more than what we are," but upon images which convey nature "as she is," as we see her, as we respond to her with feelings of mutuality and respect. Thus, in "Pastoral Poesy," Clare writes:

> True poesy is not in words
> But images that thoughts express
> By which the simplest hearts are stirred
> To elevated happiness
> ...
> But poesy is a language meet
> & fields are every ones employ
> The wild flower neath the shepherds feet
> Looks up & gives him joy
>
> A language that is ever green
> That feelings unto all impart
> As awthorn blossoms soon as seen
> Give may to every heart
> ...
> An image to the mind is brought
> Where happiness enjoys
> An easy thoughtlessness of thought
> & meets excess of joys
> ...
> & such is poesy its power
> May varied lights employ
> Yet to all mind it gives the dower
> Of self creating joy
>
> & wether it be hill or moor
> I feel where e'er I go
> A silence that discourses more
> Then any tongue can do   (*MC*, 291-2)

The last stanza appears to be subversive of language and literature – indeed, subversive of the very poem in which it is placed. For if it is true that the silence of nature is more meaningful than the language of men, then what is the point of writing or speaking at all? But this is our question, not Clare's, and the sweet-tempered and peaceful tone of the poem suggests that he was neither fighting language nor denying its eloquence but trying to discover new forms of eloquence, a new way of conveying meaning less clamorous in its assertion of "what we are," more receptive to the influences of nature "as she is." "To look on nature with a poetic eye," he wrote, "magnifies the pleasure she herself being the very essence & soul of Poesy" (*Prose*, 176). And this work of looking at nature was not for Clare a matter of merely reacting to nature, but of interacting with it. Poetic receptivity was not to be confused with inert passivity, for it depended upon the active functions of the "poetic eye," the tactful mind, the alert and respectful sensibilities of conscious men. The man who "hears the sound / When beauty fills the mind," who discovers "as some strange melody / A poem of the woods," was more truely creative than the man who drowned out nature with his own self-proclaiming cries:

> Unruffled quietness hath made
> A peace in every place
> & woods are resting in their shade
> Of social lonliness
> ...
> So would I my own mind employ
> & my own heart impress
> That poesy's self's a dwelling joy
> Of humble quietness   (*MC*, 292, 294)

Nature as the locus of "social loneliness," the place where we give and receive more than is possible within society, where we can find company and still be alone; poetry as "green language," as the meeting ground between nature and humanity, the place where "all men" give and receive the "dower of self creating joy": these are the crucial terms and definitions with which Clare challenged the words and concepts of a literary and social elite which was for him neither sociable nor eloquent enough.

In "The Voice of Nature," as in "Pastoral Poesy," the "voice," "melody," "music," "language," and "speech" that Clare celebrates are "not in words / But images" which speak eloquently to the mind not grown inured to the rich unity that is "heard and felt and seen" in nature. "The Voice of Nature" is not, I think, as fine or as disarming a poem as "Pastoral Poesy." It is a little too self-

consciously lofty and wise, and as a result it almost looks like a
piece of lyric hyperbole cluttered with old saws (words are cheap;
silence is golden; there is more poetry in life than in a book). That
the poem, nonetheless, possesses thematic depth and unity is due
to its poignant autobiographical reference and to the richness of its
synesthetic imagery. This kind of imagery (well suited to a work
which celebrates the special expressive power of the poetic image)
affirms the importance of sensuous experience at the expense of
analytic knowledge. It insults the mind that reasons and dissects,
and poses a challenge to those of us who cannot hear visual beauty,
or feel a sound, or see into the silence. The challenge is posed quite
explicitly in "The Voice of Nature." Though the poem speaks of
the fundamental unity in nature, though it suggests that there are
no discreet categories of perception in the fluidity of natural experience, it speaks of humanity in categorical and polarizing terms.
There are "the few" and there are "the crowd"; those who can feel
magic in nature and those for whom the magic does not exist; those
who can "see melody in nature's laws," hear the sun shine, and
"read its language and its speech," and then again those "heedless
worldlings" who have wilfully excluded themselves from participation in the green language of nature. These divisive categories are
put to rhetorical use in "The Voice of Nature," since, as readers of
the poem, we can only escape the ignominy of being consigned to
the insensible, unseeing, "heedless crowd" if we give ourselves over
to the synesthetic experience which Clare's imagery conveys:

> There is a language wrote on earth and sky
> By God's own pen is silent majesty;
> There is a voice that's heard and felt and seen
> In spring's young shades and summer's endless green;
> There is a book of poesy and spells
> In which that voice in sunny splendour dwells;
> There is a page in which that voice aloud
> Speaks music to the few and not the crowd;
> Though no romantic scenes my feet have trod,
> The voice of nature as the voice of God
> Appeals to me in every tree and flower,
> Breathing his glory, magnitude and power.
> In nature's open book I read, and see
> Beauty's rich lesson in this seeming-pea;
> Crowds see no magic in the trifling thing;
> Pshaw! tis a weed, and millions came with spring.
> I hear rich music whereso'er I look

But heedless worldlings chide the brawling brook;
And that small lark between me and the sky
Breathes sweetest strains of morning's melody;
Yet by the heedless crowd 'tis only heard
As the small warbling of a common bird ...
The many look for sound – 'tis silence speaks,
And song like sunshine from her rapture breaks.
I hear it in my bosom ever near;
'Tis in these winds, and they are everywhere.
It casts around my vision magic spells
And makes earth heaven where poor fancy dwells.
I read its language, and its speech is joy;
So, without teaching when a lonely boy,
Each weed to me did happy tidings bring,
And laughing daisies wrote the name of spring,
And God's own language unto nature given
Seemed universal as the light of heaven
And common as the grass upon the plain,
That all may read and meet with joy again,
Save the unheeding heart that, like the tomb,
Shuts joy in darkness and forbids its bloom   (*II*, 39)

When Clare describes his world as a place "where poor fancy
dwells," he is referring not to the paucity of his imagination but to
his poverty, to the fact that he is at once a poor man and an imaginative man. But though he is poor, he is also a poet made wealthy
by the "rich music" and "rich lesson" he receives from nature. He is
an uneducated man ("without teaching when a lonely boy") who
is also a scholar in the green language of nature, a fine textual
critic of "nature's open book." And though he is denied the travelling experience of the gentleman-poet, who can take for granted
the mobility which permits him to travel through Europe or Britain, taking in the sublime sights at Mont Blanc or Mount Snow-
don, he recognizes that staying at home has not robbed him of his
"passions of sublimity," nor has it affected his capacity to bear witness to the "glory, magnitude, and power" which he finds in nature
"wheresoe're I look." In these formulations one hears again the
paradoxical formulations of "The Village Minstrel" with its uneducated, inexperienced, economically poor hero who is tutored,
enriched, and broadened by his relationship to the limitless
natural world of his own local landscape. In both poems nature
gives to the poet what is denied to him because of his social circumstances. But there is a crucial difference between them. In "The

Voice of Nature" Clare does not apologize for his background. Nor does he plead for the poetic aspirations he is so desperate to fulfil. He speaks, not of the poetry he longs to write, but of the poetry he does write, in a green language which does not depend upon learning or wealth or social prestige to be spoken or understood. When Clare wrote about this "language meet," that "is evergreen," and "unto nature given," he was referring not to what he said through his own words, but to what nature said to him, to anyone with keen eyes and an open heart. And he believed that this language could only be conveyed through the medium of images which did not have to be translated. If we speak of the green language of his poems it is, perhaps, because we can have more confidence in the mediating and memorializing capacity of his words than Clare could ever have himself.

CHAPTER SEVEN

The Society of Nature: The Bird Poems

In 1824, Clare wrote to Taylor:

When I have done with the 'Shepherds Calendar' I shall make up my mind to publish no more for 8 or 10 years & in that interval I intend ... to write one hundred Sonnets as a set of pictures on the scenes of objects that appear in the different seasons.   (*Letters*, 156)

These proposed sonnets (written "soly for amusement") were to be "attempts" or experiments on subjects "gentle and simple as they come," and since Clare did not intend them for immediate publication, they were to give him the opportunity to develop his art of natural observation untroubled by the question of how his work would be received. The bird poems, which he began to write in 1824, were the most interesting product of that happy creative impulse.[1] Their subject is indeed gentle and simple; the pictorial element and the topic of seasonal variation figure significantly in them; and though several of the best ones are considerably longer than fourteen lines, the majority are recognizable in form and length as sonnet variations.

Perhaps because of their subject-matter and because many of them are so starkly descriptive, the bird poems have been associated with the later phases of the georgic tradition.[2] On first thought the tradition of James Grahame and Erasmus Darwin (with their apparently exhaustive, quasi-scientific accounts of rural life and scenery) certainly seems the most likely one in which to place one-hundred-odd poems which describe in minute and factual detail the nesting and feeding habits of a natural species. However, the bird poems (individually or as a sequence) actually have little in common with the late eighteenth-century georgic.

The didactic concerns, generally impersonal point of view, ency-clopedic procedures, and (when all the flourishes are allowed for) turgid and euphemistic style which are characteristic of poets such as Grahame and Darwin are nowhere to be seen in Clare's auda-ciously singular, sharply focused, episodic poems. In fact, the whole idea of man in relation to nature upon which the georgic is predicated – the belief that our "works" take precedence over our "days," "*ponos*" over "*otium*," that perceptions are engendered by the need to know nature, and the need to know by the desire to claim nature and harness its productive potentialities – is diame-trically opposed to the tactful, unpossessive attitudes Clare brought to the act of natural observation.[3] As we shall see, Clare's ornitho-logical expertise was rather impressive, his curiosity even more so. But he was not especially interested in connecting his natural observation to a larger theory of physical creation. It was always the sheer aesthetic momentousness of hearing a robin in a silent wood or catching sight of a lone heron circling an empty sky that most mattered to him, and his starkest poems testify to the value of individual perception emancipated from the concerns engendered by intellectual or material utility.

The bird poems are a practical application of the beliefs and principles articulated in the vocational writings and enclosure elegies – perception for its own sake; nature for its own sake; the rich literary possibilities found in the most ordinary human experi-ence. But in many ways they also represent a sharp departure from the works we have explored thus far. They are not haunted by a sense of audience. We find in them no gestures of deference nor defiant interventions. They touch only in the most general way upon the topics of social injustice and cultural exclusivity. Celebra-tion rather than protest appears to be their formal motive, and the subject of their celebration is not only birds in particular and nature in general, but Clare's retreat from society into nature. Indeed, if one were to draw a portrait of their author, it would be of a man intent upon escaping the brute realities of his society and the problems and responsibilities created by his consciousness of his place within its organization. And the sense of imaginative release which many of these poems convey tempt one to say that Clare had made good his escape, had found a subject, form, and point of view which allowed him to forsake the concerns and preoccupa-tions which inform his other work. Standing within and writing about the "woodland privacy" where the robin made its nest, Clare could put poverty, enclosure, prejudice, his whole social experi-ence and identity, momentarily behind him and become just a pair of clear, human eyes staring at a bird. But he had to know what he was escaping from in order to make good his escape, and in the very idea that these poems were the product of his longing to put his social experience behind him, the question of that experience and its relation to his imagination immediately asserts itself.

Among the poets who preceded Clare and whom he most admired, examples abound of those who counselled retreat from the noisome concerns of society and who justified their own forms of escape, whether temporary or permanent (to Olney or The Leasowes, Grasmere or Hagley Park), by describing society as an impossible environment in which to realize their humanity. It is no less true of Clare than of Thomson, Gray, Cowper, and Words-worth, that his motives for retreat were developed and articulated as responses to his society. The thematic interest of the finest bird poems, their formal tensions, and their centrality within the canon depend, to a considerable extent, upon their pastoral duality. One could say that they are songs of pastoral innocence into which the complexities of social experience are always intruding, for the characteristic pattern of memory, thought, anticipation, and feeling which Clare brought to the act of natural observation caused him, in the very moment of proclaiming his escape from the burdening carapace of his social knowledge, to draw upon it. Moreover, the sense of liberty he found in the pastoral world of his beloved birds contains within itself a strong criticism of the non-pastoral realities of his society. The implicit social content of his natural observation is evident in "The Robins Nest," for example, when Clare describes the hidden reaches of nature as a world immune to "interest industry and slavish gain" and untouched by the "meddling toil," "trivial things," and "artificial toys / That men call wealth" (*JCOA*, 223-4).

On first thought one can scarcely imagine a theme more accessible to Clare and more conducive to his creative poise than the theme of rural retreat. The greatest poets had written, in the greatest poems of the English tradition, about the countryside in terms of the imaginative and emotional release it afforded from the airless cloisters, the politics of the court, the anxieties and perverse sophis-tications of the city. Clare, most fortunate of men, was already there. But the countryside to which "the glorious host" retreated was very different from the countryside in which Clare lived and worked - the difference was less a function of Clare's historical period than of his class. The grottoes, gardens, and expansive estates through which the eighteenth-century poets ambled and ruminated were part of the rural landscape (and emblems of a social order) Clare was not invited to linger in long enough to write about. More significantly, his circumstances precluded him from participating in or giving complete assent to the form of rural retreat which most appealed to those poets – Horatian retirement. One thinks of Cowper, for example, who expounded upon the pleasures of retirement more systematically and in more detail than any other poet of his century. His primary intention in writing *The Task* was, in his words, "to discountenance the modern enthusiasm after a London life, and to recommend rural ease and leisure, as friendly to the cause of piety and virtue."[4] There is, I should think, no need to be detained by an examination of the retirement theme in eighteenth-century poetry: its importance has long been recognized. But we should remember that in that time the Horatian ideal recommended by poets like Cowper could have been cherished and realized only by those men and women who possessed the means to live in "ease and leisure." Cowper believed that for a man who could fully exercise his options the country was the best of all possible worlds:

> Had I the choice of sublunary good,
> What could I wish that I possess not here?
> Health, leisure, means t'improve it, friendship, peace,
> No loose or wanton, though a wand'ring muse,
> And constant occupation without care.[5]

But, of course, from Clare's perspective Cowper did possess "the choice of sublunary good"; his retirement was purchased without personal sacrifice. Cowper himself admitted as much, and with characteristic urbanity confessed:

> If solitude make scant the means of life,
> Society for me![6]

The very way the choice is posed suggests that Cowper took for granted what Clare could only long for: the opportunity to decide for himself how and where he would live and the freedom to retire from the mundane necessity of "getting and spending."

The convention of retirement presupposes that one has a place to retire to, that the "nature" one has chosen over "society" will be accessible. The pleasures which the advocates of rural retirement found in gazing and musing upon the landscape very much depended upon their freedom to wander anywhere and everywhere through it and find no paths barred to them. Thomson could wander through Marlborough and Eastbury, stand within or outside the gates of Hagley Park, as he chose. Cowper could turn off the public path, confident in his belief that no landowner would challenge his right as a gentleman to have access to all parts of the countryside:

> The folded gates would bar my progress now,
> But that the lord of this enclos'd demesne,
> Communicative of the good he owns,
> Admits me to a share; the guiltless eye
> Commits no wrong, nor wastes what it enjoys.[7]

But Clare was not able to write so blithely about his right to take in, with a "guiltless eye," a landscape which belonged to another man. In an early poem, "Narrative Verses, Written After an Excursion from Helpstone to Burghley Park," he recorded an occasion when, swept away by his longing to find a perfect place from which to view the environing landscape, he stole over the walls of the Cecil estate. But instead of taking pleasure from the prospect, he felt "troubled thoughts" and "ills almost beyond belief" arising from his knowledge that the walls of Burghley Park existed to keep out people like him:[8]

> No spire I caught, nor woody swell,
> My eye confin'd to lower bounds,
> Yet not to mark the flow'ret's bell,
> But watch the owners of the grounds;
> Their presence was my only fear,
> No boughs to shield me if they came,
> And soon amid my rash career
> I deem'd such trespassing to blame.   (I, 33)

At issue here is not an isolated event in the long history of Clare's landscape involvement, but rather the enormous impact which the denial of lawful access to large parts of the countryside had upon his sense of personal freedom. He hated the "fence of ownership" for turning him into an intruder in his own locality and for making it quite literally impossible for him to follow in the footsteps of the poets he most admired.

"Trespass," probably written shortly before Clare was admitted to the asylum, testifies most sharply to the impact of this denial. This is a sad poem to read, not only because it gives symptomatic

warning of the delusions and paranoid obsessions from which Clare
was to suffer in his later years, but because it shows the extent to
which he felt traumatized and dispossessed by those who exercised
their property-rights to the countryside. The mood of the poem is
determined by the harsh negative constructions with which it
begins and ends:

> I dreaded walking where there was no path
> And prest with cautious tread the meadow swath,
> And always turned to look with wary eye,
> And always feared the farmer coming by;
> Yet everything about where I had gone
> Appeared so beautiful, I ventured on;
> And when I gained the road where all are free
> I fancied every stranger frowned at me,
> And every kinder look appeared to say,
> 'You've been on trespass in your walk to-day.'
> I've often thought, the day appeared so fine,
> How beautiful if such a place were mine;
> But having naught I never feel alone
> And cannot use another's as my own.   (*II*, 373)

There is no shock of recognition in this poem, and the absence of
anger is disturbing. But "Trespass" is not about a new wound, but
an old one whose history is implied in the general and inclusive language of a man who distrusted "every look" and "every stranger,"
"always looked" and "always feared," and recognized (though had
not grown inured to the fact) that his deepest longings and most
innocent experiences would be met by the "no," "naught," "never"
of the master class.

It is ironic that Clare, who was born and bred in the country,
should write poems in which he cast himself in the role of an
intruder. (The irony deepens when one thinks of a poet like Cowper – educated at Westminster, called to the Bar, tested in the
examination halls of London – walking through the countryside
and writing about it as though it belonged to him.) Clare's awareness that because of the rights and values of a few members of rural
society much of the countryside was closed off to the majority of
countrymen made it difficult for him to posit the conventional
antithesis of rural retreat vs. life in society. He could – indeed, he
did – posit the antithesis, but never with the innocent confidence of
one who believed that the boundaries between nature and society,
retirement and engagement, could be easily defined or crossed. In

this respect he differs significantly from Cowper. Cowper took for granted the hierarchy of privilege upon which the gentleman's option of retirement was based, but he was by no means indifferent to the historical and social character of the countryside. When he looked out through "the loopholes of retreat" he saw that violence and suffering, corruption and greed, were as powerfully entrenched there as in the "proud and gay and gain-devoted cities" from which he had fled.[9] However, unlike Clare, who was reminded daily of the way "gain-devoted people" affected his life, Cowper did not feel personally involved (through complicity or victimization) in rural polity. Social injustice in the countryside was a literary topic not a personal experience, and so the act of bearing witness to injustice did not stop him from feeling that his rural home was a place of "blessed seclusion from a jarring world" where "rumour of oppression and deceit, / ... Might never reach me more."[10] At Olney he was able

> to see the stir
> Of the great Babel, and not feel the crowd;
> To hear the roar she sends through all her gates
> At a safe distance, where the dying sound
> Falls a soft murmur on th'uninjured ear.
> Thus sitting, and surveying thus at ease
> The globe and its concerns, I seem advanc'd
> To some secure and more than mortal height,
> That lib'rates and exempts me from them all.[11]

For Cowper, the country was the place to go to get away from the world. For Clare, it *was* the world and he could escape its deceits and oppressions only by willing himself into a state of partial amnesia. Only by forsaking all knowledge of and connection to the social character of the countryside and losing himself in the rapt contemplation of its natural character was he able to find the liberty and peace of mind Cowper had found at Olney.

If Clare was to retreat from the social world into the natural world, it was necessary to search for a topography that was empty not only of the totemic emblems of ownership - the great houses and noble gates, the property signs and farmer's fences - but of any object or activity that connected the countryside to the economic life of the nation and, beyond that, to the cruel and inequitable organization of its production and distribution. The very sight of a fence would evoke the traumatic reaction recorded in "Trespass," and so Clare sought the hidden corners of his local landscape, the small enclaves "for secresy and shelter rightly made" (*JCOA*, 208),

Where nature her own feelings to effect
Is left at her own silent work for years.   (*II*, 326)

The grazing meadows could remind him that enclosure had taken away the labourer's cottage and cow, and so he preferred to wander the wild,

unsocial heath,
That gives man no inviting hopes to come
To fix his dwelling and disturb the scene.   (*II*, 305)

A working landscape could remind him that the labour of "the thousands" supported the privileges of "the few" and so Clare preferred the fallow fields to the planted ones:

the fallow fields appear so fair
The very weeds make sweetest gardens there
And summer there puts garments on so gay
I hate the plough that comes to disarray
Her holiday delights – and labours toil
Seems vulgar curses on the sunny soil
And man the only object that distrains
Earths garden into deserts for his gains
Leave him his schemes of gain – tis wealth to me
Wild heaths to trace ...   (*JCOA*, 220)

Perhaps part of the pleasure one takes from the bird poems derives from the feeling that Clare had found his "wealth," had escaped a "world where pride and folly taunts" and reached a "still and quiet home" where "security pervades." The motives and motifs of retreat are caught vividly in the poem from which these phrases are taken, "To the Snipe":

The trembling grass
Quakes from the human foot
Nor bears the weight of man to let him pass
Where he alone and mute

Sitteth at rest
In safety neath the clump
Of hugh flag-forrest that thy haunts invest
Or some old sallow stump
...

And here may hap
When summer suns hath drest
The moors rude desolate and spungy lap
May hide thy mystic nest

Mystic indeed
For isles that ocean make
Are scarcely more secure for birds to build
Then this flag-hidden lake

Boys thread the woods
To their remotest shades
But in these marshy flats these stagnant floods
Security pervades

From year to year
Places untrodden lye
Where man nor boy nor stock hath ventured near
– Nought gazed on but the sky
...
From dangers reach
Here thou art safe to roam
Far as these washy flag-word marshes stretch
A still and quiet home

In these thy haunts
Ive gleaned habitual love
From the vague world where pride and folly taunts
I muse and look above

Thy solitudes
The unbounded heaven esteems
And here my heart warms into higher moods
And dignifying dreams

I see the sky
Smile on the meanest spot
Giving to all that creep or walk or flye
A calm and cordial lot   (*JCOA*, 205–7)

These carefully alliterated stanzas capture the moment when the
retreat from "there" to the "here" of "this flag-hidden lake" has
already been achieved. (The preponderance of "s" and "sh" sounds

could be interpreted as an imperative to respect the secrecy and silence Clare has penetrated.) Here in the "remotest shades" of nature, he has found a place impregnable – by virtue of its very uselessness – to the "vile invasions" of greed. A wasteland of "mud and rancid streams" to the profiteer, to the poet it is a small Eden where enclosure had not come, prejudice cannot touch him, and the responsibilities of social protest can be set aside for the private pieties of "a calm and cordial lot."

The bird poems have various settings, but almost invariably they are places (like the snipe's quagmire home) where other men do not choose to go. "I feel myself a monarch here," Clare wrote in "Lone Happiness," and "here" was reached by going past the "fence of ownership" down a path "not wide enough for two to pass" that brought him into the presence of "hermit living things" (*II*, 238). Like the places he discovers, the birds he describes are usually solitary. Among others, one notes the "oddling crow," " the old Heron from the lonely lake," the "lone occupiers of a naked sky," the sedge-bird whose ways are "as secret as a crickets song," the mavis who "sang and felt himself alone," the robin who lives in a "quiet glen / Hidden from fame and all the strife of men," and the nightingale whose nest is like a "hermits mossy cell" found in "pathless solitudes."[12] The sense of mutuality felt between poet and solitary bird is probably the most important element in the bird poems, but I would stop short of saying that Clare's birds function merely as objective correlatives of his solitude. In "Sand Martin," for example, the characteristics of the bird – its delitescence, its fear of men, its preference for remote and secret places – mirror the character of the poet. But though his state of mind and the situation of the sand martin are connected and coterminous, they are not fused in the compact of metaphor. The structure of address (and Clare's refusal to sentimentalize) ensures the discrete integrity of both species seen, the perceiver and the object of his perception:

Thou hermit haunter of the lonely glen
And common wild and heath – the desolate face
Of rude waste landscapes far away from men
Where frequent quarrys give thee dwelling place
With strangest taste and labour undeterred
Drilling small holes along the quarrys side
More like the haunts of vermin than a bird
And seldom by the nesting boy descried
Ive seen thee far away from all thy tribe
Flirting about the unfrequented sky

And felt a feeling that I cant describe
Of lone seclusion and a hermit joy
To see thee circle round nor go beyond
That lone heath and its melancholly pond   (*JCOA*, 208)

To say that the birds in Clare's poem are Selbornian objects of perception rather than Keatsian symbols of imaginative transcendance is not to imply that there was anything coldly rational about Clare's response to them, nor that he failed to exploit their natural symbolism. But he usually resisted the urge to humanize them, and their symbolic function within his poems has much less to do with the attributes he lent to them than those he borrowed from them. The reason he was so fascinated by birds (in life and as a literary subject) is that they were so strangely, emphatically, unhumanly themselves. Unlike him they were free and unburdened by complexity; to watch them was to forget that he was a creature of society and imagine himself a creature of the sky able to "sail about the world,"

And build on nothing but a passing cloud
As free from danger as the heavens are free
From pain and toil   (*JCOA*, 216)

They were endowed with the cunning to flourish in their environment but, unlike the men he most despised, their needs were simple and unchanging, and their territorial concerns normally did not cause the dispossession of other living things. Moreover, birds were democratic creatures: they did not distinguish between aristocrats, farmers, or ploughmen but feared alike all types of humanity. In writing about them Clare could momentarily forget about the "wider space / Between the genteel and the vulgar race" precisely because he was so consumed by his interest in the still wider space that separated humanity and nature.

The only poems in which Clare quite clearly did humanize the object of his perception are those about singing birds. Understandably he could not resist the urge to find in the thrush's "hymns to sunrise" (*JCOA*, 210) or the hedge sparrow's "inward stir of shadowed melody" (*JCOA*, 212) the inspiration for and reassuring echo of his own songs, and though he was as fascinated by silent birds as by singing ones, the resemblance between the song of a bird and the work of the poet provided the basis for a special lyricism. In some poems, the likeness was offered in the explicit terms of simile. Thus, of the yellow hammer we learn that

she dwells
A poet-like – where brooks and flowery weeds
As sweet as Castaly to fancy deems
And that old molehill like as parnass hill
On which her partner haply sits and dreams
Oer all his joy of song   (*JCOA*, 230)

In other poems, an identification was achieved through the richer terms of metaphor and allusion. Thus in "The Autumn Robin" Clare paid tribute to the robin's song in language reminiscent of the tribute paid to his brother bard in "To the Memory of Robert Bloomfield":

Sweet favoured bird! thy under-notes
In summer's music grow unknown,
The concert from a thousand throats
Leaves thee as if to pipe alone;
No listening ear the shepherd lends,
The simple ploughman marks thee not,
And then by all thy autumn friends
Thou'rt missing and forgot.

The far-famed nightingale, that shares
Cold public praise from every tongue,
The popular voice of music heirs,
And injures much thy under-song:
Yet then my walks thy theme salutes;
I find thee autumn's favoured guest,
Gay piping on the hazel-roots
Above thy mossy nest.

'Tis wrong that thou should'st be despised,
When these gay fickle birds appear;
They sing when summer flowers are prized –
Thou at the dull and dying year.
Well! let the heedless and the gay
Bepraise the voice of louder lays,
The joy thou steal'st from sorrow's day
Is more to thee than praise.   (*II*, 218)

And just as in the sonnet to Bloomfield Clare preferred the "green memorials" of the "humblest bard" to "the dazzling fashions of the day" (*I*, 527), so in his sonnet to the wren, he promoted the bell-

like song of the plainest wren or robin over the gaudy songs of more
famous birds:

> Why is the cuckoos melody preferred
> And nightingales rich song so fondly praised
> In poets ryhmes   Is there no other bird
> Of natures minstrelsy that oft hath raised
> Ones heart to extacy and mirth as well
> I judge not how anothers taste is caught
> With mine theres other birds that bear the bell
> Whose song hath crowds of happy memories brought
> Such the wood Robin singing in the dell
> And little Wren that many a time hath sought
> Shelter from showers in huts where I did dwell
> In early spring the tennant of the plain
> Tenting my sheep and still they come to tell
> The happy stories of the past again   (*JCOA*, 211)

But Clare must have been thinking of his own situation as much
as of Bloomfield's when he raised this question of the relationship
between the worth of a song and the value of public acclaim. His
own sense of being forsaken by his audience and his friends ("the
thresher in the onset & neglected ryhmer in the end," *Letters*, 126)
may have prompted him to remind the robin that "by all thy
autumn friends / Thou'rt missing and forgot." His desperate need
to believe, though his own poems could find few contemporary lis-
teners, that they would yet "surpass / The cobweb praise of
fashion" may have led him to commend the wren and the robin,
whose songs are vindicated by nature's favour, and to scorn the
"popular voice" of the "far-famed nightingale," whose songs are
vindicated only by "cold public praise." If no comfort from men,
then comfort from the birds and from one's own integrity. And
integrity tends to wear a humble dress in these poems. The birds
with whom Clare identifies are usually the most common, the least
colourful and least praised of the species, for these are the ones
that invite him

> To think that I in humble dress
> Might have a right to happiness
> And sing as well as greater men   (*JCOA*, 155)

Thus, in "The Nightingales Nest," he finds comfort in the observation that the nightingale, whose fame normally precludes any act of identification, is the plainest of birds:

> Ive nestled down
> And watched her while she sung – and her renown
> Hath made me marvel that so famed a bird
> Should have no better dress than russet brown
> Her wings would tremble in her extacy
> And feathers stand on end as twere with joy
> And mouth wide open to release her heart
> Of its out sobbing songs   (*JCOA*, 213–4)

But Clare's pleasure did not blind him to the darker side of the identification. Though the nightingale singing in solitude may have been a natural symbol of the poet's solitary work and of his commitment to his own creative capacity, it was also a reminder of the prejudice and indifference with which his commitment had been met: his birds always sang to an audience of one.

That Clare could be reminded by the song of a solitary bird of his own difficulties within the literary market-place suggests just how incapable an escape-artist he was. He could eschew the company of men for the company of birds, and go past the fences and worked fields into "the deliciousness of solitude" where

> The air we breathe seems void of every trace
> Of earth and all its trouble, and the mind
> Yearns for a dwelling in so sweet a place,
> From trouble's noise, such stillness seemeth by.   (*II*, 324)

But the stillness of such places and the psychic withdrawal they represented were often unsettled by his memory of the noisome realities he tried to leave behind. In a sense, his inability to forget why he so ardently longed for the "social loneliness" of retreat subverted his retreat, not by denying him the peace of mind he truly found within nature, but by reminding him of how precarious and temporary it was. Hiding in the place where the moorhen made its nest allowed for the aesthetic appreciation of an experience in which no sensation was too fleeting to be felt, no perception too small to be recorded:

> I walk and swing my stick for joy
> And catch at little pictures passing bye
> A gate whose posts are two old dotterel trees
> A close with molehills sprinkled oer its leas
> A little footbrig with its crossing rail
> A wood gap stopt with ivy wreathing pale
> A crooked stile each path crossed spinney owns
> A brooklet forded by its stepping stones
> A wood bank mined with rabbit holes – and then
> An old oak leaning oer a badgers den   (*JCOA*, 220-1)

A catalogue of most simple pleasures – but "tis wealth to me," Clare wrote, and one feels almost mean-spirited in suggesting that this was the only wealth a man in his circumstances was ever likely to possess. But one cannot dismiss the feeling that the pleasures, deep or spontaneous, which Clare found in the society of nature were not sufficient recompense for the nature of the social experience from which he had fled and to which, inevitably, he had to return. "Pain shadows on," he wrote in "The Moorehens Nest," and all such pleasures leave me is their praise" (*JCOA*, 219). In the apostrophe to poetry with which this poem begins, he describes himself as a man seeking sanctuary in the real world of nature and in the "fairy visions" of the mind. But the refuge proves too frail, and his heart

> warms and chills and burns and bursts at last
> Oer broken hopes and troubles never past
> I pay thee worship at a rustic shrine
> And dream oer joys I still imagine mine
> I pick up flowers and pebbles and by thee
> As gems and jewels they appear to me
> I pick out pictures round the fields that lie
> In my minds heart like things that cannot die
> Like picking hopes and making friends with all
> Yet glass will often bear a harder fall
> As bursting bottles loose the precious wine
> Hopes casket breaks and I the gems resign ...
> And thus each fairy vision melts away
> Like evening landscapes from the face of day   (*JCOA*, 219)

The creative spontaneities of the present were not all that broke like glass against the never-entirely-evaded memories of the past. To some extent the very landscapes in which Clare sought refuge became tainted by his inability to forget his knowledge of society. He always emphasized the remoteness and inaccessibility of the bird-world he had penetrated. The snipe builds its nest where "security pervades" (*JCOA*, 216). The moorhens lay "in safetys mood" –

> though danger comes
> It dares and tries and cannot reach their homes
> And so they hatch their eggs and sweetly dream
> On their shelfed nests   (*JCOA*, 221)

The robins live in a "woodland privacy":

> Where old neglect lives patron and befriends
> Their homes with safetys wildness – where nought lends
> A hand to injure – root up or disturb
> The things of this old place – there is no curb
> Of interest industry or slavish gain
> To war with nature so the weeds remain
> And wear an ancient passion that arrays
> Ones feelings with the shadows of old days
> The rest of peace the sacredness of mind
> In such deep solitudes we seek and find
> Where moss grows old and keeps an evergreen
> And footmarks seem like miracles when seen
> So little meddling toil doth trouble here
> The very weeds as patriarchs appear
> And if a plant ones curious eyes delight
> In this old ancient solitude we might
> Come ten years hence of trouble dreaming ill
> And find them like old tennants peaceful still   (*JCOA*, 224)

Yet the celebration of safety is expressed so constantly and, as it were, defensively, that the mind inevitably raises the spectre of its opposite – the danger that these "ancient solitudes" will be invaded and destroyed by society's "interest industry or slavish gain." The "age sublime" of Clare's "music making Elm" (*JCOA*, 98) could not save it from the depredations of improvement, and so, why should the ancientness of these solitudes save them? It may be argued that this idea can only be teased out of the bird poems by distorting what Clare insisted upon: that he had finally found places which would not be lost to him as Round-Oak Waters and Swordy Well had been. But there is an epitaphic cast to the tone and language of these poems which conveys the impression that Clare was celebrating not the secured permanence of the enclaves he discovered but their mode of surviving, year by year, against a threatening, imminent end. The birds are safe for now, one feels, but, as Clare said about the snipe, "dangers reach" is "scarcely one stride" away:

> Free booters there
> Intent to kill and slay
> Startle with cracking guns the trepid air
> And dogs thy haunts betray   (*JCOA*, 207)

Clearly, he was troubled by society's capacity to "meddle," "curb," "injure," "harm," and "war with nature," and (despite his protestations to the contrary) by the possibility that "come ten years hence of trouble dreaming ill" his sanctuary would be changed and fenced against him. He expressed (perhaps inadvertently) his consciousness of that possibility by claiming that the moorhen lived in a place that "nature *tries* / To keep alive for poesy to prize" (*JCOA*, 220, my emphasis).

It is the poet's inability to escape his knowledge of society that makes the bird poems – if only by default – socially engaged. This is not to say that society and its vices figure largely in these poems. To read them after one has read the poverty poems, enclosure elegies, and vocational works is to feel that social protest, anger, and outrage are conspicuous by their absence. But the social experience which informed those other works also haunts the bird poems. Their small but sharply felt intimations of disruption and loss recall the enclosure elegies, and though they do not specifically refer to enclosure or oppressive landlords, poverty or prejudice, they challenge (sometimes directly, more often indirectly) the specific values which gave sanction to those pernicious realities.

It is no accident that "The Robins Nest" is set, like the most famous pilgrimage in literary history, in the renewing springtime, for the journey of retreat this poem records is an act of spiritual devotion. Indeed, although there are important variations within the sequence, each bird poem records a separate episode which may be placed within the continuum of Clare's lifelong pilgrimage to nature's "rustic shrine." His journey to the places where birds made their nests was at once a flight away from the prevailing values of the age and a quest for the simpler yet nobler values by which he wanted to live. In "The Moorehens Nest" he seeks the "angel answers" of nature to escape the "vulgar curses" of a society obsessed by "schemes of gain" (*JCOA*, 220). In "The Robins Nest" he flees "far from the ruder world's inglorious din" and from a social dispensation which

> sees no glory but in sordid pelf
> And nought of greatness but its little self
> Scorning the splendid gift that nature gives
> Where natures glory ever breathes and lives

And what he finds in the tutelary presence of nature are lessons in humanity. "Each ancient tree" he sees

> Becomes a monitor to teach and bless
> And rid me of the evils cares possess
> And bid me look above the trivial things
> To which prides mercenary spirit clings
> The pomps the wealth and artificial toys
> That men call wealth beleagued with strife and noise
> To seek the silence of their ancient reign
> And be my self in memory once again   (*JCOA*, 223-4)

The self he longs to find in memory may be that of his own childhood. But I think more is implied, that the memory he wants to explore belongs not to himself alone but to the history of the race. Though the idea of childhood is consonant with the imagery of birth and renewal (nests, eggs, fledglings, young grass, tender shoots, opening flowers) with which the poem begins and ends, the emphasis falls upon the great and enduring age of the self-renewing world and upon the way it evokes "an ancient passion that arrays / Ones feelings with the shadows of old days." The poem admonishes us to recover that ancient passion, to see with Adam's grateful, wondering eyes, and to live at one and not at war with nature. The admonition belongs to conventional pastoral, but it is quickened by Clare's historically specific disaffection for the selfish, reductive economism of his age. Its conventionality did not blind him to its radically transforming power.

In the idea of Clare's lifelong pilgrimage to nature's "rustic shrine" we possess the principle which unites and organizes the bird poems. But a question arises: is it always possible to define this pilgrimage as a quest for the best self, the humanity, the range of feeling, which the poet fears will be lost or destroyed if he remains in society as he knows it? Not all of the bird poems have the symbolic resonance of "The Robins Nest" or "The Moorehens Nest," in which the character of the poet is lit with interiority and the liberating society of nature is so sharply contrasted to the oppressive nature of society. Indeed, even in those poems which do invite symbolic interpretation, in "The Nightingales Nest," for example, where the nightingale represents a quality and range of experience which the poet cannot find within society ("Her joys are evergreen her world is wide"), the bird always retains its objective identity. The nightingale exists as a natural fact, as an object of the poet's perception, but also as the agent of its own capacity to perceive, as an image that does not entirely give itself up to its signifying functions in the poem. In the central passage of the poem, the bird as observed object is almost lost in the sweep of the poet's subjective response:

> See there shes sitting on the old oak bough
> Mute in her fears our presence doth retard
> Her joys and doubt turns all her rapture chill
>   Sing on sweet bird may no worse hap befall
> Thy visions than the fear that now decieves
> We will not plunder music of its dower
> Nor turn this spot of happiness to thrall
> For melody seems hid in every flower
> That blossoms near thy home   (*JCOA*, 215)

But in the lines which follow, as though he fears that the object of his perception will be subsumed by the record of his reactions to it, Clare falls back from insight to sight, from signification to notation:

> How curious is the nest no other bird
> Uses such loose materials or weaves
> Its dwelling in such spots - dead oaken leaves
> Are placed without and velvet moss within
> And little scraps of grass - and scant and spare
> Of what seems scarce materials down and hair.   (*JCOA*, 215)

The image of the nightingale, which had begun to seem translucent, has now become opaque, inpenetrable to every mode of apprehension save that of the physical eye. And this movement, this stepping away from symbol and evocation, and then the falling back to the sturdy and reassuring object-world of leaves and grass, is not at all uncommon in the bird poems.

In some instances the object-world is apparently all that we are offered. About these poems, to those of us who are not Selbornians, there seems at first little to say except perhaps, borrowing from Wordsworth, that we "will look around for poetry, and will be induced to enquire by what species of courtesy these attempts can be permitted to assume that title."[13] From the time Clare first began to publish, this kind of question has been raised frequently by critics who have complained that much of his work belongs, not in a volume of poetry, but in the notebook of a naturalist, and, at least at first glance, a few of the bird poems almost seem to justify the complaint. "The Missel-Thrush's Nest" is an example:

> In early March, before the lark
> Dare start, beside the huge oak tree,
> Close fixed agen the powdered bark,
> The mavis' nest I often see;
> And mark, as wont, the bits of wool
> Hang round about its early bed;
> She lays six eggs in colours dull,
> Blotched thick with spots of burning red.　(*II*, 226)

But to the question – is this a poem? – the only answer is: it is indeed a poem, though not one that belongs in the Romantic period. Perhaps the best way to approach this work would be to read it by the light of the twentieth-century imagist aesthetic, to compare Clare and his missel-thrush to Marianne Moore with her skunks and wood-weasels, or William Carlos Williams with his woodthrush and red lily. One thinks especially of Williams for whom there were "no ideas but in things."[14] "It all depends," he observed, "on what you call profound," and for him, so much depended

> upon

> a red wheel
> barrow[15]

seen in a particular way in a particular context. For Clare, it all depended upon "six eggs in colours dull / Blotched thick with spots of burning red" seen in a particular light, in a particular time and place. Certainly in its economy of detail, the direct treatment of its subject, its surface fact – described without any reaching after deeper truth – his poem anticipates the imagist creed. But even if we agree that "The Missel-Thrush's Nest" is a poem (even an interesting one which bears some affinity to the works of a sophisticated poet in a later age), in what sense can we say that it records an episode in Clare's quest for the liberty, or peace of mind, or noble values he cannot find in his society? No questing motives are inscribed in its form. It offers no access to the character of the perceiver, evokes no mood, carries no symbolic freight, only a heavy cargo of natural observation. If read in isolation from the rest of Clare's nature poetry, it appears to celebrate no quest for an alternative system of values. Indeed it presents no values at all unless it is read as one poem within the sum of poems which make up the bird poem collection.

But if we place it within the context of the collection as a whole it suddenly seems to be about something after all. It presents the kind of concrete and particular act of mental experience from which all the imagery, the symbol, the evocation, and the meaning of the bird poems arise. It records a beginning, the point of perception from which Clare works outwards in other poems, such as, to take but one example, his lyric sonnet to "Pastoral Liberty":

> O for the unshackled mood as free as air
> & pleasure wild as birds upon the wing
> The unwronged impulse won from seasons fair
> Like birds perrenial travels with the spring
> Come peace & joy the unworn path to trace
> Crossing ling-heaths & hazel crowded glen
> Where health salutes me with its ruddy face
> & joy breaths freely from the strife of men
> O lead me any where but in the crowd
> On some lone island rather would I be
> Than in the world worn knowledge noising loud
> Wealth gathering up & loosing – leave with me
> Calm joy & humble hope for quiet won
> To live in peace unhurt & hurting none   (*MC*, 455)

Nothing is directly seen in these lines, not even the "ling-heaths and hazel-crowded glen," which are only invoked. It is the poet's mood or state of mind which shapes this poem, not his natural observation, and the mood alone prevails until it gives way to the articulation of specific values. And the values expressed in this sonnet should be familiar to us by now. Here, as in so many of the enclosure elegies, the poet can best state his ideas about human need and desire by rejecting the morality of a society where wealth is always being gathered up by some men and lost by others, where common knowledge is clamorous but not to be trusted, where men cannot live without either victimizing or becoming the victims of other men. The pastoral of solitude, liberty, and joy which is presented in this poem is wrestled from Clare's ironic vision of his society. If we turn from "Pastoral Liberty," so resonant with values and ironies, back to "The Missel-Thrush's Nest," we hear more clearly the thematic silences of the earlier poem. But there is a sense in which we are also now in a position to fill those silences, since the sonnet offers the subjective mediations which have been withdrawn in "The Missel-Thrush's Nest," leaving us in the austere object-world of "six eggs," "powdered bark," and "bits of wool."

If Clare's lyrics deepen our appreciation and understanding of his purely descriptive poems, the reverse is also true: the complement, one could say, is mutual. "The Missel-Thrush's Nest" complements "Pastoral Liberty" by offering what is missing from that thematically richer poem – perceptual immediacy. The sparse and tough "Missel-Thrush's Nest" can be read as a record of the radical encounter between human eye and natural object from which arises the "ancient passion" to live at one with nature, and the act of unmediated perception it records may be understood as the beginning of an arduous quest for better values. But it may also be read as the end of the quest, the point reached when the poet has already achieved the "unwronged impulse" of his pastoral liberty, has already found the real place or the place in the mind where he can live and sing "unhurt and hurting none," and can feel that he is a happy man in a generous world. I appear to be claiming that "The Missel-Thrush's Nest" and "Pastoral Liberty" cannot stand alone as discreet poems, but this is not quite what I intend. "Pastoral Liberty" is a well-structured sonnet built upon the convention of pastoral retreat, though the convention is recast in Clare's idiomatic terms. And "The Missel-Thrush's Nest" can stand alone as a testament to the uniqueness of every act of vision, as an image of the mind arrested by a natural image upon which "so much depends." Nevertheless, we are richer, the poems are richer, if we read them together, as products of the same impulse developed in one poem as a structure of feeling, in the other as a structure of perception, and in the best of the bird poems, in "The Robins Nest," "The Nightingales Nest," and "The Moorehens Nest," as developments within both structures.

More than any other grouping within Clare's canon, more than the enclosure elegies or the vocational poems, the bird poems have to be read and understood as a unified set of variations upon a theme: first, because they were all written from the same complex of motives; secondly, because only by reading them as we find them – grouped together in the manuscripts but also in the collections edited by the Tibbles and by Robinson and Summerfield – can we catch the nature and the value of the experiences they convey. If we are to appreciate how absorbing and how valuable these experiences were for Clare, we almost have to relive them as Clare lived them, to read the separate poems as he composed them, poem after poem, written "to the moment" of encounter after encounter between the poet and one bird after another. These manifold encounters are always the same yet always different; the same poet is invariably coming across a bird, but the bird is always changing – now it is a robin, now a landrail, now a snipe – and the poet's modes of apprehension are numerous and varied. The remarkable variety of ways in which Clare sees and describes the birds he meets with in the landscape should command the respect of a generation of readers who have fed upon the poetry of William Carlos Williams and Wallace Stevens and have washed it down with liberal quantities of perception-theory. We discover in these poems of Clare's, not "Thirteen Ways of Looking at a Blackbird," but dozens of ways of looking at dozens of different kinds of birds. And the sheer quantity of these poems, I want to suggest, may be almost as important as the quality of individual pieces within the group. Like the quantity of good things to which Adam points in *Paradise Lost*, the number of birds described by Clare conveys a complex image of nature's abundance and its teeming profusion of kinds. The large quantity also serves as testimony to what was for Clare one of our most important and inexhaustible human resources, our capacity to see. "We always suppose that we see what we only know," wrote Ruskin.[16] But for the author of the bird poems, the work of seeing took precedence over his considerable knowledge of his subject-matter, and the reflexes of his familiarity with the habits of the nightingale or robin were always checked by his tactful curiosity and willingness to be surprised.

In some of the bird poems, as we have seen, the act of recording the physical aspects of perception also took precedence over the act of self-disclosure. "I hear," I see," "I look," "I love to hear," and "I love to see" are characteristic phrases in these poems, and the fact that he loves to see whatever he happens to see is sometimes all one explicitly learns about this particular "I." It could be argued that through careful reading we learn much more, that in a poem like "Emmonsails Heath in Winter," for example (which begins with a characteristically stark predicate phrase), we are given access to the wintry thoughts and melancholy feelings of the poet through the pattern and selection of the images:

I love to see the old heaths withered brake
Mingle its crimpled leaves with furze and ling
While the old heron from the lonely lake
Starts slow and flaps his melancholy wing
And oddling crow in idle motions swing
On the half rotten ash trees topmost twig
Beside whose trunk the gipsy makes his bed
Up flies the bounding woodcock from the brig
Where a black quagmire quakes beneath the tread
The fieldfares chatter in the whistling thorn
And for the haw round fields and closen rove
And coy bumbarrels twenty in a drove
Flit down the hedgerows in the frozen plain
And hang on little twigs and start again   (*JCOA*, 212)

But it is, after all, not the poet but the crow that is "oddling," the plain that is "frozen," the lake that is "lonely," and the heron's wing that is "melancholy." The contrast between the slow flight and idle motion of the heron and crow and the nervous, vigorous action of the woodcock and "coy bumbarrells" may tell us something about the pattern of the poet's mind, may suggest the contrarieties of reflection and creative release. The simultaneity of action, the incessant chatter and circular flight, may be a symbol of nature's unity and of its comic capacity to wither, freeze, rot, and yet endure. The poem is intriguing and comes to us begging for ingenious explanation. But, in the end, its formal and thematic significance depends upon our ability to take it for what it is: simply a record of what Clare saw on Emmonsail's Heath in winter, a record which eschews pathetic fallacy and symbolism, does not turn natural objects into objective correlatives of human feeling, and is indifferent to the very idea of ideas. It belongs to what Geoffrey Hartman has described as the "kind of poetry [that] does not wish to become thought or afterthought" but is "happy to be 'the cry of its occasion', something heard, or at best something that cleanses the doors of the senses."[17]

Yet we should be wary of ascribing to Clare a more single-minded concern with the cold, clear data of physical sensation than he in fact possessed. One agrees entirely with Barrell when he sharply challenges the very stale critical assumption "that for a descriptive poem to have content, it must pass beyond itself into meditation or whatever."[18] But acknowledging that a poem need be nothing more than the description of a single sensation or natural object should not hinder us from recognizing that human values may be attendant upon and expressed through the simplest act of perception, and that natural description is always in some sense prescriptive, offers a way of seeing and a set of convictions, based upon the way of seeing, about the proper relationship between man and nature. By abstaining from symbolic practice in describing the missel-thrush, the sand martin, and the birds on Emmonsails Heath, by stressing the opacity of these birds, their otherness, their remoteness from the compulsions of ordinary human life, and by allowing their solid features to take their position in his poems without any lateral sliding into the complex corners of memory or association, Clare gave formal expression to his belief that we must see nature "as she is," and come to her without prejudice and without the desire to remake her in our image. No less than Clare's most impassioned enclosure elegies, his most starkly descriptive bird poems must be related to his lifelong defence of nature, and beyond that to the particular historical circumstances and social commitments which made this defence so difficult and necessary.

Conclusion

Edmund Blunden understood the intimate connection between Clare's social experience and imagination, though I have some reservations about the way he expressed this understanding when he said that Clare's writings "are nothing else but the record of a strife with circumstance for the privilege of the child's clarity through years that obscure it."[1] "Child's clarity" may be a felicitous pun, but "nothing else but the record" is much too severe, and I am troubled by the suggestion (and all it implies of emotional regression and intellectual immaturity) that Clare's great goal was to see life on the child's level. The vision of the child was indeed important to him, but the point of his nostalgic recreations of childhood was precisely that the fall from the spontaneous pleasures of early sensuous experience into the conscious life was inevitable and irreversible:

> Summer pleasures they are gone like to visions every one
> And the cloudy days of autumn and of winter cometh on
> I tried to call them back but unbidden they are gone
> Far away from heart and eye and for ever far away   (*JCOA*, 258)

With increasing force in the asylum years he expressed a longing to

> sleep as I in childhood, sweetly slept,
> Untroubling, and untroubled where I lie,
> The grass below - above the vaulted sky.   (*JCOA*, 361)

By then he had become "the self-consumer of my woes," a man living "like vapours tost

Into the nothingness of scorn and noise, –
    Into the living sea of waking dreams,
Where there is neither sense of life or joys,
    But the vast shipwreck of my lifes esteems.   (*JCOA* , 361)

From the prospect of that shipwreck, childhood was remembered as an island of blessed safety and joy. But the quality of the memory was hardly new. From his earliest days, in his very first poems, childhood was a symbol for Clare of the secure and easy life he never had.

There is nothing childish about the desire to recover the joy and spontaneity of the child, and it goes without saying – one would have thought – that Clare's longing to escape the winter fields of experience for the "summer pleasures" of innocence is proof that he was acutely, painfully conscious of the burdens of mature consciousness. Yet among the critics (Blunden included) who rediscovered Clare in the 1920s, one finds a marked tendency to characterize Clare as not merely childlike, but childish, unconscious, "strangely simple," untouched by ideas of any kind. The fact that the characterization was often offered in the spirit of kindness and compliment should not blind us to its condescension or inaccuracy. J. Middleton Murry, for example, argued that for this "child-man," the sort of aesthetic problems which interested Keats would have seemed "like a problem of metaphysics to a ploughboy." And in discussing the natural objects in Clare's poetry, he wrote: "he seems ... to have lived on the same level of existence as they ... We feel that it is only by an effort that he manages to make himself conscious of his emotion towards them or of his own motive in singing of it."[2] Thus Murry moves us from Clare as ploughboy to Clare as plant. His comments were made in 1921, but for all that they differ from what was said by Clare's most condescending contemporaries, they belong to 1821. What Murry said sixty years ago would not especially concern me were it not that the legacy of his idea of Clare is still very much with us. The terms have changed, the interests have varied, but one continues to find evidence of an imperious refusal to credit Clare with the most basic intellectual skills. For all the sophistication and sympathy of his insight into Clare's sense of place, Barrell recalls Murry when he suggests that the "knowledge" conveyed in the poetry of 1822 to 1832 is so purely and entirely local that no larger, more abstract ideas (about man or nature or society or the relations between them) can be deduced from it. More troubling still is the recent claim of J.R. de J. Jackson that "Clare's weakness, at least in the poetry he published before

1836 ... is that he has so little to say, he is so ineffectively reflective."[3]

In part it was to counter the impression of Clare as an unthinking and unreflective man, unconscious of what he wrote about, or why, or where it belonged in literary tradition, or how it challenged the values of the genteel class, that I have drawn attention to the evolution of his literary principles and to his self-consciousness about his role as poet. I do not mean to claim Clare as a literary theorist, and it's quite possible that he would have been delighted by those who have characterized him as a purely instinctive, spontaneous, natural poet, another version of fancy's child warbling his native wood-notes wild. But it is surely a measure of the condescension which has characterized Clare studies in the past that one has to insist that he *knew* what he was talking about, that he *thought* about what it meant to be a "natural" poet, that he worked his way through to *ideas* which could validate the poetry he wrote and compel popular acceptance of it. Though he seems at times to back into ideas and then back out again, and though, one need hardly say, he did not bring to the task the philosophical brilliance and profundity of a Keats or a Wordsworth, he was, in his own way and with his own terms, no less interested in defining the quality and meaning of his work, and no less vehement in telling us what a poet ought and ought not to be doing.

Clare's capacity for critical reflection is equally apparent in his writings upon the market-place, property, poverty, education, electoral reform. In this study, reasons of space have precluded a full exploration of his social criticism, but one hopes future studies will continue to bring to light his ideas on political orthodoxy and dissent, rampant commercialism and old corruption, the relations between the disenfranchised and the elite, and the role of rustic culture within the culture of the nation as a whole. There is a great deal of exposed ideological bone in the flesh of Clare's poetry, and historians seeking to understand how, for example, the arguments of reform were received in the small country villages, or how the rural workingman responded to his hard and necessary labour, would do well to turn to *The Parish* and *The Shepherd's Calendar*. We have often been warned that to search for social reference or scrutinize a poem for the access it affords into the consciousness of a nation or a class or a generation is to reduce it to the status of an historical document. One understands the motive from which such warnings flow: the need to recognize, in Lukács' phrase, "the peculiarity of the aesthetic."[4] But I fail to see how one can under-

mine or obscure the aesthetic merits of Clare's poetry by acknowledging that he is a figure of epitomizing significance to other forms
of discourse and enquiry than those which properly belong to
literary criticism.

The need to explore Clare's rhetorical strategies and clarify his
meanings in context seems all the more pressing because in writing
of his own social experience he was also writing of the experience of
a people who left few records of their struggles with circumstance.
This is not to say that he was, any more than Shelley or Byron, the
passive bearer of the habits and views of the class into which he was
born. We should approach with extreme scepticism those who
would argue, as W.K. Richmond has done, that Clare was primarily a folk-poet, and, as such, "constitutionally unfitted" for individualism and idealism, that he could express himself fully only
"through contacts with people like himself," and that his poetry
was "written as a labourer might hoe a field of turnips, with no eye
on the ending, no thought of what is to come next, but with a mas-
sive, unquestioning patience."[5] Here again is the refusal to grant
the capacity of critical thought to a poet who questioned and challenged some of the most basic values of his society. But what I find
most alarming about this sort of argument is its tendency to assume
that individualism was an alien notion or reality to Clare and
"people like him." For such an assumption must cut off access to
Clare's profoundest recognition: that he was subject to social deter-
mination, but free to decide the way he responded to its controlling
will, that he could not choose the class into which he was born, but
chose for himself the way he would relate as man and poet to that
class. As Clare well knew, the city publisher to whom he expressed
himself most fully, the "glorious host" he so admired, even the critics he most despised were more "like himself" in inclination and
aspiration than the illiterate rustics of Helpston. But his relationship to these people – forged in full consciousness of what he lost
and gained by it – was not one of similarity, but identification. He
was as self-absorbed and as preoccupied as any other poet with the
specificity of his poetic problems, but from the very beginning he
understood that he would not solve his problems by cutting himself
off from his past or by failing to situate himself in the history of his
era. Thus he challenged class-prejudice not only because it made
the passage from creative inspiration to execution more arduous
than it ought to have been, but because it intensified the already
severed conditions of his society. He argued against enclosure not
only because it destroyed "the poets visions of lifes early days," but
because it "trampled on the grave / Of labours rights and left the

poor a slave." He celebrated the hidden enclaves of the natural landscape not only as his greatest creative resource, but as the last resort of the workingman, the only place and pleasure and token of freedom left to him. And in intimating in the bird poems that this last resort would soon be invaded and appropriated by a rapacious master class, he gave a fully intended pathos to his celebrations.

One cannot argue for the expressive significance of that pathos nor for the social protest it implicitly carried without being aware that one has to argue against those who believe that transcendence and abstraction are the mark of a great poet, that poets of enduring achievement stand free of personal and historical circumstance, universalize their material, and write upon subjects that are central to mankind. But it all depends, of course, upon what one thinks of as central and universal. I do not mean to claim for Clare the greatness of his most famous contemporaries, nor do I wish to challenge Aristotelian verities which have been affirmed even by the most committed practitioners of a socially informed criticism. But to suggest that Clare doomed himself to an irredeemably minor position in the literature of his country by writing about his struggles as workingman and working-class poet may well tell us less about Clare's limitations than it does about the limits of the tradition to which he so ardently hoped to belong.

In his last years, in Northampton Asylum, Clare looked back upon his life and himself suggested that he had failed to realize his imaginative potential and that his failure had been caused by his inability to escape the bounds of circumstance:

Earth's prison chilled my body with its dram
Of dullness, and my soaring thoughts destroyed,
I fled to solitudes from passions dream,
But strife persued - I only know, I am,
I was a being created in the race
Of men disdaining bounds of place and time: -
A spirit that could travel o'er the space
Of earth and heaven, - like a thought sublime,
Tracing creation, like my maker, free,
A soul unshackled - like eternity,
Spurning earth's vain and soul debasing thrall
But now I only know I am, - that's all.   (*JCOA*, 361-2)

Paradoxically, the language of these lines suggests the very capacity for transcendence that Clare here laments having never fully realized. All the palpable memories, circumstantial distinctions, and particular experiences which shaped the identity of the younger poet have been transcended, and the poet who speaks to us from this and other asylum poems is no longer John Clare, the expert on class and its cruelties, the village child, the seeker of "pastoral liberty," the defender of labour's rights, the challenger of genteel prejudice, but is rather - in words which are Wordsworthian in their abstraction - "a being created in the race of men," "a soul," "a spirit," "a thought sublime." I do not believe that this movement away from the colourful particulars of circumstance into the white light of abstraction represents an advance in profundity or centrality or formal execution upon the work of the early or middle years. Though Clare, looking back upon the ruins of his past, may have regretted his failure to escape the bounds of his social identity and experience, his poetry is inimitable and fascinating, his story is instructive and, in the clearest sense, heroic, precisely because he stayed within those bounds and, making them his central theme, mined their possibilities and traced the hard contours of their cruelest limitations.

A Note on Texts

As yet there is no standard edition of Clare's collected works though an Oxford English Texts edition, first projected almost twenty years ago, is now in the making. Until that edition appears Clare's readers must depend upon the various texts edited by Eric Robinson and his co-editors, Margaret Grainger, David Powell, Kelsey Thornton, and George Deacon. The text I use most often is the Oxford Authors *John Clare* which contains the fullest and most useful selection of Clare's poems yet to appear. It has now become something of a convention among Clare scholars to quote from the texts of the five editors above and, when that is not possible, to fall back upon the manuscripts. I have not chosen to follow this procedure for two reasons. First, I believe one's readers ought to be able to assess the validity of one's critical opinions or the aptness of the lines one has adduced as evidence by looking at the entire poem from which one has quoted. This seems especially important when one is offering an argument about a poem's structure or meaning. But this is not really possible (and certainly not for North American readers) if one is quoting from the manuscripts.

Secondly, as anyone who has perused the manuscripts will know, the work of deciphering the poems, already made difficult by Clare's handwriting, the quality of his ink, his habit of crowding his pages and margins with lines and stanzas of disparate poems, is further compounded by the multiplicity of scattered texts for single poems. I am concerned by the possibility that, by having different critics select and edit passages from the manuscripts to support the evidentiary needs of their own arguments, we will end up with a wild and far too numerous assortment of readings for one poem. Such a scenario will not form the basis for sound and fruitful critical debate and would, paradoxically, undermine the very thing everyone is seeking to defend: the integrity of Clare's poems.

The procedure I have chosen to follow when recent editions do not contain a poem I wish to consider is to fall back upon *The Poems of John Clare* edited by J.W. Tibble in 1935. Scholars have long and justifiably complained about Tibble's occasional misreadings, his habit of grievously over-punctuating the lines, and his tendency to make unnecessary alterations (such as changing Clare's "o" to "oh!"). My own experience has been that, once the necessary allowances have been made for Tibble's need to correct Clare's grammatical errors and misspellings, his edition is not quite as poisonously unreliable as has been supposed. For most of Clare's poetry, his readings do not substantially vary in word or line from Robinson and Summerfield's readings in *Selected Poems and Prose of John Clare*. But I do not wish to appear to be defending Tibble; his edition has long cried out to be superseded and I am grateful that I have had to resort to it very rarely. I have also had to rely on his selection of the letters because Mark Storey's new edition, *The Letters of John Clare* (Oxford: Clarendon Press 1985), appeared only after my work had been completed.

Notes

INTRODUCTION

1 Robinson and Summerfield, "A Poet in his Joy," 194.

2 Hazlitt, *Lectures on the English Poets*, 251.

3 Reprinted in Storey, *Critical Heritage*, 30. Wherever possible, letters to Clare, early reviews, and other critical material will be quoted from this collection.

4 See *SC*, 18-21, 40-1, 128 for the only autobiographical references in this long poem. The references are interesting but brief and apparently incidental.

5 However, as Ian Watt has observed in *Rise of the Novel*, the rural labouring poor continued to play a negligible role in the composition of the reading public in the eighteenth century: "despite a considerable expansion it still did not normally extend much farther down the social scale than to tradesmen and shopkeepers, with the important exception of the more favoured apprentices and indoor servants" (53). For the history of the working-class reader in the nineteenth century see Altick, *English Common Reader*; Webb, *British Working Class Reader*; and Harrison, *Learning and Living*.

CHAPTER ONE

1 *Letters*, 41, 52; *Prose*, 69; *SPP*, 171.

2 For the Georgians who rediscovered Clare in the 1920s, Clare's specific class-identity was less imporant than his general character as a countryman bearing witness to a way of life and quality of landscape to which they longed to return. In recent criticism, the best discussion of Clare's ruralism and how it distinguished him from his contemporaries is in Swingle, "Stalking the Essential John Clare,"

273-84. The fullest treatment of Clare's localism is to be found in Barrell, *The Idea of Landscape*.

3 *SPP*, xviii.

4 Letter to Edward Rippingille, May 14, 1826, as quoted in Storey, "Some Previously Unpublished Letters," 183.

5 *I*, 145 and 542; *SC*, 68-9. Also see the prose-fragment on the vicar and Ralph Wormstall ("one of the last of the opulent Farmers of the Old School") in *SPP*, 24-30.

6 His distrust, not of reform *per se*, but of those who argued for reform purely out of self-interest figures in "To a Fallen Elm" (*JOCA*, 96-8) and, more significantly, in *The Parish*.

7 Clare's library has been preserved (though not in its entirety) in the Northampton Public Library. Its contents are listed in David Powell, *Catalogue*, 23-34.

8 Northampton Mss. 7, p. 3. The poem has never been published.

9 See *Letters*, 72-3 and 125, for references to Queen Caroline, and *Prose*, 46-50, for Clare's account of the militia experience he suffered as a consequence of anti-Bonaparte hysteria.

10 See also the fragment, "A speech from 'The Bone and Cleaver Club'," in *Prose*, 229-30.

11 Keats, *Letters*, 1:320.

12 Ibid., 224.

13 Timothy Brownlow, "A Molehill for Parnassus," 30.

14 Crabbe, *Poems*, 1:121.

15 *Critical Heritage*, 66.

CHAPTER TWO

1 Barrell, 215. For a full account of the enclosure of Helpston and its economic consequences see 98-110 and 189-215.

2 The fact that the parish of Maxey to the north and Etton, Glinton, Northborough, and Peakirk to the east were enclosed at the same time as Helpston would have contributed to Clare's feeling that enclosure was sweeping across the whole countryside. Indeed three-quarters of the nation's four thousand parliamentary enclosures occurred in two periods, first in the 1760s and 1770s, and then during the war period from 1793 to 1815, and in these two periods about one half of the land of Huntingdonshire, Leicester, and Northampton-shire was enclosed. See Hobsbawm and Rude, *Captain Swing*, 27, and Hobsbawm, *Industry and Empire*, 80.

In his poems, letters, and prose Clare does not mention any parliamentary enclosures other than Helpston's; yet we should not suppose that he did not know of them. He may well have learned about them at the Blue Bell tavern where he drank his beer, or in Stamford where he bought his books, or at Milton Park where he visited frequently with those two well-informed men, Artis and Henderson, or he might have learned of them through the many newspapers that he read so intently. (He took *The Stamford Mercury*, *The Essex Herald*, and *The Examiner*; he read *The Times* and Cobbett's *Political Register* and had access to other regional papers.) Since he passed his formative years in one of the counties (and next to another) which experienced one of the most intense periods of enclosure, it is probable that Clare had a general knowledge of enclosure and a specific knowledge of other enclosed villages, and that in articulating his protest against improvement he was dovetailing that knowledge into his local poems.

3 Barrell, 194-202.

4 The idea that England was being betrayed from within by a new polity (which allowed for enclosures, rack-renting, poor-houses, inequitable taxation, and corruption in the courts) is also developed in "England, 1830" (*II*, 117) and *The Parish*, in which the henchmen of the new order are characterized as "turks imperial of the woodland bough" (l. 2114).

5 Joanna E. Rapf, review of Barrell, *The Idea of Landscape*, and Tibble, *John Clare*, 80.

6 MacLean, *Agarian Age*, 47.

7 Barrell, 110-16, 175, and 198-202.

8 Though in principle Clare had no sympathy for mobs and mob-violence, "Remembrances" (1832) provides some evidence that he was sympathetic to the labourers who rioted and set fires in the disturbances of 1830 - and then were imprisoned, transported, or hanged. In the poem it is "mouldywharps" and not labourers who are exiled or executed "as traitors," but the form of their suffering recalls the harsh punishments handed down by the Special Commission which tried the followers of Captain Swing. Though there are no specific references to Captain Swing in Clare's published writings, he must have known what was happening in his own vicinity: the machine-breaking riots spread into the Soke of Peterborough, occurring at Oundle and southeast of Kettering. See Hobsbawm and Rude, 146-8.

9 Wordsworth, *Poetical Works*, 2:83.

10 Ibid., 4:388.

11 Ibid., 2:387.

12 Barrell, 200.

13 Ibid., 106.

14 Ibid., 116.

CHAPTER THREE

1 See *Prose*, 86-93, for Clare's impressions of the "Londoners" he met at Taylor's table.

2 Bloom, *Anxiety of Influence* 5, 12, 21.

3 *Critical Heritage*, 50.

4 Ibid., 196.

5 Ibid., 115.

6 Clare's opinion of Wordsworth may be gleaned from the *Letters*, 133 and *Prose*, 118, 142, 210, 217.

7 Bloomfield, *The Farmer's Boy*, 4; *The Banks of Wye*, 80.

8 Burns, *Poetical Works*, 1:v.

9 Ross, *Early Critical Reviews*, vii.

10 Burns, *Poems, Chiefly in the Scottish Dialect*, 199.

11 Renwick, *English Literature 1789–1815*, 216.

12 Burns, Kilmarnock ed., iii-iv.

13 Wordsworth, *Prose Works*, 3:123.

14 Clare's tributes to Byron are to be found in the *Prose*, 99-100, 209, 223-4.

15 Southey, *Lives and Works of the Uneducated Poets*, vii, 11-12.

16 Had Clare had the chance to read Southey's whole book rather than just the preliminary essay, he would have been somewhat mollified by Southey's claim (163) that he did not categorize Bloomfield as an uneducated poet because his work merited presentation for its own sake.

17 Quoted in Southey, 128.

18 *Critical Heritage*, 91.

19 Ibid., 90.

20 Ibid., 95.

21 Ibid., 111.

22 Ibid., 105.

23 Ibid., 54.

24 Ibid., 112.

25 Ibid., 112.

26 *Gentleman's Magazine* (February 1820), as quoted in the end-papers of *The Village Minstrel*, 1st ed.

27 *Critical Heritage*, 170.

28 Ibid., 51.

29 Ibid., 152.

30 Ibid., 154.

31 Ibid., 168.

32 See Irene H. Chayes's discussion of the dramatic structure of the Romantic crisis-lyric in "Rhetoric as Drama: An Approach to the Romantic Ode, 67-79.

33 The lyric situation and self-portraiture are not all that recall Shelley. Verbal echoes of *Adonais* (stanzas 42 and 43 especially) can be found in "To the Rural Muse," most notably in the last lines of the third stanza ("To me a portion of thy power be given ...").

CHAPTER FOUR

1 Beattie, *The Minstrel*, vi.
2 De Selincourt, *Letters of William and Dorothy Wordsworth*, 1:586.
3 Wright, *English Dialect Dictionary*, 5:862.
4 Clare's pronouncements on religious experience and doctrine are found in the *Prose*, 220, 226-7, and *Letters*, 150, 159-61, 249. Also see Mark Minor, "John Clare and the Methodists," 31-50.
5 *Critical Heritage*, 168.
6 Howitt, *The Rural Life of England*.
7 See Malcolmson, *Popular Recreations in English Society 1700-1850*, 89-95, 137-46, 158-61.
8 One exception to the rule is found in the description of the harvest feast (*I*, 145, third stanza).
9 One could argue, however, that the phrase "Crusoe's lonely isle" contains an allusion not only to Defoe's text but to Bloomfield's *The Farmer's Boy* (65) in which the rural labourer is described as "the Crusoe of his lonely field."
10 King, "Beattie and Keats: The Progress of the Romantic Minstrel," 180.
11 *Critical Heritage*, 170.
12 Shelley, *Complete Poetical Works*, 2:44.
13 Ibid., 43, 46.

CHAPTER FIVE

1 See *Letters*, 365n.
2 Clare's contempt for men and women of the middle and upper middle classes who pretended to more learning and sophistication than they in fact possessed is a persistent theme in the first half of *The Parish* and in his prose. See *Letters*, 85 and *Prose*, 72, 76-78, 173, 208-9, 222-3.
3 See, for example, "The Braggart" (*II*, 345), "The Lout" (*II*, 347-8), and "The Thresher" (*II*, 350).
4 See the *Autobiography* (*Prose*, 23-5) in which Clare writes of muttering, but not uttering, his responses to natural beauty: "I observd all this with the same raptures as I have done since but I knew nothing of poetry / it was felt & not uttered."
5 Gray, *Complete Poems*, 39.

6 Blackwood's 3 (August 1818): 519–24.
7 In *A Grammar of the English Language*, 16, Cobbett argued that

> *pronunciation* is learned as birds learn to chirp and sing. In some counties of England many words are pronounced in a manner different from that in which they are pronounced in other counties; and, between the pronunciation of Scotland and that of Hampshire the difference is very great indeed. But, while all inquiries into the causes of these differences are useless, and all attempts to remove them are vain, the differences are of very little real consequence. For instance, though the Scotch say *coorn*, the Londoners *cawn*, and the Hampshire folks *carn*, we know they all *mean* to say *corn*.

8 Cobbett, *Advice to Young Men*, 48.
9 Davie, "John Clare," 964; and Robinson and Summerfield, "John Taylor's Editing of Clare's *The Shepherd's Calendar*," 359–69.
10 Chilcott, *A Publisher and his Circle*, 86–128, 195, passim. Ian Jack has not looked closely at the relationship between Clare and Taylor but has suggested that Taylor made some improvements in Clare's text – most notably in *The Shepherd's Calendar*. See *English Literature 1815–1832*, 30, and "Poems of John Clare's Sanity," 232n.
11 See *Critical Heritage*, 47–9, 160–2.
12 Quoted in *SC*, xii.
13 Brownlow argues that "the evidence of Clare's letters is that he resented Taylor's alterations of his manuscripts" (40n). But only a very few of the letters allow for such a conclusion (see, for example, *Letters*, 71, 96; *Prose*, 152); the majority give the overwhelming impression that Clare not only agreed with Taylor's alterations but often was thrilled by them. Disagreements certainly arose over *The Shepherd's Calendar*, and the years in which Clare was writing the poem and Taylor was editing it show neither poet nor publisher at his best. But the disagreements were caused not so much by Taylor's emendations as by his failure to edit the work with proper dispatch and by Clare's uncertainties as to how the poem and the volume as a whole should be organized. The letters written before and after this episode indicate that Clare neither resented nor distrusted Taylor's editorial procedures. The following letter, to Taylor of March 1821, is characteristic:

> your alterations in 'Solitude' are capital & this poem is now one of the best in the Vols: – your omissions in the 'Woodman' are very good & the poem reads now uncommonly well so be sure dont take them in again – your omission of the Verse in Sunday is after a second thought very appropriate & very just – your wishing to make one verse of the 2 is right – so be sure send me a copy of

the 2 verses & the way you would have them done / your assistance in such things I find very nessessary & in fact will not do without it - so in future when you want any alterations you'll know how to get them - your omissions in the other poems are capital / I saw their defects & wondered I never saw them before you crossd them out ... I am very fearful your turning your mind to take the original readings as you hinted in your last letter ... they cannot read better than they do in your alterations (*Letters*, 106-7)

Similar proof of Clare's confidence in Taylor's editorial decisions and literary taste can be found in *Letters*, 46, 51, 68, 74-5, 81, 84, 95-6, 103, 111, 115, 120-1, 125, 154, 172, 180, 184-6, 257. His lack of confidence in *other* editors to whom he submitted his work ("my contributions are so mutilated that I do not know them again") is recorded in *Letters*, 179-80, *Prose*, 146.

14 See Brownlow, 31 and 35; Barrell, 158-9, 170; and Strang, "John Clare's Language," 160-1.
15 Barrell, 123.
16 Ibid., 147, 188.
17 Ibid., 182.
18 Ibid., 128.
19 Ibid., 126-7 and passim.
20 Goody and Watt, "The Consequences of Literacy," 63.
21 Ibid., 29.
22 Barrell, 126; *Letters*, 67.
23 The fact that Clare used "lilac" and "princifeather" in the same poem (*II*, 231) strongly supports the idea that he used dialect-words because he consciously chose to do so.
24 Stevens, *Collected Poems*, 38.
25 *JCOA*, 25; ibid., 198; *SPP*, 95.
26 *JCOA*, 212; ibid., 128; *SPP*, 82.
27 *II*, 133.
28 *JCOA*, 128.
29 Ibid., 158.
30 Ibid., 212.
31 Ibid., 167-8.
32 Ibid., 162.
33 Ibid., 213.
34 *I*, 326; *JCOA*, 127; ibid., 163; *SPP*, 96.
35 *JCOA*, 198-9.
36 Ibid., 17; ibid., 13; ibid., 24.
37 Baker, *Glossary of Northamptonshire Words and Phrases*. Even Baker cannot always help us to know for certain whether Clare's words were inherited from the language of his community or were

invented, since in noting the use and defining the meanings of some dialect-words, Clare is her sole authority.

38 The exceptions to the rule only support the idea that dialect-words were associated with the lower class. For example, Mr Yorke in *Shirley* moves easily between dialect and standard English but when he uses dialect it is for the rhetorical purpose of declaring his identification with the lower class: his bilingualism is proof of his ability to bridge class divisions. In a similar way Clare's old-style master in *The Shepherd's Calendar*, "whose speech was vulgar as his clown" (69), proves through his language that he does not wish to separate himself from the rustic community. Henchard in *The Mayor of Casterbridge*, who speaks dialect but is angered when his daughter does, reveals the consciousness of a parvenu.

39 George Eliot, *Works*, 1:11-12.

40 B.M.H. Strang as quoted in Wakelin, *English Dialects: An Introduction*, 153.

41 Barrell, 63.

42 See *Early Critical Reviews on Robert Burns*, 282; and McKillop, "Local Attachment and Cosmopolitanism," 191-218.

43 See Mary Russell Mitford's celebration of local experience in *Our Village*, 1-2.

44 *Critical Heritage*, 142.

45 Ibid., 103.

46 Ibid., 71.

47 Ibid., 55.

48 Ibid., 207.

49 Leavis, *The Common Pursuit*, 189-90.

50 Dryden, *Essays*, 2:233.

51 *Critical Heritage*, 175.

52 Quoted in J.W. and Anne Tibble, *John Clare: A Life*, 124.

53 *Critical Heritage*, 154.

54 Wade, "John Clare's Use of Dialect," 84.

CHAPTER SIX

1 Empson, *Some Versions of Pastoral*, 12.

2 Gombrich, *Art and Illusion*, 12, 23, 56-63, 73-7, 331, and passim.

3 As quoted in Gombrich, 150.

4 *Critical Heritage*, 120.

5 *Blackwood's* 3 (August 1818): 519-24.

6 See "Shadows of Taste" (*JCOA*, 170-4) for Clare on changing metrical fashions.

7 Yeats, *The Variorum Edition*, 425.

8 Stevens, 497.

9 Hazlitt, 318-22.

10 *SPP*, xxv.

11 Wordsworth, *Poetical Works*, 2:386.

12 Ibid., 392.

13 Ibid., 386.

14 Ibid., 5:5.

15 Ibid., 327.

16 Jacobus, *Tradition and Experiment in Wordsworth's 'Lyrical Ballads'*, 9.

17 J.W. and Anne Tibble, *John Clare: A Life*, 311.

18 Coleridge, *Complete Poetical Works*, 364.

19 J.W. Tibble has suggested that Clare was not "interested in words as words ... The unit for him was the short phrase or clause - the verbal expression of the image upon which his attention was focused" (*I*: viii).

20 Hartman, *Beyond Formalism*, 232.

CHAPTER SEVEN

1 Clare wrote five poems about birds before 1824, and the bird (as image or symbol) figures importantly in poems on other subjects written before this date. But 1824 is the year in which Clare began to take the subject of birds seriously enough to commit his energies to writing extended groups - one is tempted to say sequences - of bird poems. J.W. Tibble and Robinson and Summerfield clearly understood the importance of reading the bird poems as a unified set, for both their editions print most of the bird poems one after another. Two volumes dedicated solely to bird poems have also been printed: *Bird's Nest: Poems by John Clare*, in which all but one of the twenty poems included are published for the first time; and *John Clare: Bird Poems*, which reprints eighty-six poems from Tibble's 1935 edition. If we add to these eighty-six poems "The World's End" (*II*: 213), which J.W. Tibble expressly included in his bird poem grouping, the nineteen poems first published by Anne Tibble in her 1973 collection, and "The Moorehens Nest," which Robinson and Summerfield have been the first to publish, we find a total of 107 bird poems. However, since no consensus has been reached about what exactly constitutes a bird poem, it's impossible to be dogmatic about this number. "Winter's Walk," for example, is included in the Folio Society edition, though I do not consider it a bird poem, while "Emmonsails Heath in Winter," in which birds play an important role, has not been categorized by any editor as a bird poem.

2 J.W. and Anne Tibble, *John Clare: His Life and Poetry*, 132; Todd, *In Adam's Garden*, 45–6.

3 The terms *ponos* (hardship, effort) and *otium* (freedom, escape from work or business, vacation) are fully defined in Rosenmeyer, *The Green Cabinet*, 22–6, 65–73. I am also indebted to Renato Poggioli's discussion of the differences between the georgic and the pastoral dispensation in *The Oaten Flute*, 1, 4, 6, 246, and passim.

4 Cowper, *Correspondence*, 253.

5 Cowper, *Poetical Works*, 179.

6 Ibid., 134.

7 Ibid., 136.

8 Earlier, when Clare laboured in the gardens of Burghley Park, the walls had served a different but no less troubling function. See above, 25–6.

9 Cowper, *Poetical Works*, 184, 144.

10 Ibid., 178, 146.

11 Ibid., 184.

12 *JCOA*, 97, 165, 208, 212, 215, 222.

13 Wordsworth, *Poetical Works*, 2:386.

14 Williams, *The Autobiography*, 390.

15 Williams, *Selected Poems*, 30.

16 As quoted in Gombrich, 251.

17 Hartman, 257.

18 Barrell, 130.

CONCLUSION

1 *Critical Heritage*, 381.

2 Murry, *John Clare and Other Studies*, 9.

3 Jackson, *Poetry of the Romantic Period*, 23.

4 Quoted in Williams, *Marxism and Literature*, 151.

5 Richmond, *Poetry and the People*, 162, 176–7.

Select Bibliography

The following bibliography lists all works cited in the text or notes and the most important or useful of the works consulted during the writing of this study. A complete bibliography of writings on Clare up to 1977 (including reviews, books, articles, dissertations, reference books, and reviews of studies of Clare) is provided by H.O. Dendurent in *John Clare: A Reference Guide* (Boston: G.K. Hall 1978). Dendurent's annotations are idiosyncratic and, on occasion, misleading, but in every other respect his bibliography is reliable.

WORKS AND SELECTED EDITIONS

Poems Descriptive of Rural Life and Scenery. London: Taylor and Hessey, and E. Drury 1820.

The Village Minstrel, and Other Poems. London: Taylor and Hessey, and E. Drury 1821.

The Shepherd's Calendar; with Village Stories. London: Taylor and Hessey 1827.

The Rural Muse. London: Whittaker 1835.

The Poems of John Clare, ed. J.W. Tibble. 2 vols. London: Dent 1935.

The Later Poems of John Clare, ed. Eric Robinson and Geoffrey Summerfield. Manchester: Manchester University Press 1964.

The Shepherd's Calendar, ed. Eric Robinson and Geoffrey Summerfield. London: Oxford University Press 1964.

Selected Poems and Prose of John Clare, ed. Eric Robinson and Geoffrey Summerfield. London: Oxford University Press 1967.

John Clare: Selected Poems, ed. Elaine Feinstein. London: University Tutorial Press 1968.

Bird's Nest: Poems by John Clare, ed. Anne Tibble. Northumberland: Mid Northumberland Arts Group 1973.

The Midsummer Cushion, ed. Anne Tibble. Northumberland: Mid Northumberland Arts Group 1979.

John Clare: Bird Poems. London: Folio Society 1980.

The Rural Muse, Poems by John Clare, ed. R.K.R. Thornton. Ashington: Mid Northumberland Arts Group and Carcanet New Press 1982.

John Clare, ed. Eric Robinson and David Powell. The Oxford Authors: Oxford University Press 1984.

The Later Poems of John Clare, eds. Eric Robinson and David Powell. 2 vols. London: Oxford University Press 1984.

Sketches in the Life of John Clare by Himself, ed. Edmund Blunden. London: Cobden-Sanderson 1931.

The Letters of John Clare, ed. J.W. and Anne Tibble. London: Routledge and Kegan Paul 1951.

The Prose of John Clare, ed. J.W. and Anne Tibble. London: Routledge and Kegan Paul 1951.

John Clare: The Journals, Essays, and the Journey from Essex, ed. Anne Tibble. Manchester: Carcanet New Press 1980.

John Clare's Birds, ed. Eric Robinson and Richard Fitter. Oxford: Oxford University Press 1982.

The Natural History Prose Writings of John Clare, ed. Margaret Grainger. Oxford: Oxford University Press 1983.

John Clare's Autobiographical Writings, ed. Eric Robinson. Oxford: Oxford University Press 1983.

OTHER SOURCES

Altick, Richard D. *The English Common Reader: A Social History of the Mass Reading Public*. Chicago: University of Chicago Press 1957.

Baker, Anne Elizabeth. *Glossary of Northamptonshire Words and Phrases*. London: John Russell Smith 1854.

Barrell, John. *The Idea of Landscape and the Sense of Place 1730–1840: An Approach to the Poetry of John Clare*. Cambridge: Cambridge University Press 1972.

- "John Clare, William Cobbett and the Changing Landscape." *From Blake to Byron*, New Pelican Guide to English Literature, ed. Boris Ford. Harmondsworth: Penguin 1982.

Beattie, James. *The Minstrel; or the Progress of Genius and Other Poems*. London: John Sharpe 1823.

Bloom, Harold. *The Anxiety of Influence: A Theory of Poetry*. New York: Oxford University Press 1973.

Bloomfield, Robert. *The Farmer's Boy; a Rural Poem*. London: Vernor and Hood 1800.

- *The Banks of Wye*. London: Vernor, Hood, and Sharpe 1811.

Blunden, Edmund. *Keats's Publisher: A Memoir of John Taylor*. London: Jonathan Cape 1936.

Brook, G.L. *English Dialects*. London: André Deutsch 1963.

Brownlow, Timothy. *John Clare and Picturesque Landscape*. Oxford: Oxford University Press 1983.

- "A Molehill for Parnassus: John Clare and Prospect Poetry." *University of Toronto Quarterly* 48 (1978): 23-40.

Burns, Robert. *Poems, Chiefly in the Scottish Dialect*. Kilmarnock: John Wilson 1786.

- *The Poetical Works*. Alnwick: Catnach and Davison 1808.

Chayes, Irene H. "Rhetoric as Drama: An Approach to the Romantic Ode." *PMLA* 76 (1964): 67-79.

Cherry, J.L. *Life and Remains of John Clare*. London: Frederick Warner 1873.

Chilcott, Tim. *A Publisher and His Circle: The Life and Work of John Taylor, Keats's Publisher*. London: Routledge and Kegan Paul 1972.

- *'A Real World & Doubting Mind': A Critical Study of the Poetry of John Clare*. Pickering: Hull University Press 1985.

Cobbett, William. *A Grammar of the English Language*. 1818. London: Charles Griffin n.d.

- *Advice to Young Men*. 1829-30. London: George Routledge 1887.

Coleridge, Samuel Taylor. *The Complete Poetical Works*, ed. Ernest Hartley Coleridge. Oxford: Clarendon Press 1912.

Cowper, William. *Correspondence*, ed. Thomas Wright. London: Hodder and Stoughton 1904.

- *Poetical Works*, ed. H.S. Milford. 4th ed. London: Oxford University Press 1967.

Crabbe, George. *Poems*, ed. Adolphus William Ward. Cambridge: Cambridge University Press 1905.

Crossan, Greg. *A Relish for Eternity: The Process of Divinization in the Poetry of John Clare*. Salzburg Studies in English Literature no. 53. Salzburg: University of Salzburg 1976.

Davie, Donald. "John Clare." *New Statesman* 67 (19 June 1964): 964.

Dryden, John. *Essays*, ed. W.P. Ker. Oxford: Clarendon Press 1900.

Eliot, George. *Works*. Vol. 1. London: William Blackwood 1901.

Empson, William. *Some Versions of Pastoral*. London: Chatto and Windus 1935.

Frosch, Thomas R. "The Descriptive Style of John Clare." *Studies in Romanticism* 10 (Spring 1971): 137-49.

Gombrich, E.H. *Art and Illusion: A Study in the Psychology of Pictorial Representation*. 3d ed. London: Phaidon Press 1968.

Goody, Jack, ed. *Literacy in Traditional Societies*. Cambridge: Cambridge University Press 1968.

Grainger, Margaret, ed. *A Descriptive Catalogue of the John Clare Collection in Peterborough Museum and Art Gallery*. Peterborough: Peterborough Museum Society 1973.

Gray, Thomas. *The Complete Poems*, ed. H.W. Starr and J.R. Hendrickson. Oxford: Clarendon Press 1966.

Hammond, J.L., and Barbara. *The Village Labourer 1760–1832*. London: Longmans, Green 1911.

Harrison, J.F.C. *Learning and Living 1790–1960: A Study in the History of the English Adult Educational Movement*. Toronto: University of Toronto Press 1961.

Hartman, Geoffrey H. *Beyond Formalism*. New Haven: Yale University Press 1970.

Hazlitt, William. *Lectures on the English Poets*. London: Taylor and Hessey 1819.

Hobsbawm, E.J. *Industry and Empire: An Economic History of Britain since 1750*. London: Weidenfield and Nicolson 1968.

Hobsbawm, E.J., and Rudé, George. *Captain Swing*. New York: Random House 1968.

Hoggart, Richard. *The Uses of Literacy*. London: Chatto and Windus 1957.

Howard, William J. *John Clare*. Boston: Twayne Publishers 1981.

Howitt, William. *The Rural Life of England*. 3d ed. London: Longman, Brown, Green, and Longmans 1884.

Jack, Ian. *English Literature 1815–1832*. Oxford: Clarendon Press 1963.

- "Poems of John Clare's Sanity," in *Some British Romantics*, ed. James V. Logan, John E. Jordan, and Northrop Frye. Columbus: Ohio State University Press 1966.

Jackson, J.R. de J. *Poetry of the Romantic Period*. London: Routledge and Kegan Paul 1980.

Jacobus, Mary. *Tradition and Experiment in Wordsworth's 'Lyrical Ballads' (1798)*. Oxford: Clarendon Press 1976.

Keats, John. *The Letters ... 1814–1821*, ed. H.E. Rollins, Cambridge: Harvard University Press 1958.

Keith, W.J. *The Poetry of Nature: Rural Perspectives in Poetry from Wordsworth to the Present*. Toronto: University of Toronto Press 1980.

King, E.H. "Beattie and Keats: The Progress of the Romantic Minstrel." *English Studies in Canada* 3 (Summer 1977): 176–94.

Leavis, F.R. *The Common Pursuit*. London: Chatto and Windus 1958.

Levi, Peter. *John Clare and Thomas Hardy.* London: Athlone Press 1975.

McKillop, Alan D. "Local Attachment and Cosmopolitanism – The Eighteenth-Century Pattern," in *From Sensibility to Romanticism: Essays Presented to Frederick A. Pottle,* ed. Frederick W. Hilles and Harold Bloom. London: Oxford University Press 1965.

MacLean, Kenneth. *Agrarian Age: A Background for Wordsworth.* New Haven: Yale University Press 1950.

Malcolmson, Robert W. *Popular Recreations in English Society 1700–1850.* Cambridge: Cambridge University Press 1973.

Martin, Frederick. *The Life of John Clare.* London: Macmillan 1865. Reprint, ed. Eric Robinson and Geoffrey Summerfield. London: Frank Cass 1964.

Mingay, G.E. *Enclosure and the Small Farmer in the Age of the Industrial Revolution.* London: Macmillan 1968.

Minor, Mark. "John Clare and the Methodists: A Reconsideration." *Studies in Romanticism* 19 (Spring 1980): 31–50.

Mitford, Mary Russell. *Our Village.* 1824–32. London: Henry G. Bohn 1848.

Murry, J. Middleton. *John Clare and Other Studies.* London: Peter Nevill 1950.

"On the Cockney School of Poetry." *Blackwood's Magazine* 2 (October 1817): 38–41: 3 (August 1818): 519–24; 5 (April 1819): 97–100.

Page, Norman. *Speech in the English Novel.* London: Longman 1973.

Poggioli, Renato. *The Oaten Flute: A Study of Pastoral Poetry and the Bucolic Ideal.* Cambridge: Harvard University Press 1975.

Powell, David, ed. *Catalogue of The John Clare Collection in the Northampton Public Libaray.* Northampton: Northampton Public Library 1964.

Rapf, Joanna E. Review of Barrell, *The Idea of Landscape and the Sense of Place,* and Tibble, *John Clare: A Life. Studies in Romanticism* 13 (Winter 1974): 79–84.

Renwick, W.L. *English Literature 1789–1815.* Oxford: Clarendon Press 1963.

Robinson, Eric, and Summerfield, Geoffrey. "John Taylor's Editing of Clare's *Shepherd's Calendar.*" *Review of English Studies* n.s. 14 (November 1963): 359–69.

– "John Clare (1793–1864): A Poet in his Joy." *The Cambridge Review* (23 January 1965): 194–9.

Rosenmeyer, Thomas G. *The Green Cabinet: Theocritus and the European Pastoral Lyric.* Berkeley, University of California Press 1969.

Ross, John D., ed. *Early Critical Reviews on Robert Burns.* Glasgow: William Hodge 1900.

Shelley, Percy Bysshe. *The Complete Poetical Works*, ed. Neville Rogers. Oxford: Clarendon Press 1975.

Southey, Robert. *The Lives and Works of the Uneducated Poets*, ed. J.S. Childers. London: Humphrey Milford 1925.

Stevens, Wallace. *The Collected Poems*. New York: Alfred A. Knopf 1968.

Storey, Mark, ed. *Clare: The Critical Heritage*. London: Routledge and Kegan Paul 1973.

- *The Poetry of John Clare: A Critical Introduction*. New York: St. Martin's Press 1974.

- "Some Previously Unpublished Letters from John Clare." *Review of English Studies* n.s. 25 (May 1974): 177-85.

Swingle, L.J. "Stalking the Essential John Clare: Clare in Relation to His Romantic Contemporaries." *Studies in Romanticism* 14 (Summer 1975): 273-84.

Thompson, E.P. *The Making of the English Working Class*. Harmondsworth: Penguin 1968.

Tibble, J.W., and Anne. *John Clare: A Life*. London: Cobden-Sanderson 1932. Revised ed. London: Michael Joseph 1972.

- *John Clare: His Life and Poetry*. London: Heinemann 1956.

Todd, Janet M. *In Adam's Garden: A Study of John Clare's Pre-Asylum Poetry*. Gainesville, Fla.: University of Florida Press 1973.

Unwin, Rayner. *The Rural Muse: Studies in the Peasant Poetry of England*. London: George Allen and Unwin 1954.

Wade, Stephen. "John Clare's Use of Dialect." *Contemporary Review* 223 (August 1973): 81-4.

Wakelin, Martyn F. *English Dialects: An Introduction*. London: Athlone Press 1972.

Watt, Ian. *The Rise of the Novel: Studies in Defoe, Richardson, and Fielding*. London: Chatto and Windus 1957.

Webb, R.K. *The British Working Class Reader, 1790–1960: Literacy and Social Tension*. London: George Allen and Unwin 1955.

Williams, Raymond. *The Country and the City*. New York: Oxford University Press 1974.

- *Marxism and Literature*. Oxford: Oxford University Press 1977.

Williams, William Carlos. *The Autobiography*. New York: Random House 1951.

- *Selected Poems*. New York: New Directions, 1968.

Wilson, June. *Green Shadows: The Life of John Clare*. London: Hodder and Stoughton 1951.

Wordsworth, William. *The Poetical Works*, ed. Ernest de Selincourt and Helen Darbishire. 2nd ed. Oxford: Clarendon Press 1952-9.

- *The Prose Works*, ed. W.J.B. Owen and Jane Worthington Smyser. Oxford: Clarendon Press 1974.
- *The Letters of William and Dorothy Wordsworth*, ed. Ernest de Selincourt. Oxford: Clarendon Press 1967.

Wright, Joseph, ed. *The English Dialect Dictionary*. London: Henry Frowde 1904.

Yeats, W.B. *The Variorum Edition of the Poems*, ed. Peter Allt and Russell K. Alspach. New York: Macmillan 1957.

Index

215